DEBBY KRATOVIL

quilter's new perpetual BLOCK-A-DAY CALENDAR

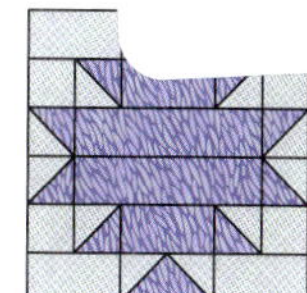

Quilter's NEW Perpetual Block-a-Day Calendar

Copyright © 2025 by Debby Kratovil

PUBLISHER: Amy Barrett-Daffin

CREATIVE DIRECTOR: Gailen Runge

COVER DESIGNER: April Mostek

PRODUCT TEAM: April Mostek, Betsy La Honta, Zinnia Heinzmann

Published by C&T Publishing, Inc., P.O. Box 1456, Lafayette, CA 94549

All rights reserved. No part of this work covered by the copyright hereon may be used in any form or reproduced by any means—graphic, electronic, or mechanical, including photocopying, recording, taping, or information storage and retrieval systems—without written permission from the publisher. The copyrights on individual artworks are retained by the artists as noted in *Quilter's NEW Perpetual Block-a-Day Calendar*. These designs may be used to make items for personal use only and may not be used for the purpose of personal profit. Items created to benefit nonprofit groups, or that will be publicly displayed, must be conspicuously labeled with the following credit: "Designs copyright © 2025 by Debby Kratovil from the product *Quilter's NEW Perpetual Block-a-Day Calendar* from C&T Publishing, Inc." Permission for all other purposes must be requested in writing from C&T Publishing, Inc.

We take great care to ensure that the information included in our products is accurate and presented in good faith, but no warranty is provided, nor are results guaranteed. Having no control over the choices of materials or procedures used, neither the author nor C&T Publishing, Inc., shall have any liability to any person or entity with respect to any loss or damage caused directly or indirectly by the information contained in this product. For your convenience, we post an up-to-date listing of corrections on our website (ctpub.com). If a correction is not already noted, please contact our customer service department at ctinfo@ctpub.com or P.O. Box 1456, Lafayette, CA 94549.

Printed in China

10 9 8 7 6 5 4 3 2

INTRODUCTION

Welcome to the Quilter's NEW Perpetual Block-a-Day Calendar! Here you will find a block for every day of the year and an extra block for leap year. With a wide variety of blocks you can challenge yourself to make them all or select your favorites and explore endless quilt design possibilities!

Featuring traditional, pictorial and original blocks in a range of sizes from 6″ × 6″ to 24″ × 24″, each block pattern includes a full-color illustration and an easy-to-use rotary-cutting key. Basic instructions and a block index are at the back of the calendar.

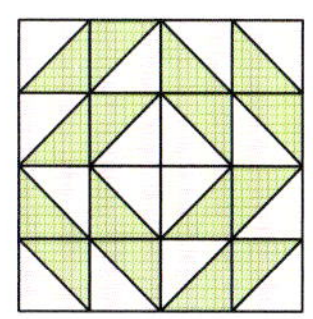

january 1

OH, MY STARS!

18″ × 18″

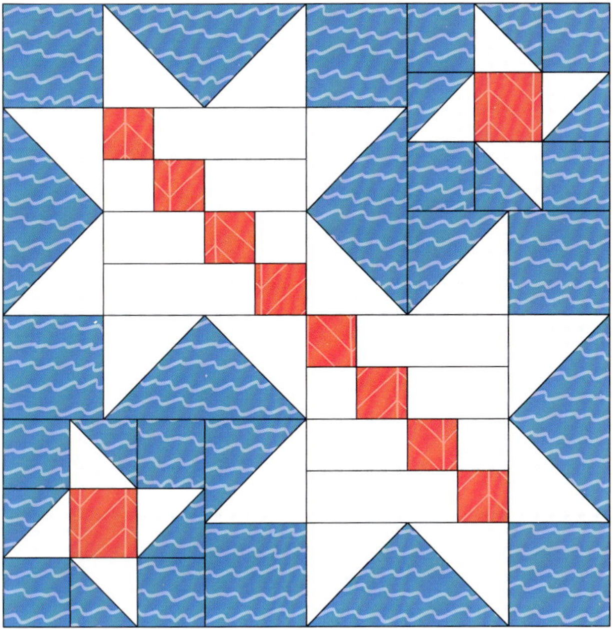

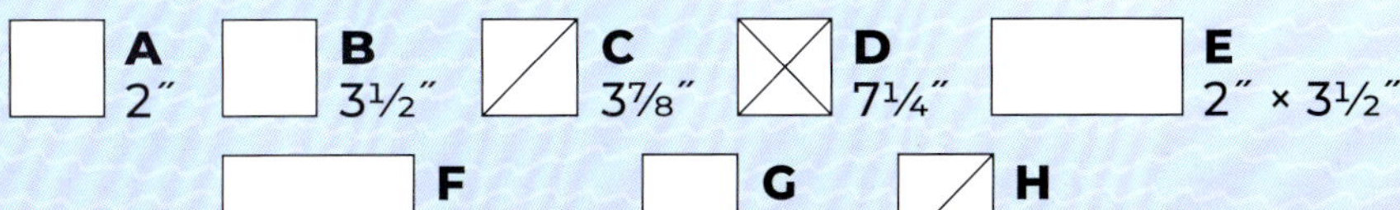

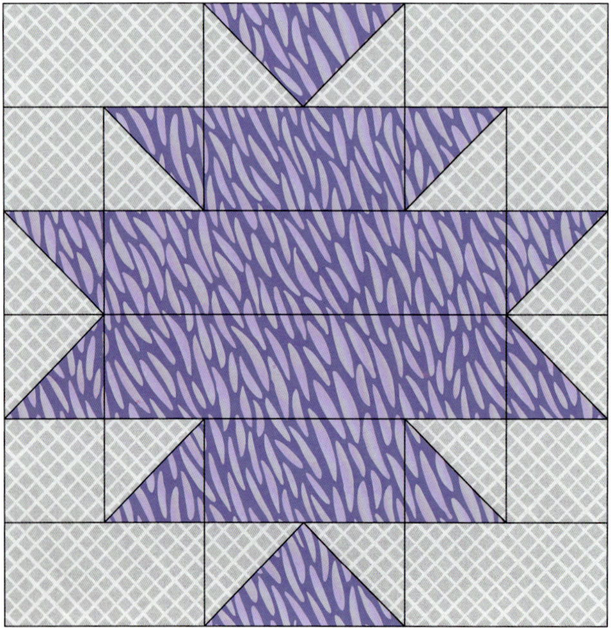

december 31

DELECTABLE MOUNTAINS

12″ × 12″

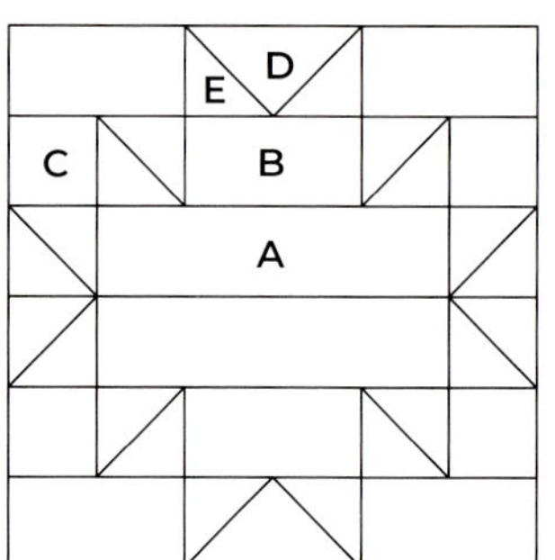

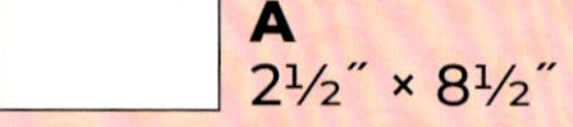

A
2½″ × 8½″

B
2½″ × 4½″

C
2½″

D
5¼″

E
2⅞″

january 2

TURNSTILE

12″ × 12″

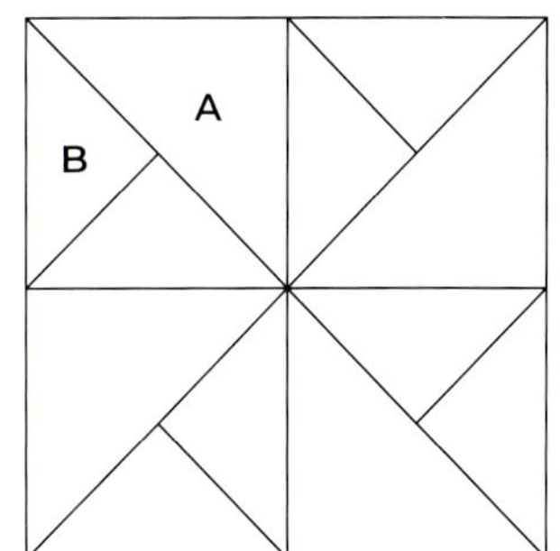

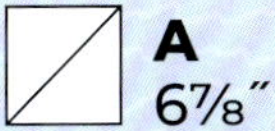

A
6⅞″

B
7¼″

december 30

ZIG AND ZAG

8″ × 8″

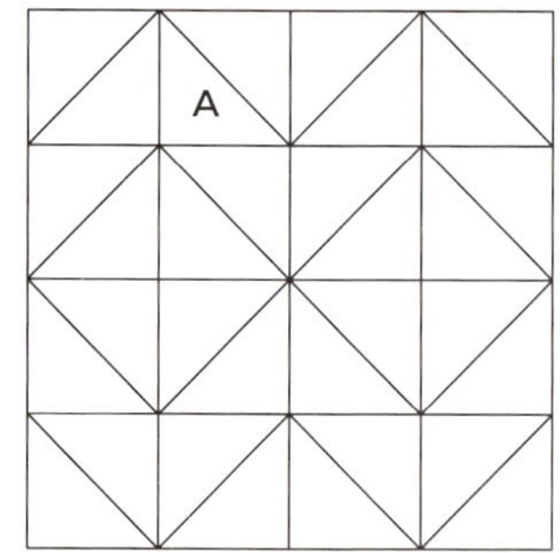

A
2⅞″

january 3

STEPPING STONES CABIN

12″ × 12″

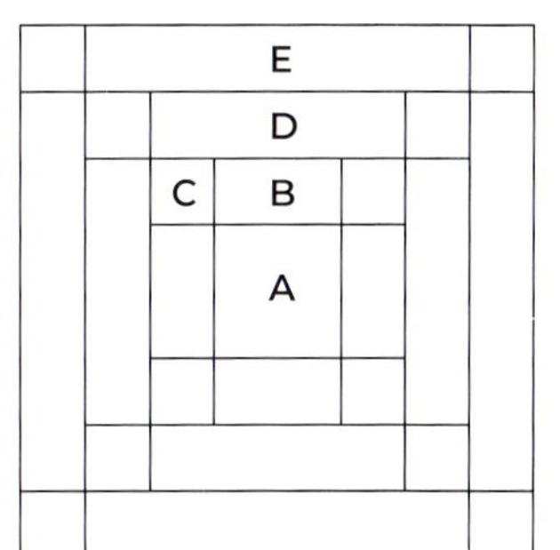

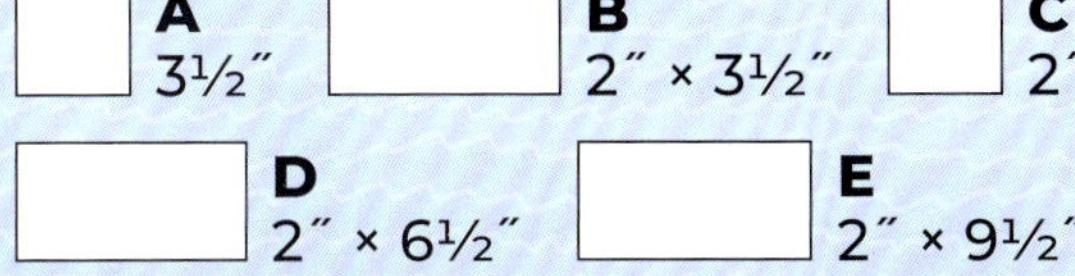

december 29

BRICK ROAD

12″ × 12″

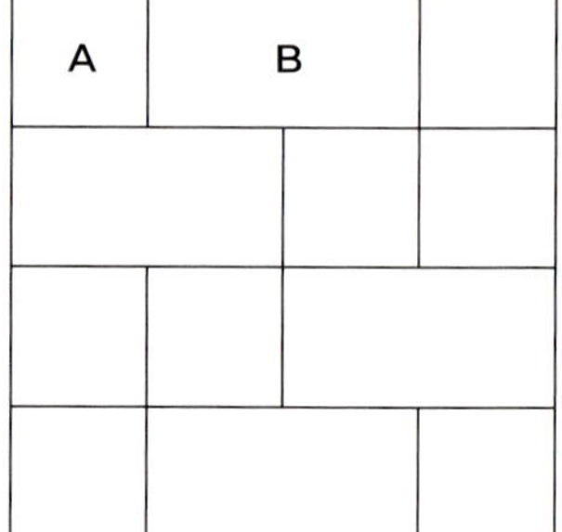

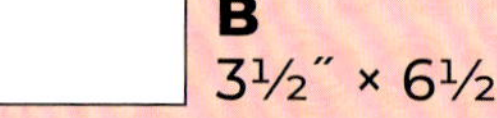

A
3½″

B
3½″ × 6½″

january 4

BLUES AND WHITES

12″ × 12″

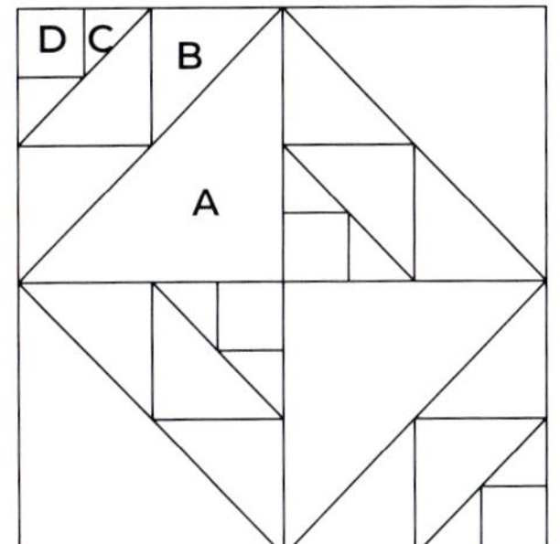

A 6⅞″

B 3⅞″

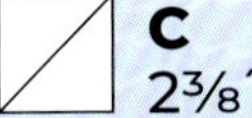

C 2⅜″

D 2″

december 28

DIAGONAL FOUR PATCH

8″ × 8″

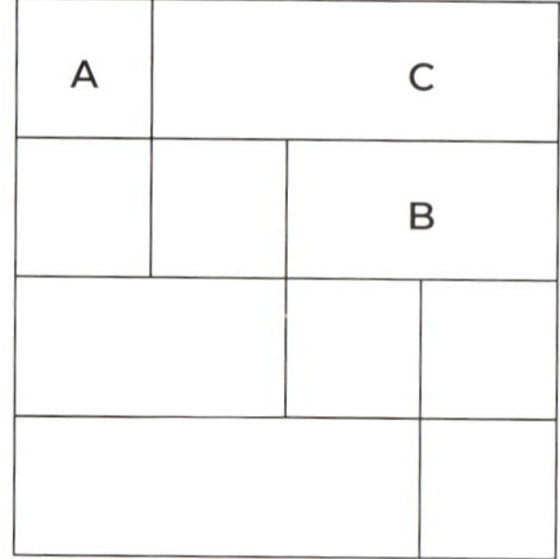

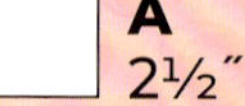

A
2½″

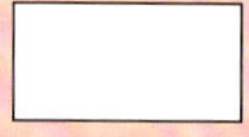

B
2½″ × 4½″

C
2½″ × 6½″

january 5

PENNSYLVANIA

12″ × 12″

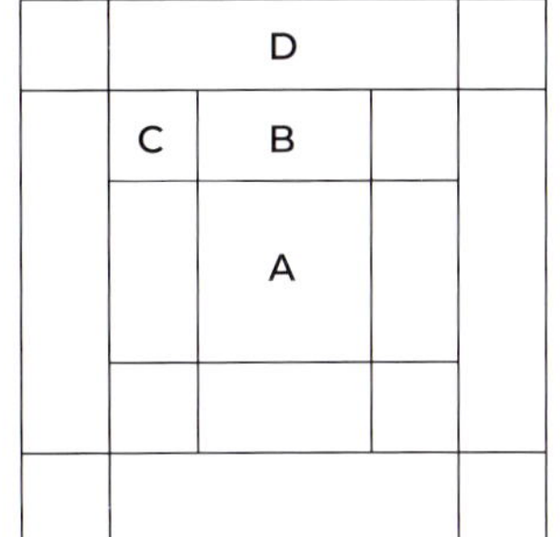

A
4½″

B
2½″ × 4½″

C
2½″

D
2½″ × 8½″

december 27

TWIN PINES
8″ × 8″

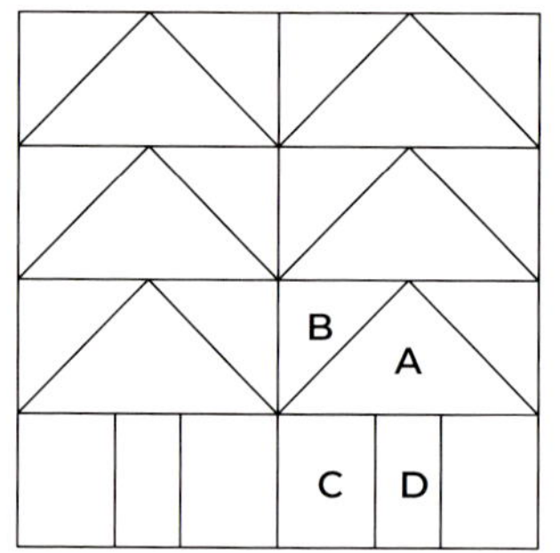

A
5¼″

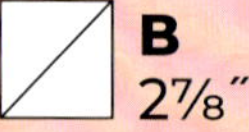
B
2⅞″

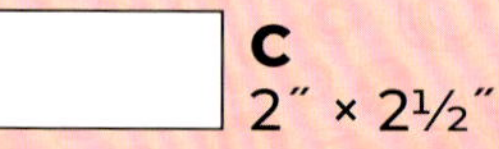
C
2″ × 2½″

D
1½″ × 2½″

january 6

ART SQUARE

12″ × 12″

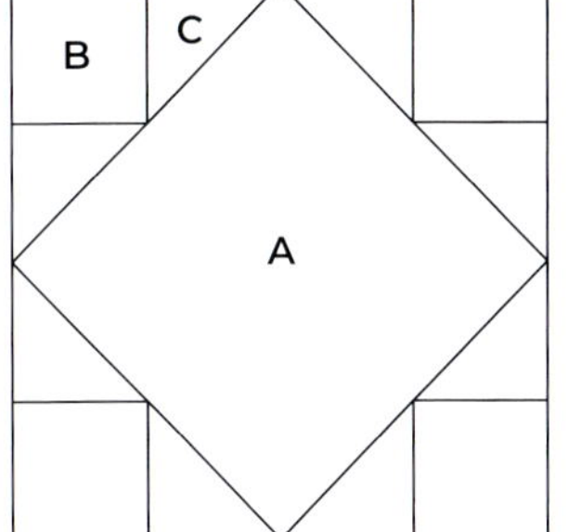

A 9″

B 3½″

C 3⅞″

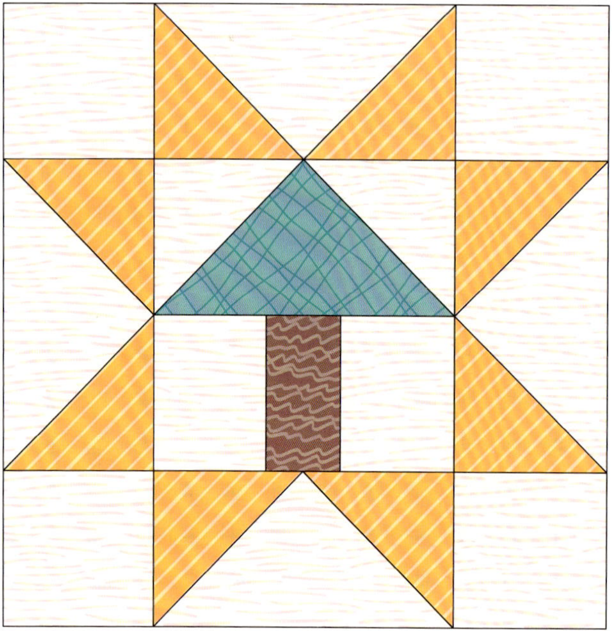

december 26

STAR AND PINE BLOCK

18″ × 18″

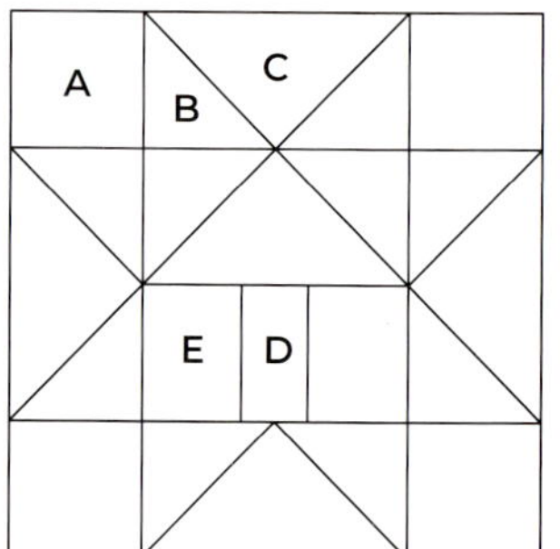

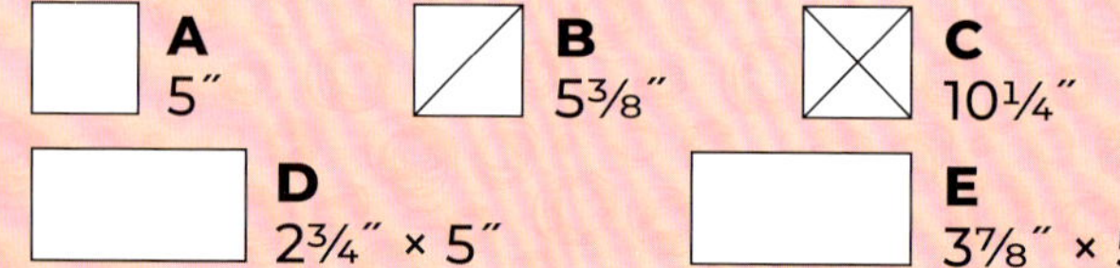

january 7

ART SQUARE VARIATION

12″ × 12″

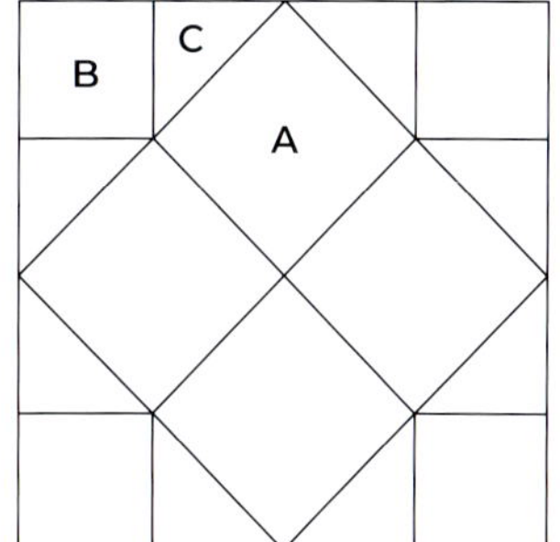

A 4¾″

B 3½″

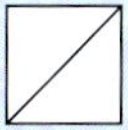

C 3⅞″

december 25

CHRISTMAS STAR

18″ × 18″

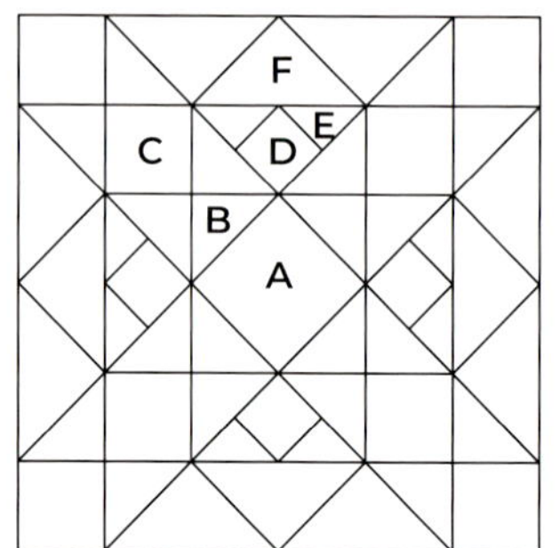

	Piece	Size
	A	4¾″
	B	3⅞″
	C	3½″
	D	2⅝″
	E	4¼″
	F	7¼″

january 8

IMPERIAL T

18″ × 18″

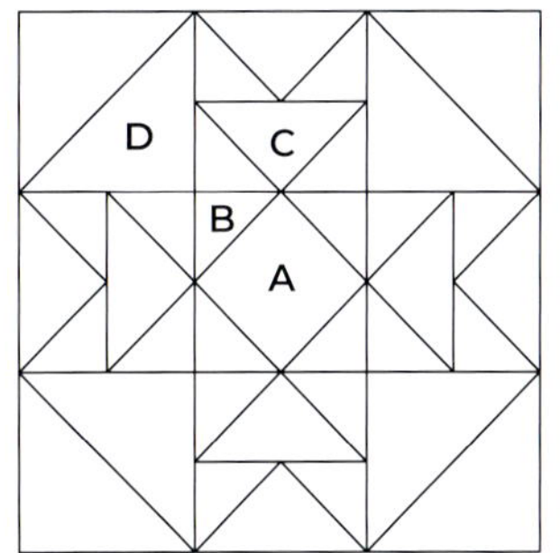

A 4¾″

B 3⅞″

C 7¼″

D 6⅞″

december 24

PRESENT #3

8″ × 8″

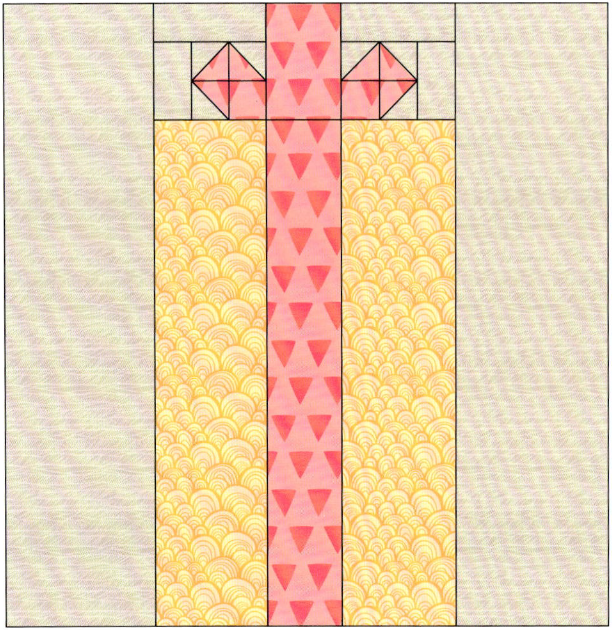

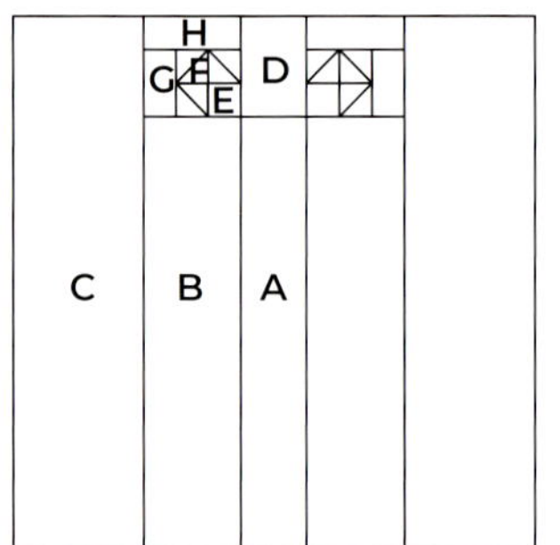

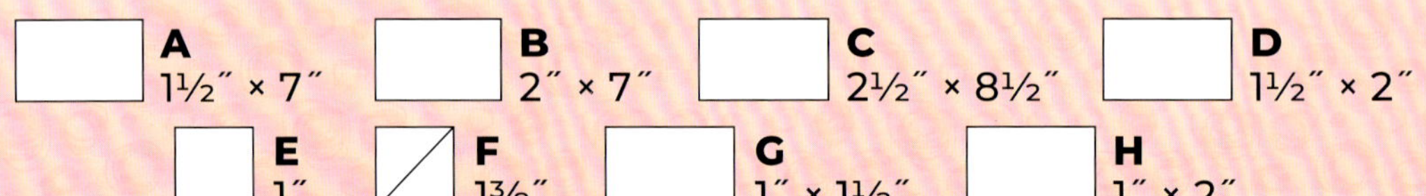

january 9

IMPERIAL T VARIATION

18″ × 18″

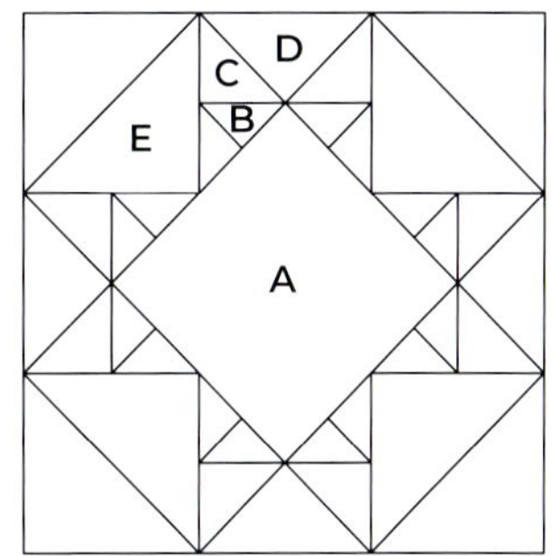

A
9″

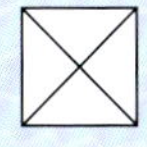

B
4¼″

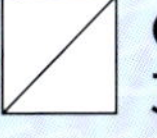

C
3⅞″

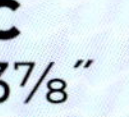

D
7¼″

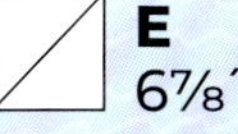

E
6⅞″

december 23

PRESENT #2

8″ × 8″

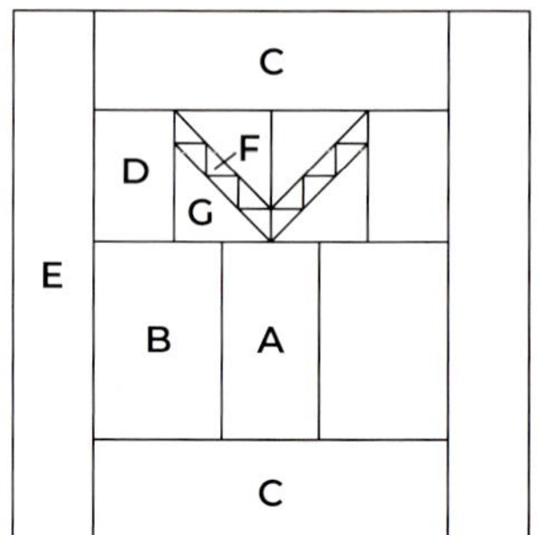

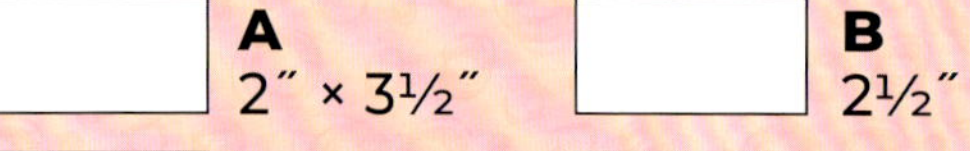

A
2″ × 3½″

B
2½″ × 3½″

C
2″ × 6″

D
1¾″ × 2½″

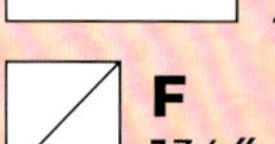

E
1¾″ × 8½″

F
1⅜″

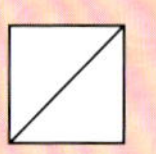

G
2⅜″

january 10

LUCKY STAR

9″ × 9″

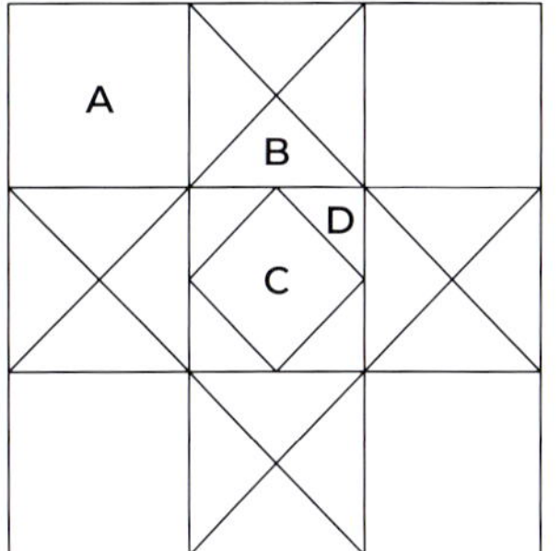

A 3½″

B 4¼″

C 2⅝″

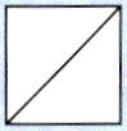

D 2⅜″

december 22

PRESENT #1

8″ × 8″

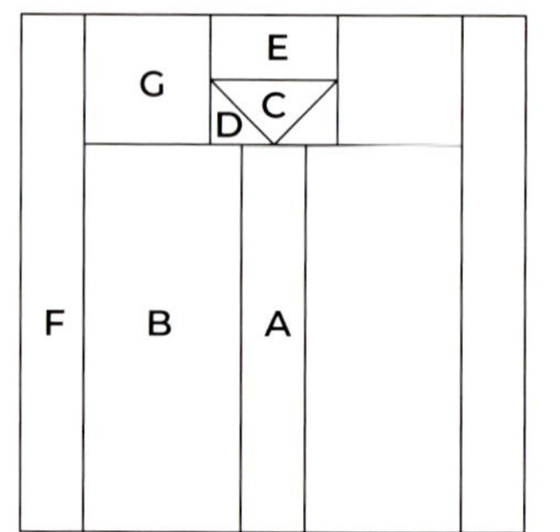

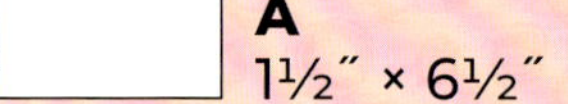

A
1½″ × 6½″

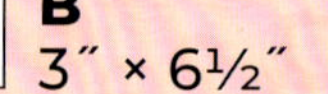

B
3″ × 6½″

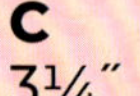

C
3¼″

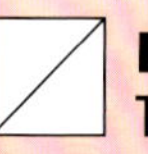

D
1⅞″

E
1½″ × 2½″

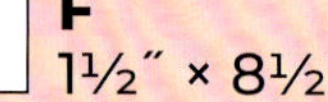

F
1½″ × 8½″

G
2½″

january 11

MOSAIC STAR
9″ × 9″

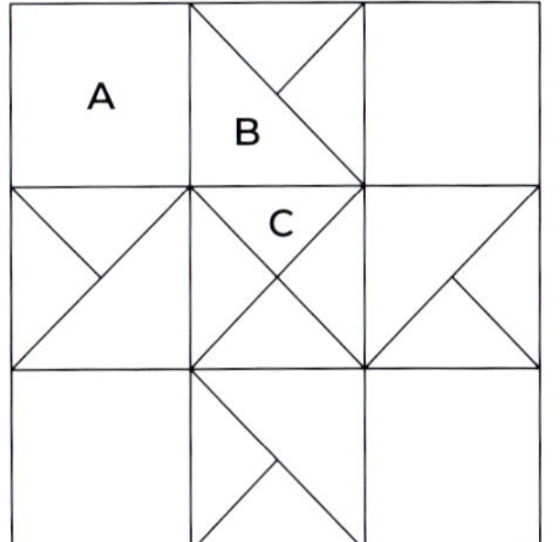

A
3½″

B
3⅞″

C
4¼″

december 21

THIS AND THAT

12″ × 12″

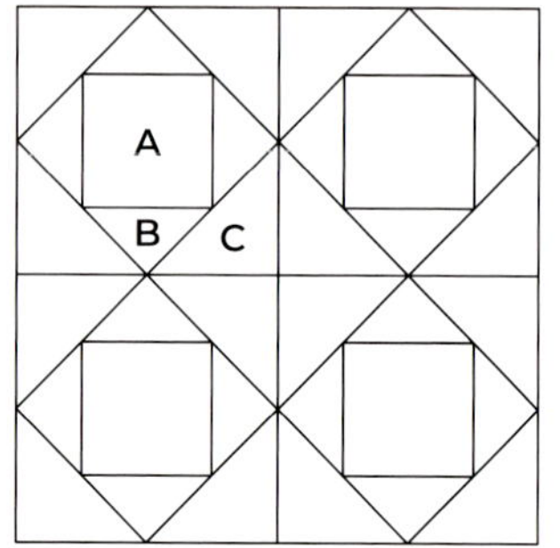

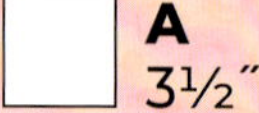

A
3½″

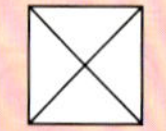

B
4¼″

C
3⅞″

january 12

BOY'S FANCY
9″ × 9″

B
C
A

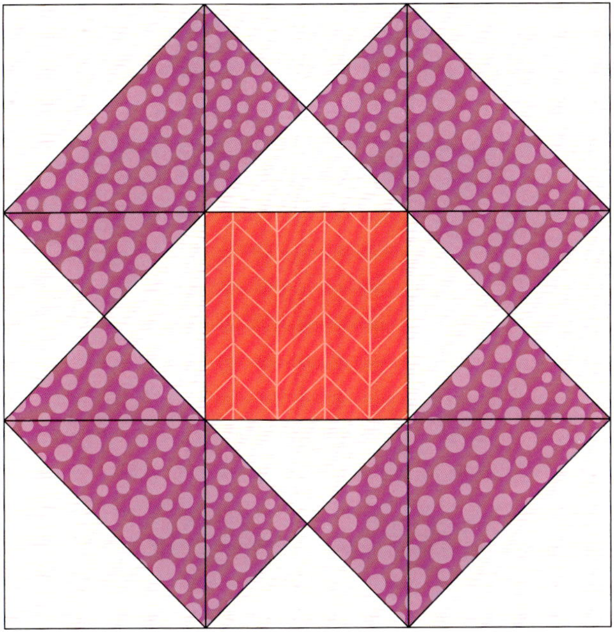

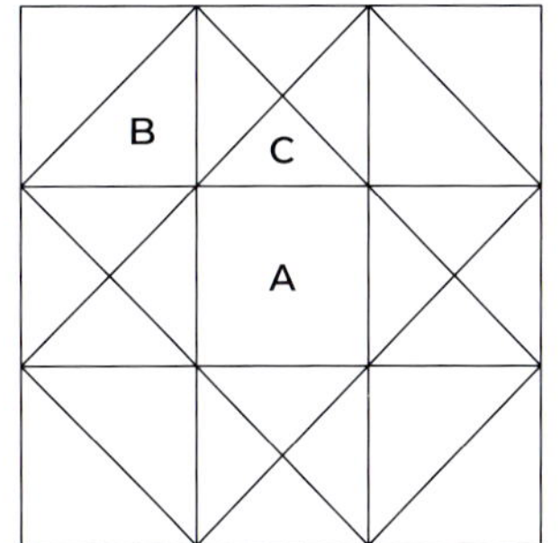

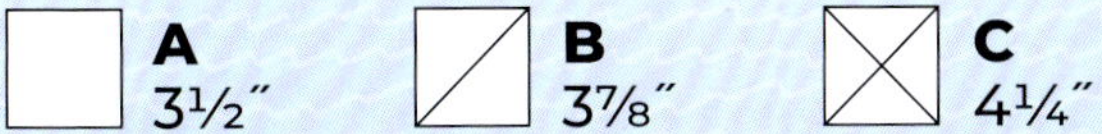

A
3½″
B
3⅞″
C
4¼″

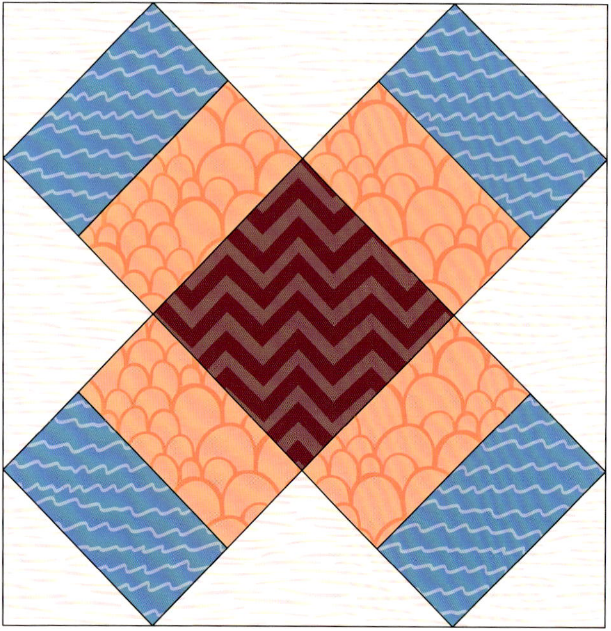

december 20

GRECIAN SQUARE

12″ × 12″

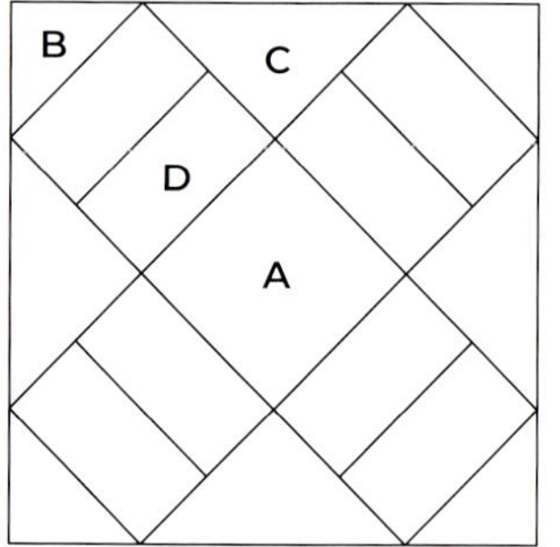

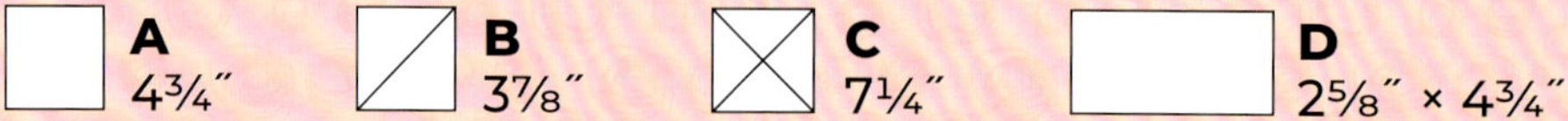

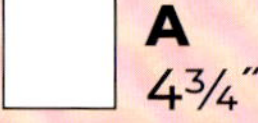

A
4¾″

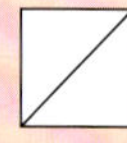

B
3⅞″

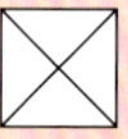

C
7¼″

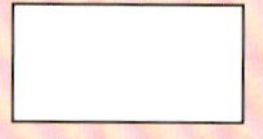

D
2⅝″ × 4¾″

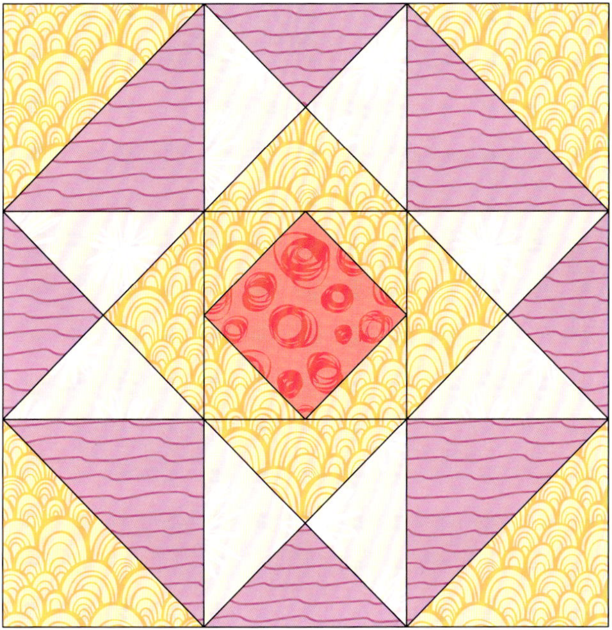

january 13

CARD BASKET
9″ × 9″

A
B
C
D

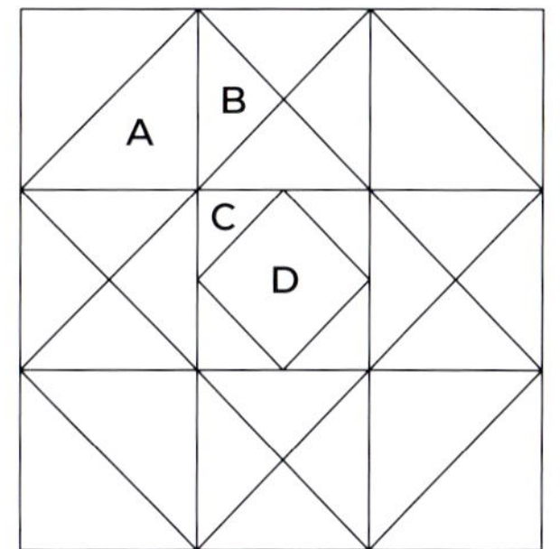

A
3⅞″
B
4¼″
C
2⅜″
D
2⅝″

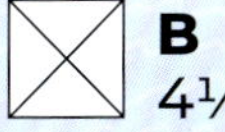

december 19

BY CHANCE

12″ × 12″

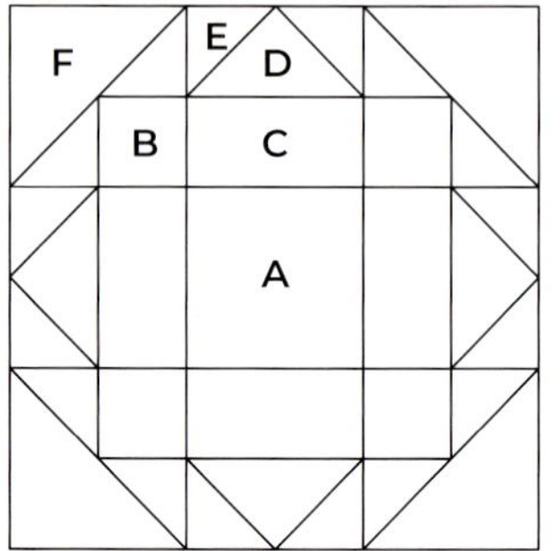

A
4½″

B
2½″

C
2½″ × 4½″

D
5¼″

E
2⅞″

F
4⅞″

january 14

SWAMP PATCH

9″ × 9″

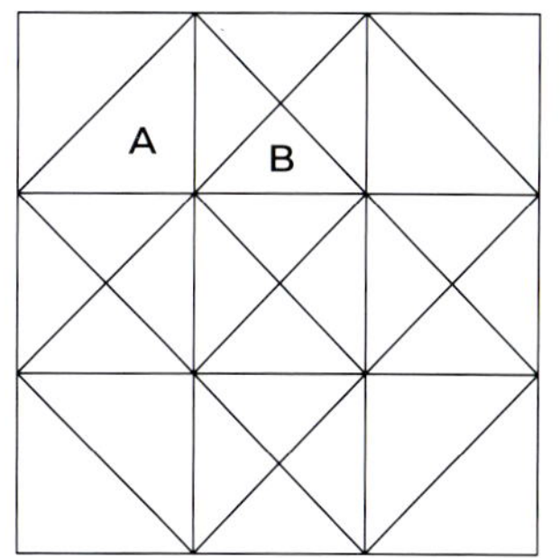

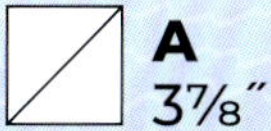

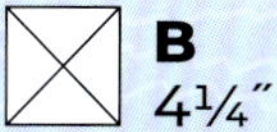

A
3⅞″

B
4¼″

december 18

BERKELEY

12″ × 12″

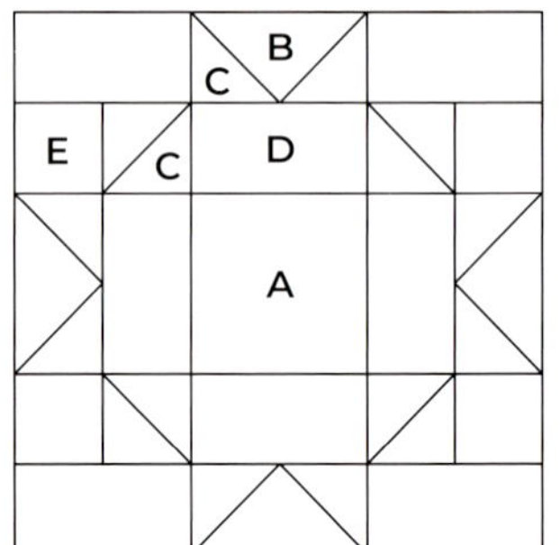

A
4½″

B
5¼″

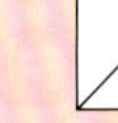

C
2⅞″

D
2½″ × 4½″

E
2½″

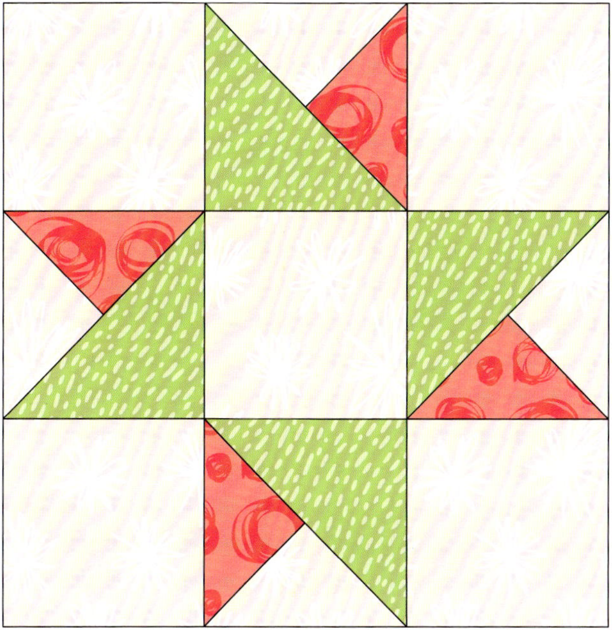

january 15

AIR CASTLE

9″ × 9″

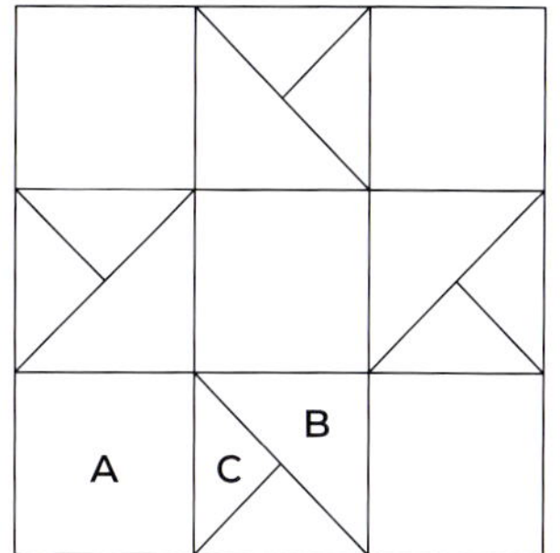

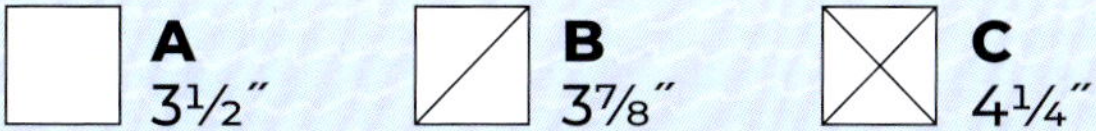

A 3½″

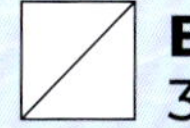

B 3⅞″

C 4¼″

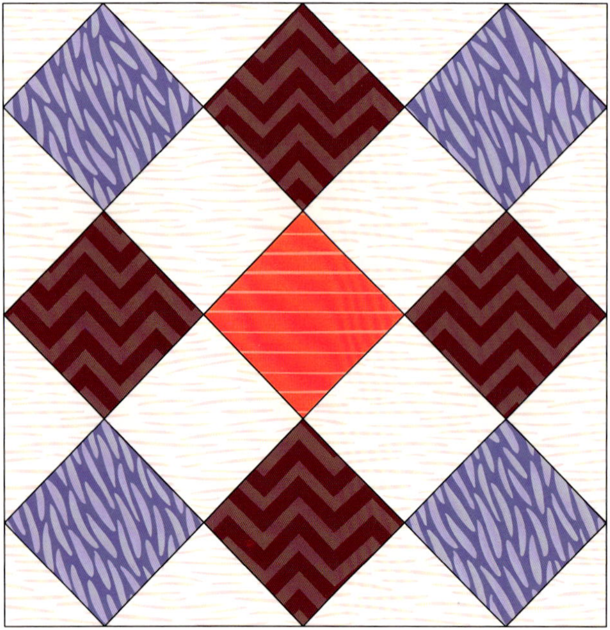

december 17

GRANDMOTHER'S PRIDE

12″ × 12″

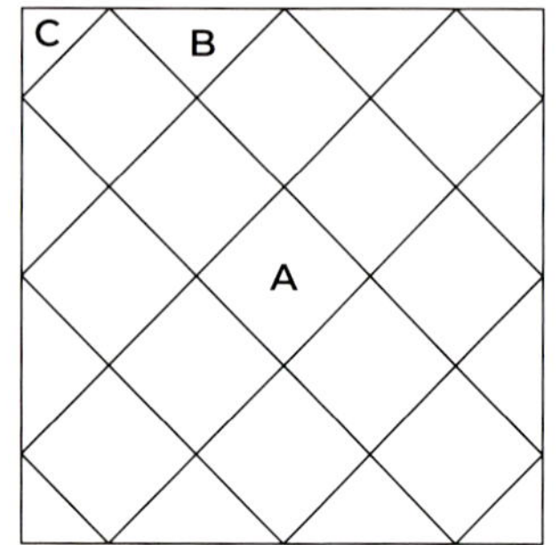

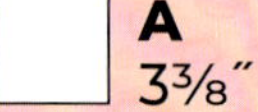

A
3⅜″

B
5¼″

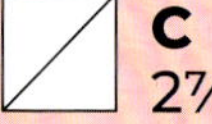

C
2⅞″

january 16

CAMELOT STAR

9″ × 9″

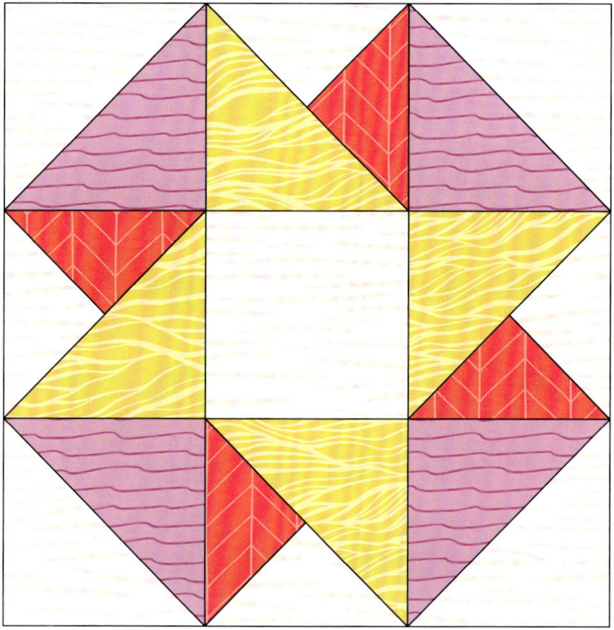

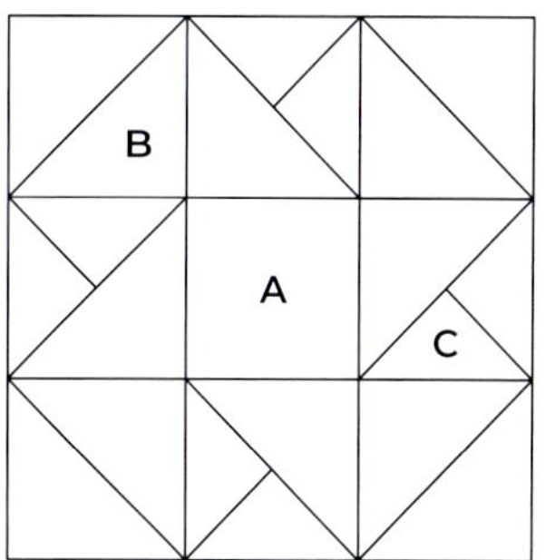

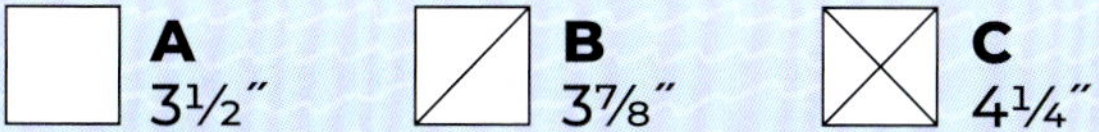

A
3½″

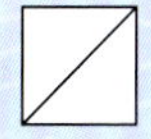

B
3⅞″

C
4¼″

december 16

CENTENNIAL

12″ × 12″

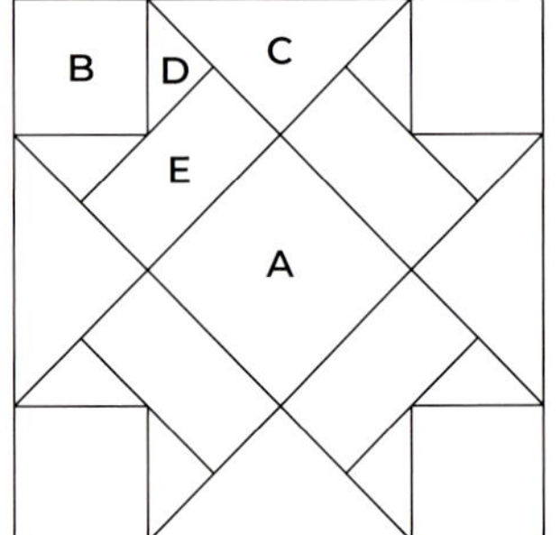

A
4¾″

B
3½″

C
7¼″

D
4¼″

E
2⅝″ × 4¾″

january 17

STEPPING STONES STAR

9″ × 9″

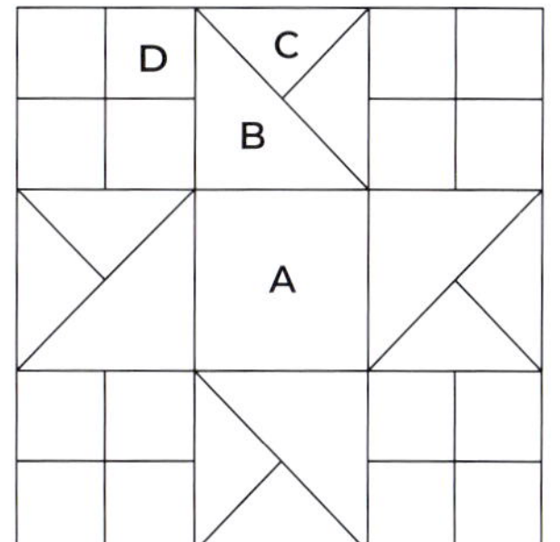

A
3½″

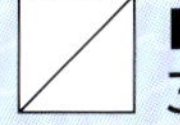

B
3⅞″

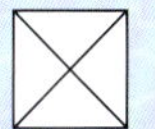

C
4¼″

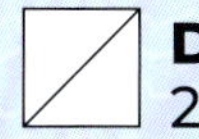

D
2″

december 15

BONNIE SCOTLAND

12″ × 12″

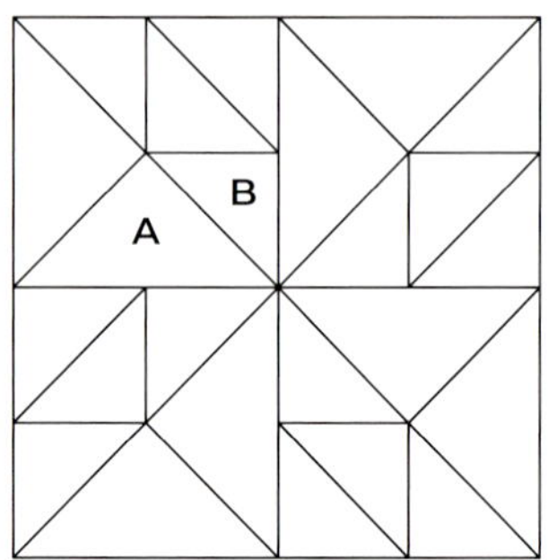

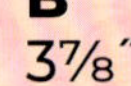

january 18

DOUBLE HEARTS

16″ × 16″

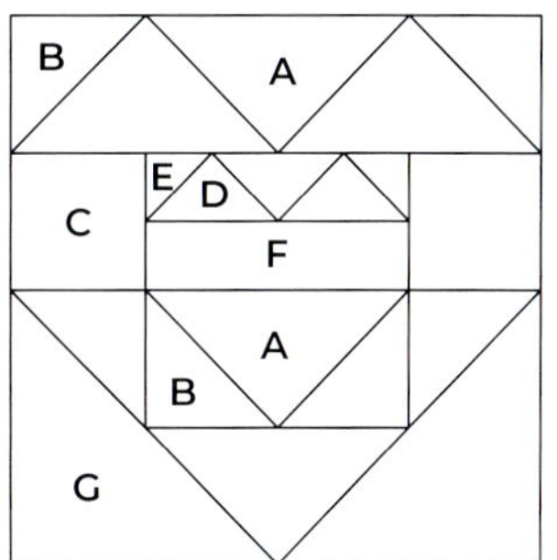

A
9¼″

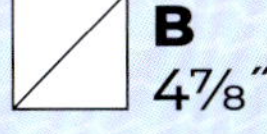

B
4⅞″

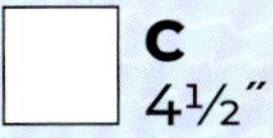

C
4½″

D
5¼″

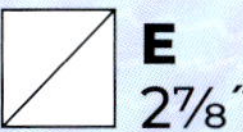

E
2⅞″

F
2½″ × 8½″

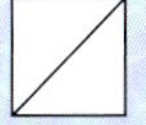

G
8⅞″

december 14

FOUR PATCH AND RAILS

8″ × 8″

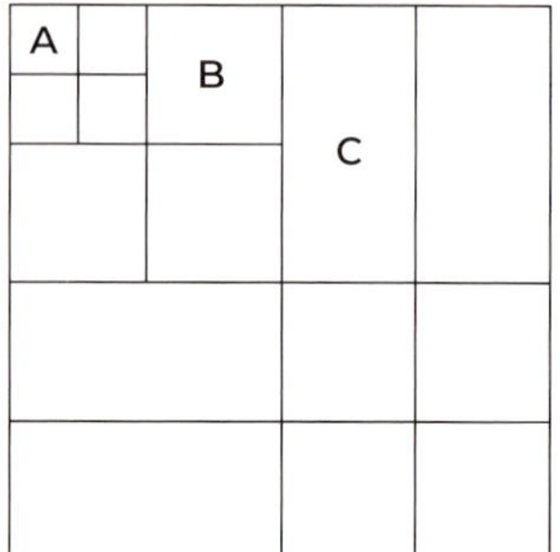

A
1½″

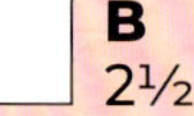

B
2½″

C
2½″ × 4½″

january 19

PARADOX

12″ × 12″

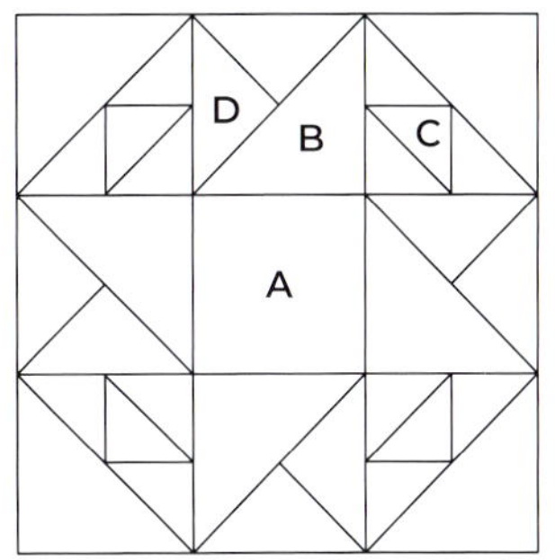

A 4½″

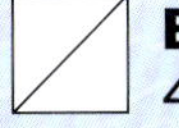

B 4⅞″

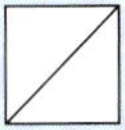

C 2⅞″

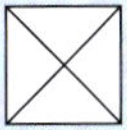

D 5¼″

december 13

MRS. KELLER'S 9 PATCH

10″ × 10″

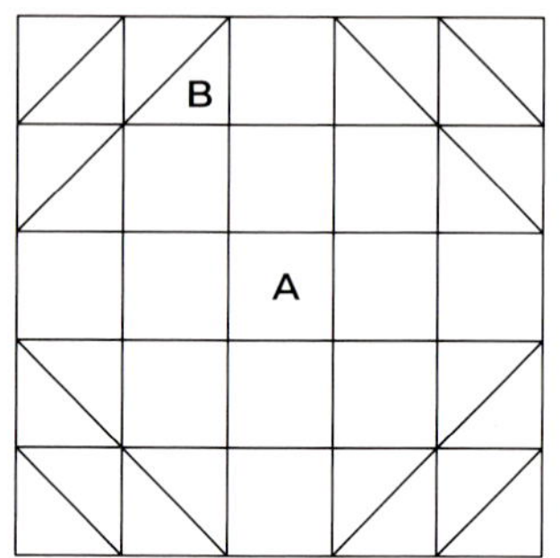

A 2½″

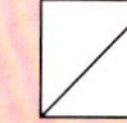

B 2⅞″

january 20

SHOOFLY MOSAIC

12″ × 12″

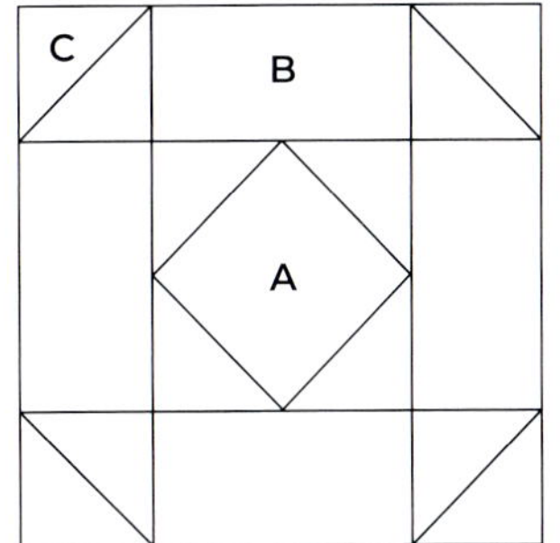

A
4¾″

B
3½″ × 6½″

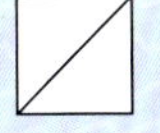

C
3⅞″

december 12

CROSSES AND LOSSES

10″ × 10″

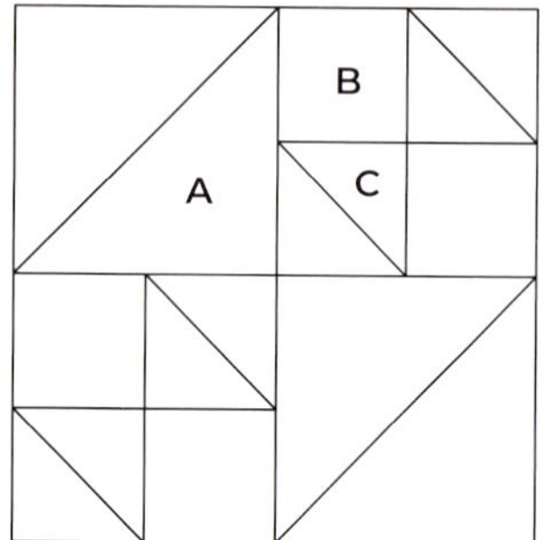

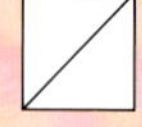

A
5⅞″

B
3″

C
3⅜″

january 21

CROWNING GLORY

12″ × 12″

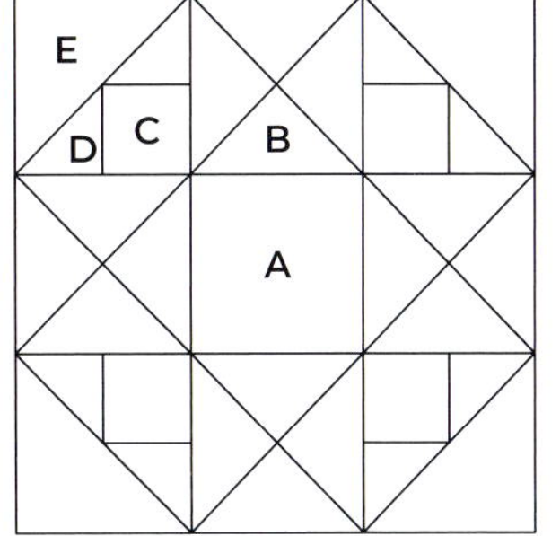

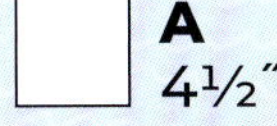

A 4½″

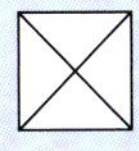

B 5¼″

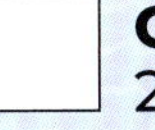

C 2½″

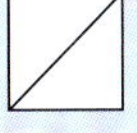

D 2⅞″

E 4⅞″

december 11

SHOOFLY AND FOUR PATCH

12″ × 12″

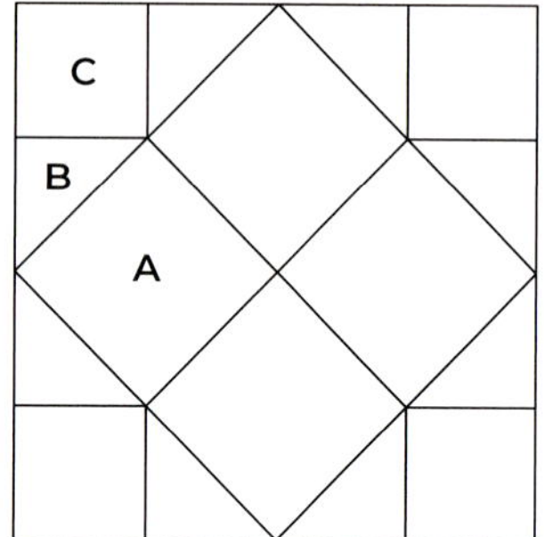

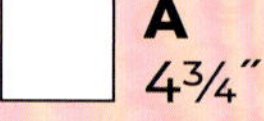

A
4¾″

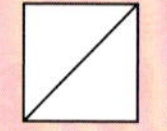

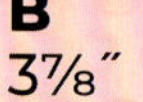

B
3⅞″

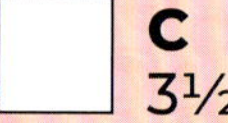

C
3½″

january 22

UNDERGROUND RAILROAD

12″ × 12″

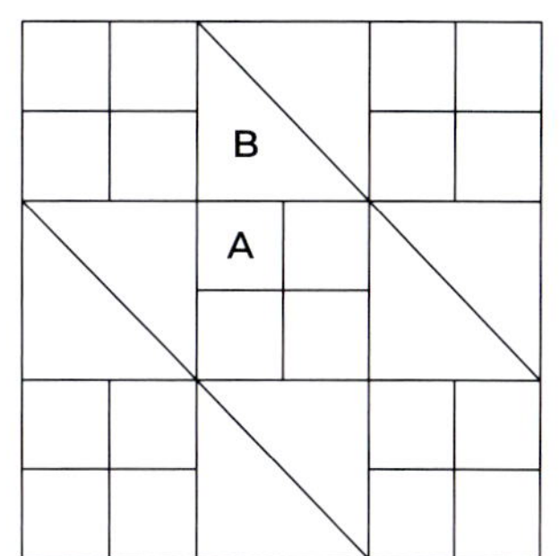

A
2½″

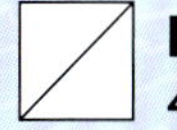

B
4⅞″

december 10

BEAR'S PAW

14″ × 14″

D
C
A
B

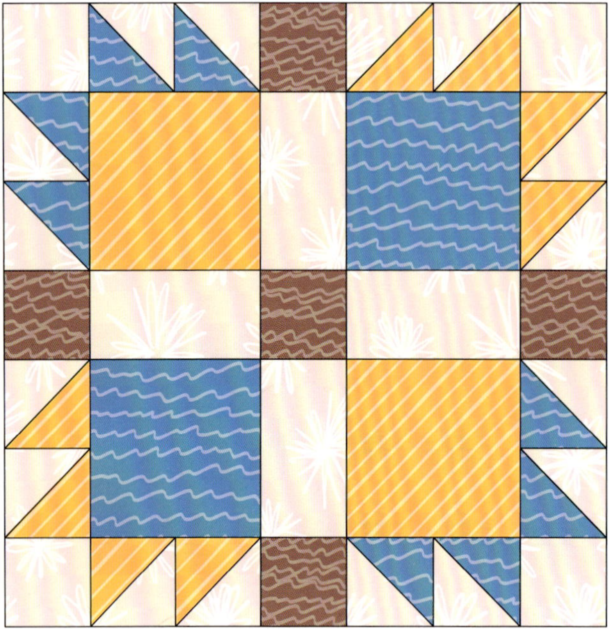

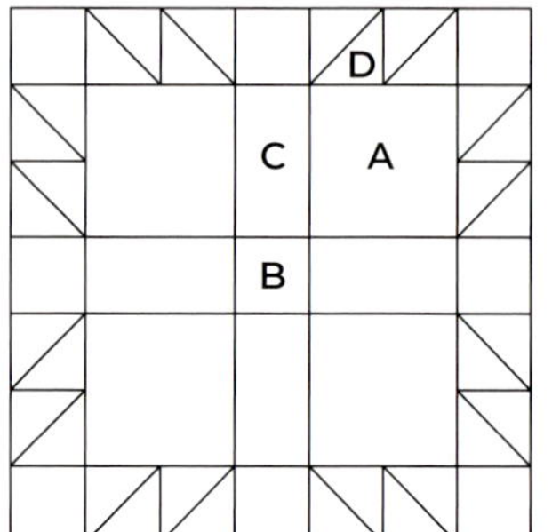

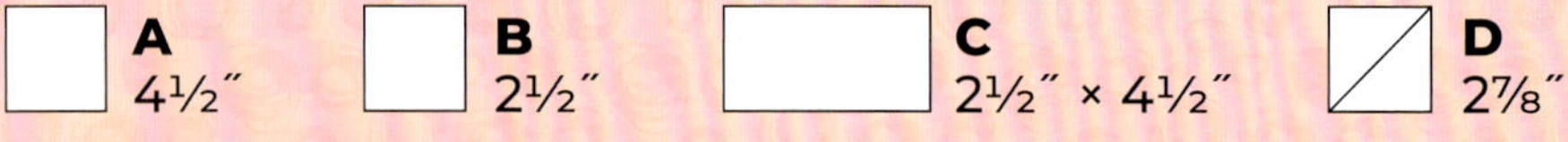

A
4½″
B
2½″
C
2½″ × 4½″
D
2⅞″

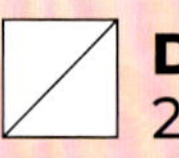

january 23

AUTOGRAPH

14″ × 14″

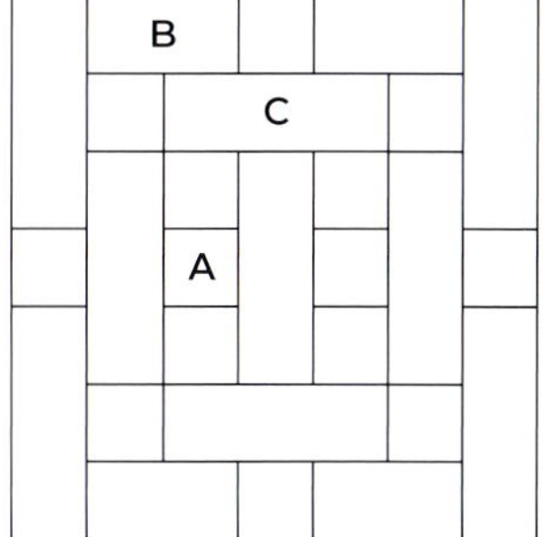

A
2½″

B
2½″ × 4½″

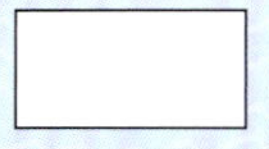

C
2½″ × 6½″

december 9

THE ROSEBUD

8″ × 8″

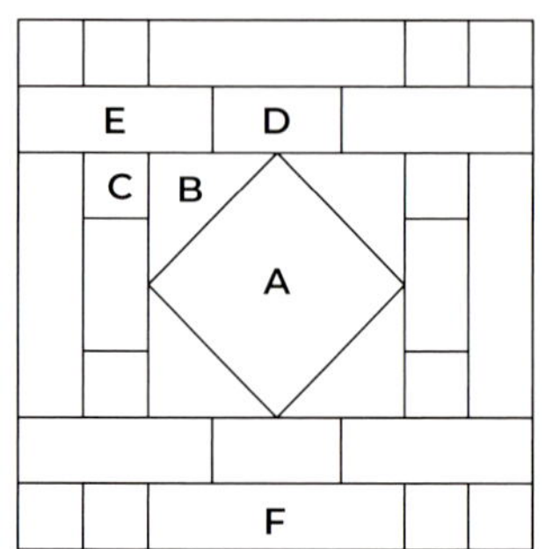

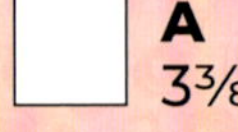

A
3⅜″

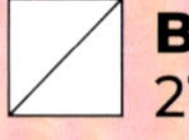

B
2⅞″

C
1½″

D
1½″ × 2½″

E
1½″ × 3½″

F
1½″ × 4½″

january 24

LOGS AND MORTAR

14″ × 14″

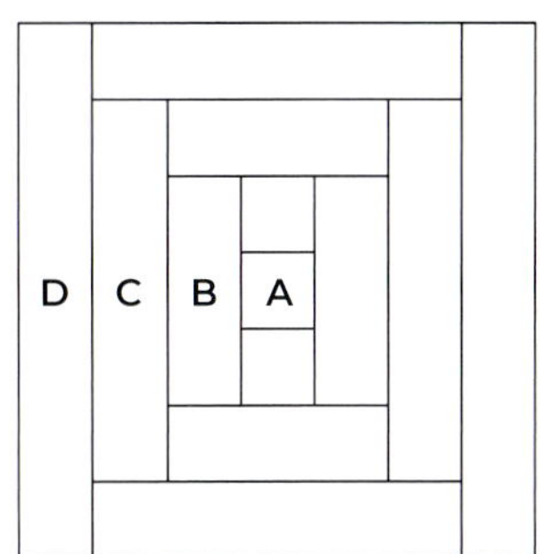

A
2½″

B
2½″ × 6½″

C
2½″ × 10½″

D
2½″ × 14½″

december 8

DOUBLE X

8″ × 8″

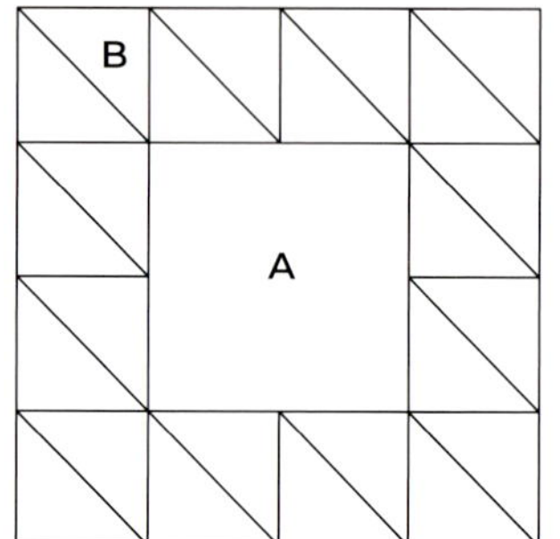

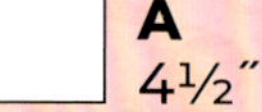

A
4½″

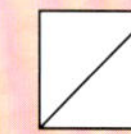

B
2⅞″

january 25

SOUTHWEST CROSS

14″ × 14″

C

B

A

A
2½″

B
2½″ × 4½″

C
4½″ × 6½″

december 7

SPINWHEEL

8″ × 8″

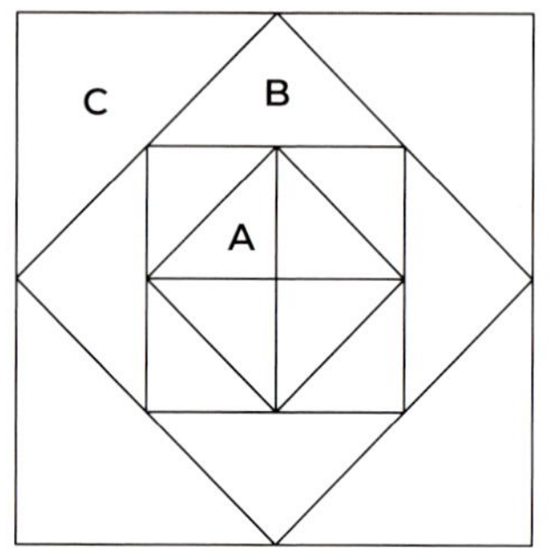

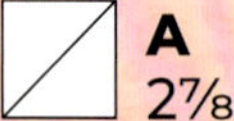

A
2⅞″

B
5¼″

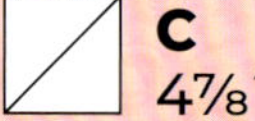

C
4⅞″

january 26

TOWN CENTER STAR

12″ × 12″

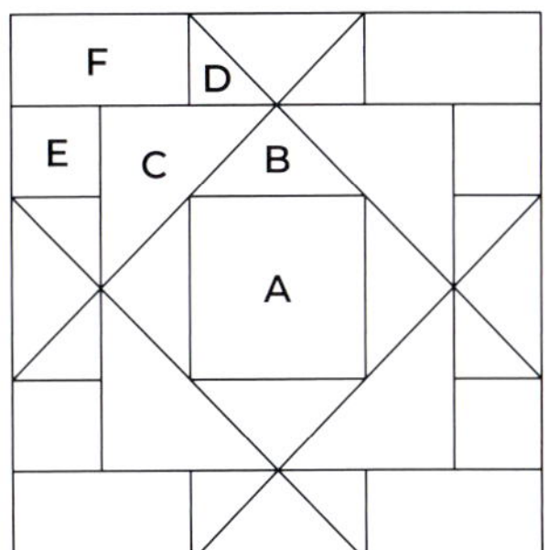

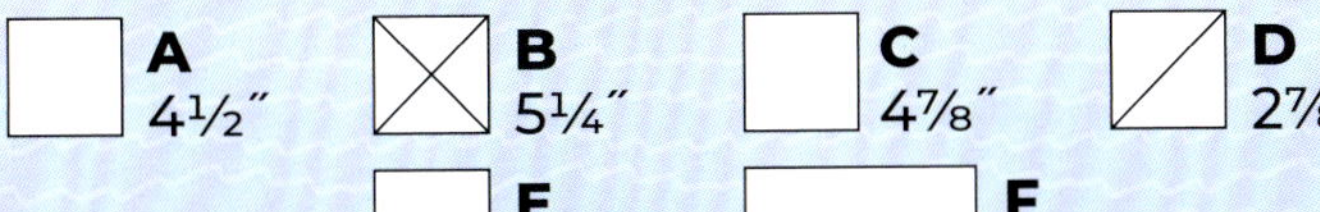

december 6

JERUSALEM BLOCK

10″ × 10″

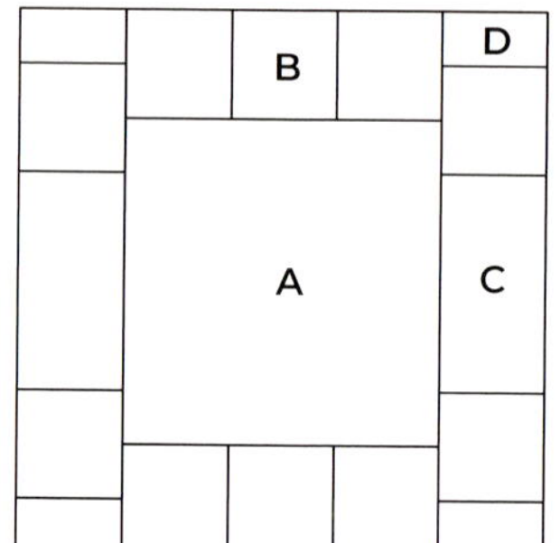

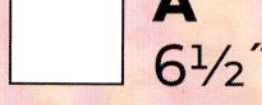

A
6½″

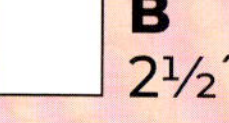

B
2½″

C
2½″ × 4½″

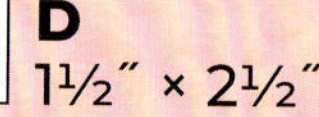

D
1½″ × 2½″

january 27

PRAIRIE FLOWER

8″ × 8″

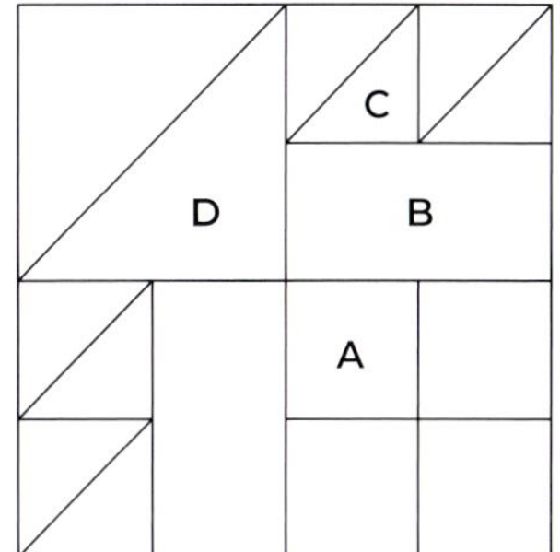

A
2½″

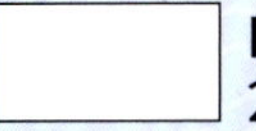

B
2½″ × 4½″

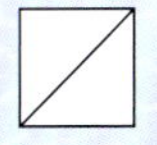

C
2⅞″

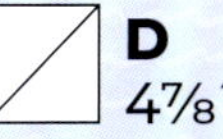

D
4⅞″

december 5

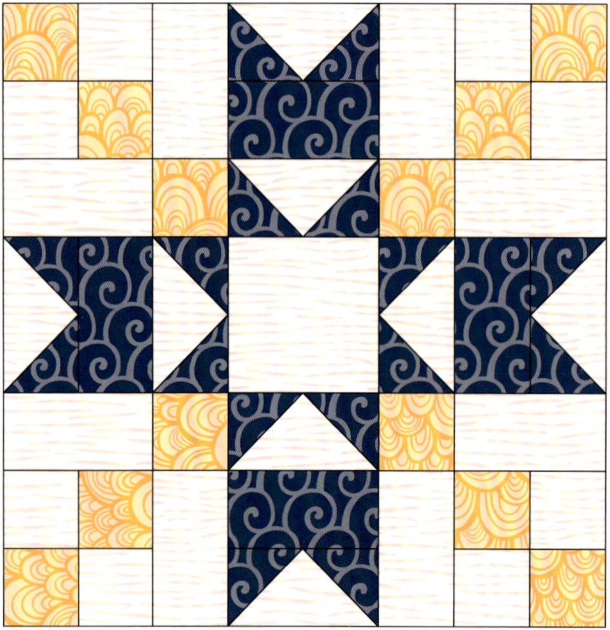

STAR OF HOPE

16″ × 16″

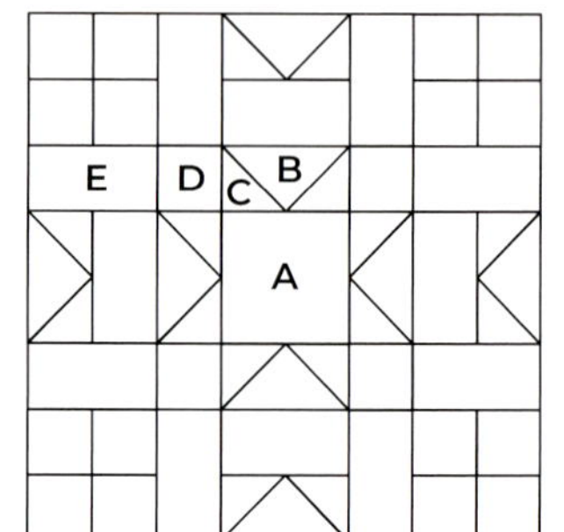

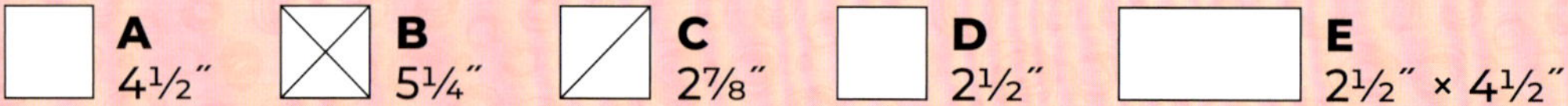

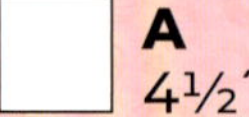

A
4½″

B
5¼″

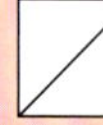

C
2⅞″

D
2½″

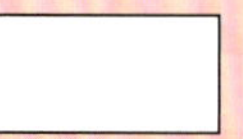

E
2½″ × 4½″

january 28

CROSS AND CROWN

14″ × 14″

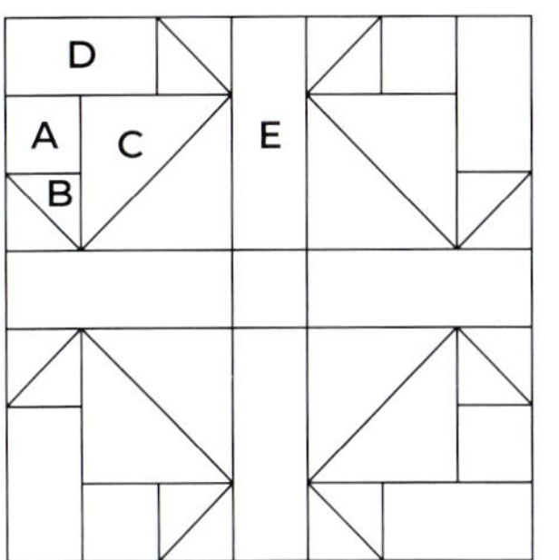

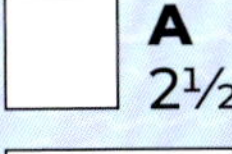

A
2½″

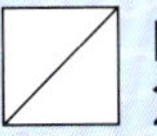

B
2⅞″

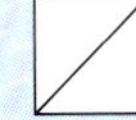

C
4⅞″

D
2½″ × 4½″

E
2½″ × 6½″

december 4

FOUR AND NINE

16″ × 16″

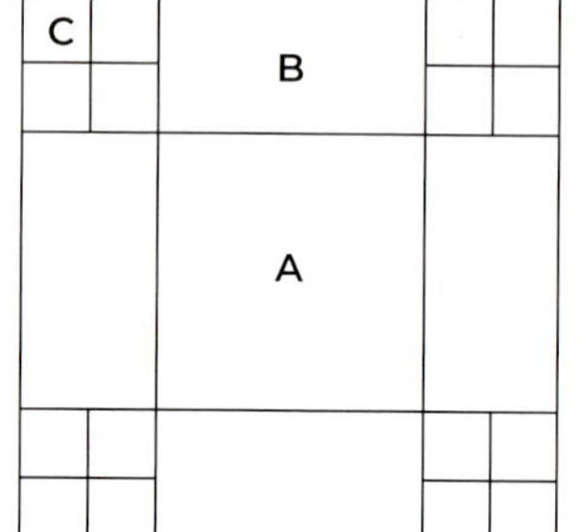

A
8½″

B
4½″ × 8½″

C
2½″

january 29

DOVE AT THE WINDOW

18″ × 18″

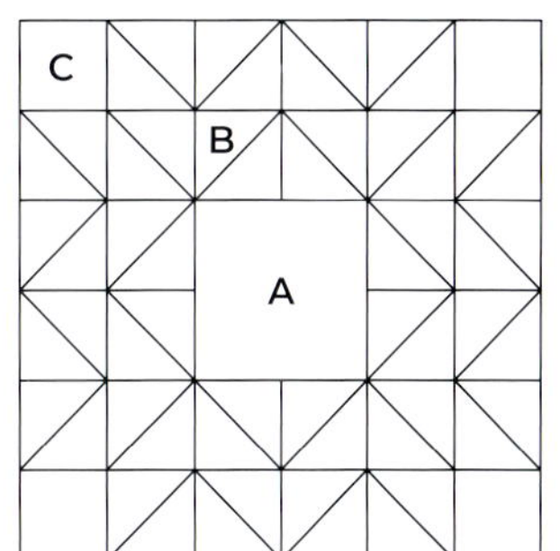

A 6½″

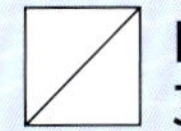

B 3⅞″

C 3½″

december 3

YULE TREE

9″ × 9″

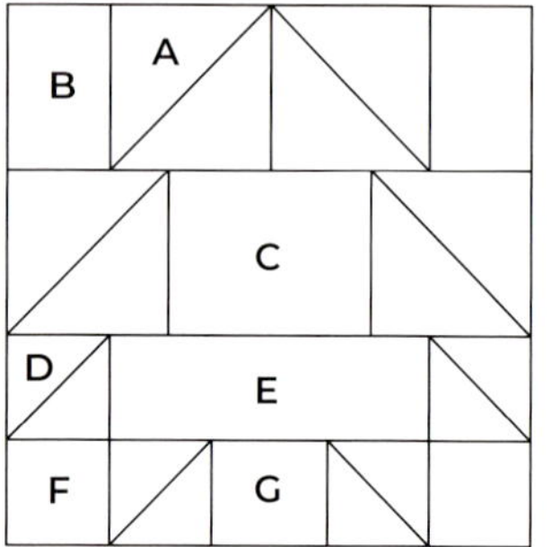

A
3⅝″

B
2¼″ × 3¼″

C
3¼″ × 4″

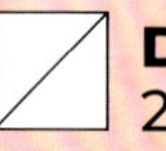

D
2⅝″

E
2¼″ × 6″

F
2¼″

G
2½″ × 2¼″

january 30

DOVE IN THE WINDOW

14″ × 14″

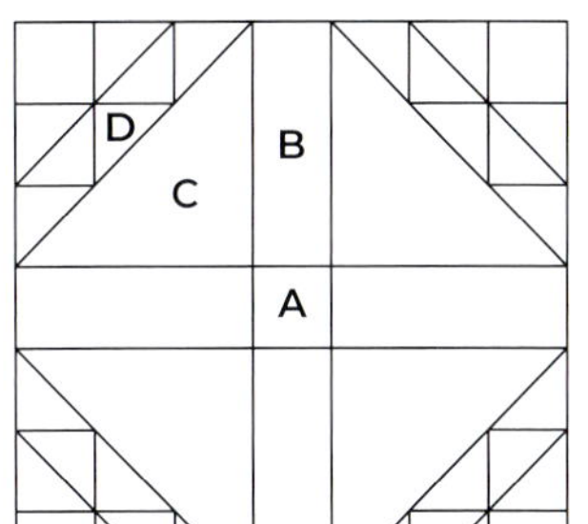

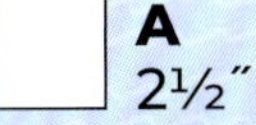

A
2½″

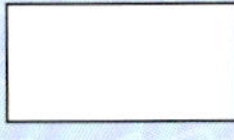

B
2½″ × 6½″

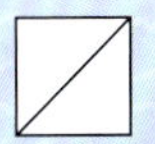

C
6⅞″

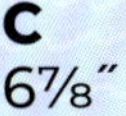

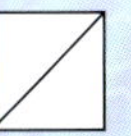

D
2⅞″

december 2

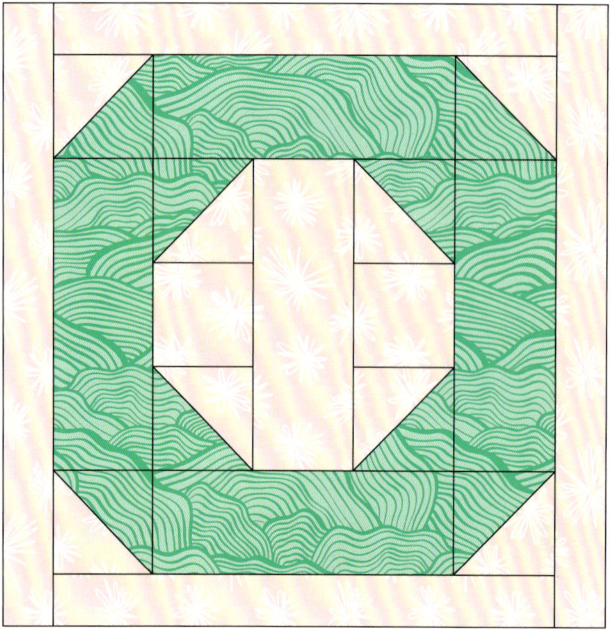

WREATH BLOCK

9″ × 9″

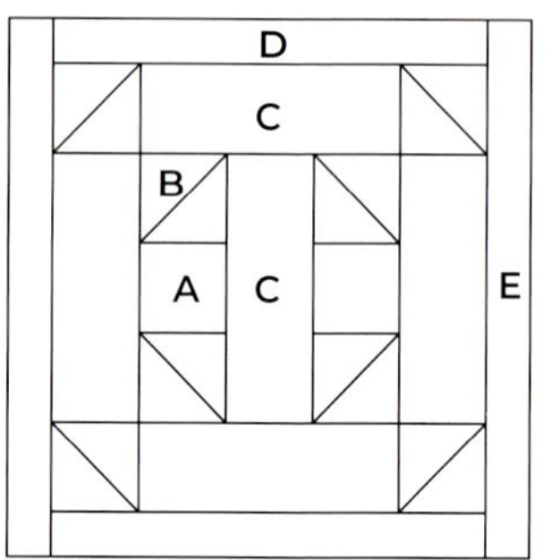

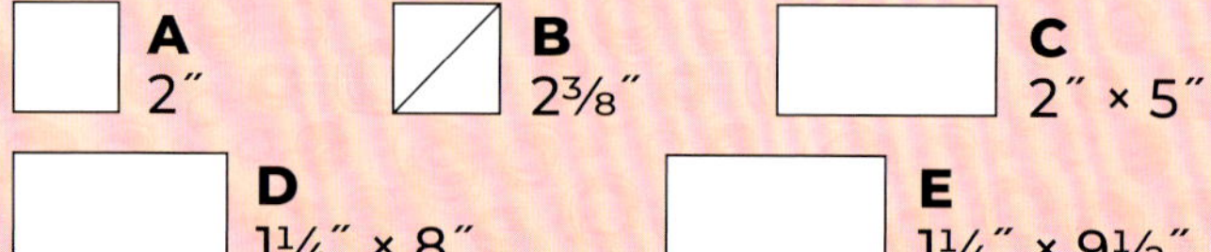

january 31

NORTHWIND BLOCK

8″ × 8″

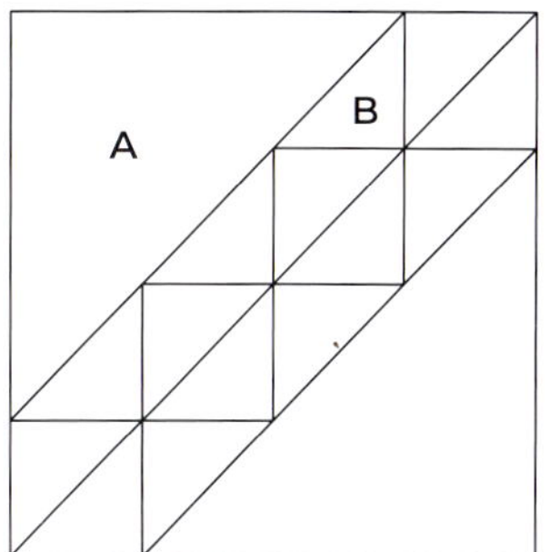

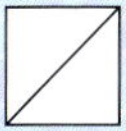

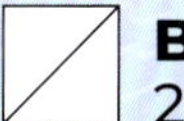

A
6⅞″

B
2⅞″

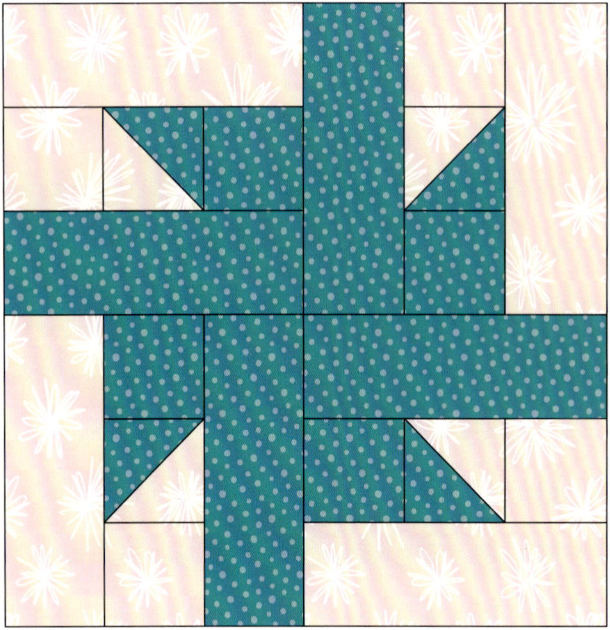

december 1

TESSELATING STAR

12″ × 12″

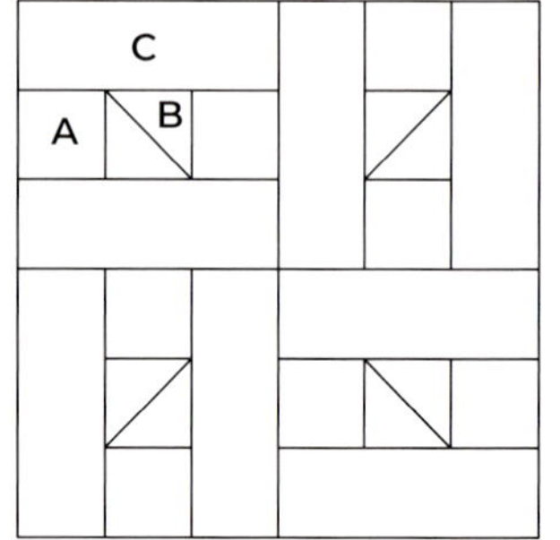

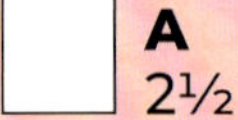

A
2½″

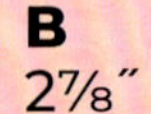

B
2⅞″

C
2½″ × 6½″

february 1

SNAIL'S TRAIL

16″ × 16″

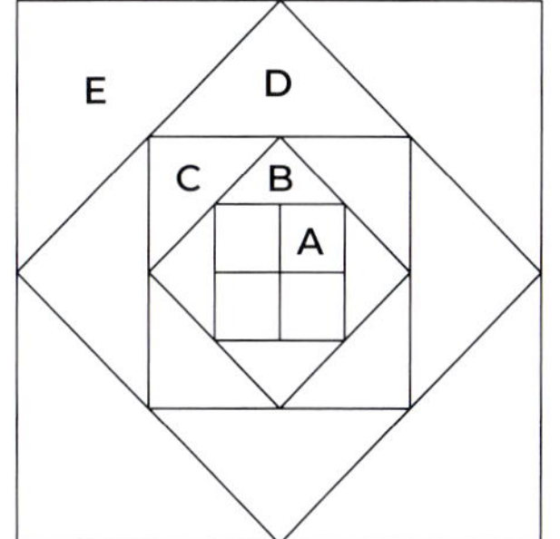

A
2½″

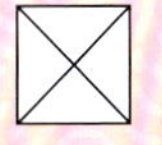

B
5¼″

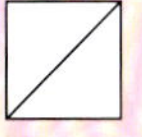

C
4⅞″

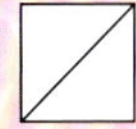

D
9¼″

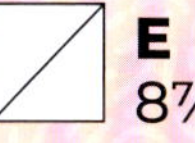

E
8⅞″

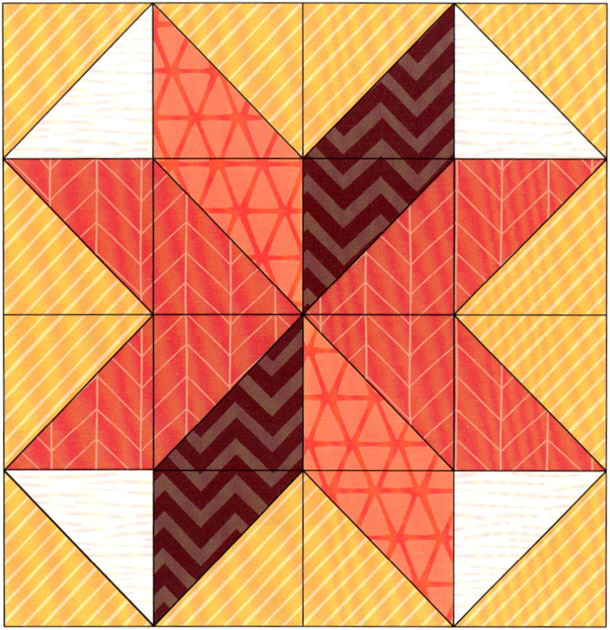

november 30

STAR PUZZLE
16″ × 16″

A
4⅞″

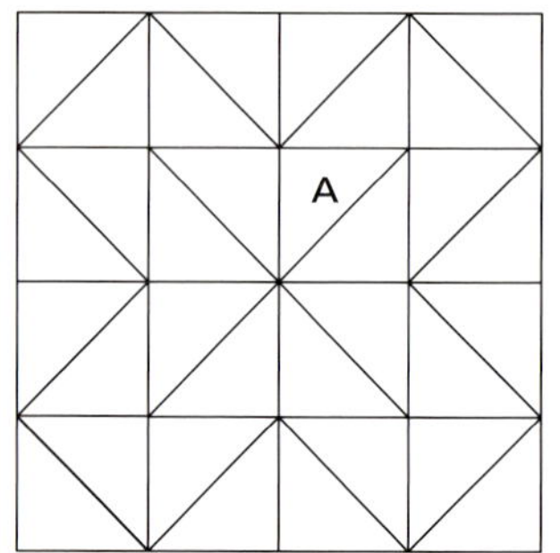

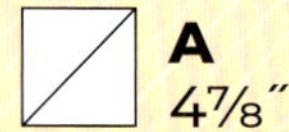

february 2

STAR AND CROSS BLOCK

15″ × 15″

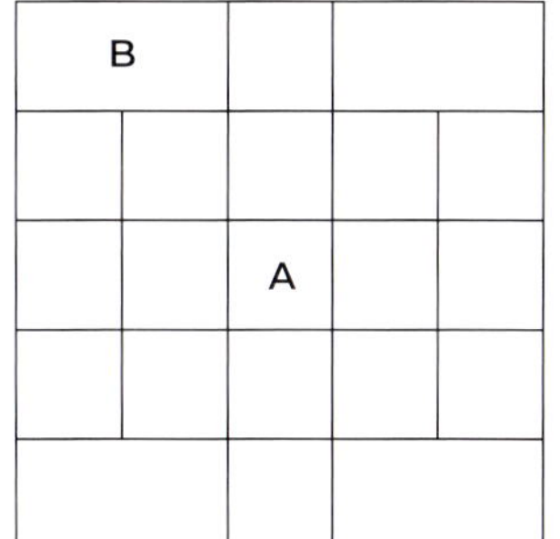

A
3½″

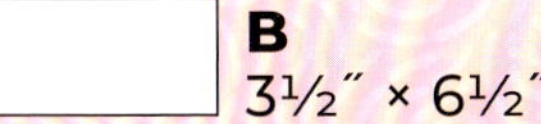

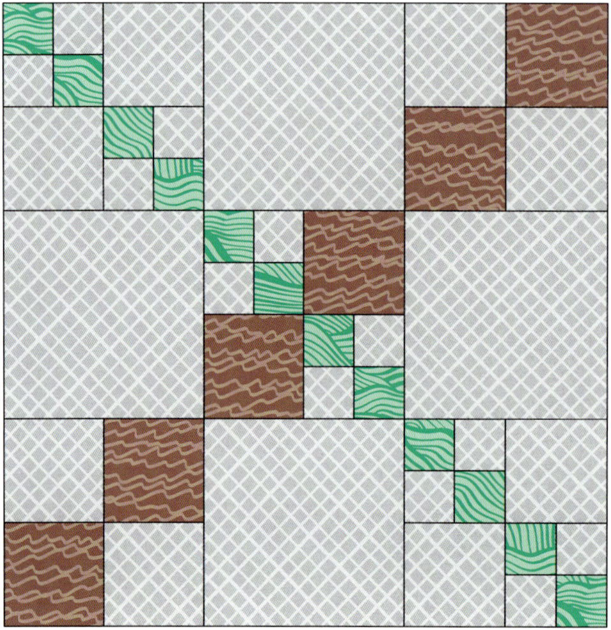

november 29

FOUR PATCH IN NINE

12″ × 12″

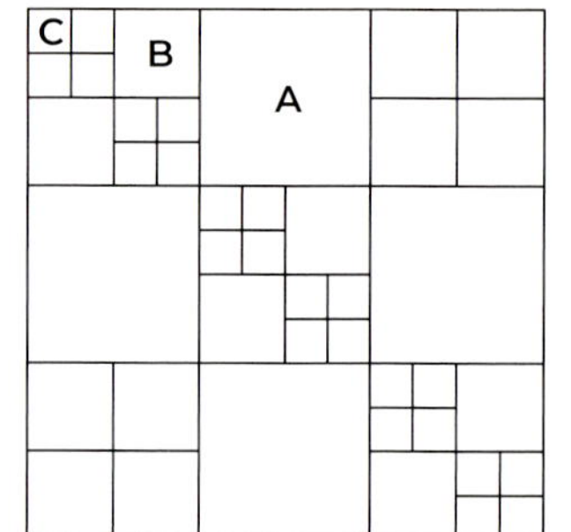

A 4½″

B 2½″

C 1½″

february 3

GARDEN OF EDEN

10″ × 10″

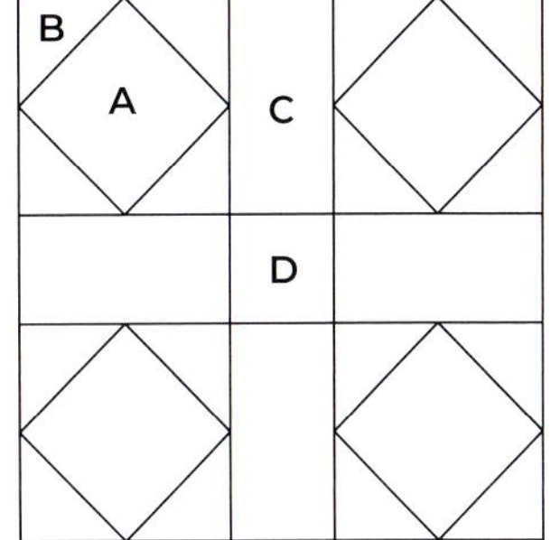

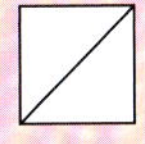

A
3 3/8″

B
2 7/8″

C
2 1/2″ × 4 1/2″

D
2 1/2″

november 28

BUILDING BLOCKS

12″ × 12″

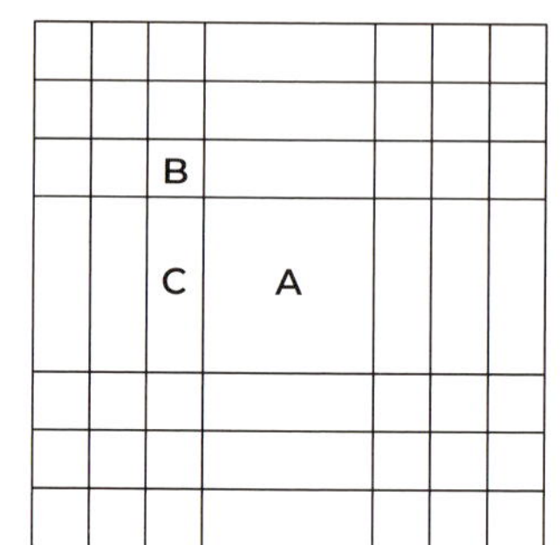

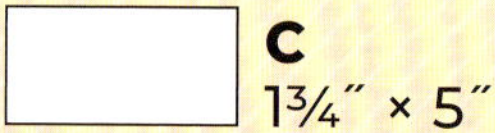

A
5″

B
1¾″

C
1¾″ × 5″

february 4

DUCK'S FOOT

10″ × 10″

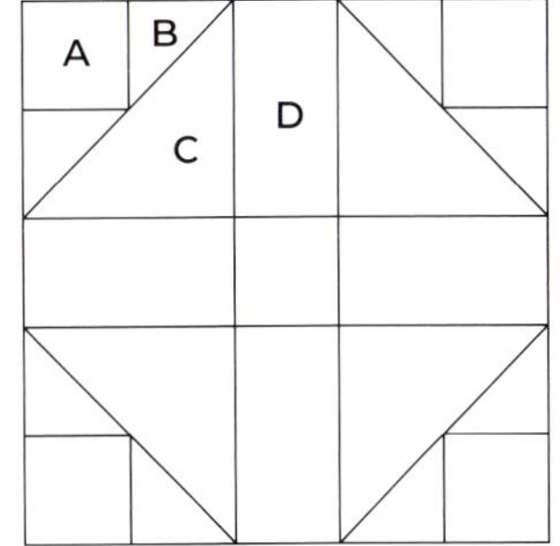

A
2½″

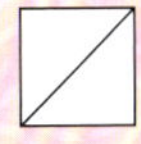

B
2⅞″

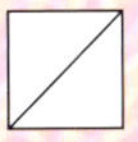

C
4⅞″

D
2½″ × 4½″

november 27

TIC TAC TOE

12″ × 12″

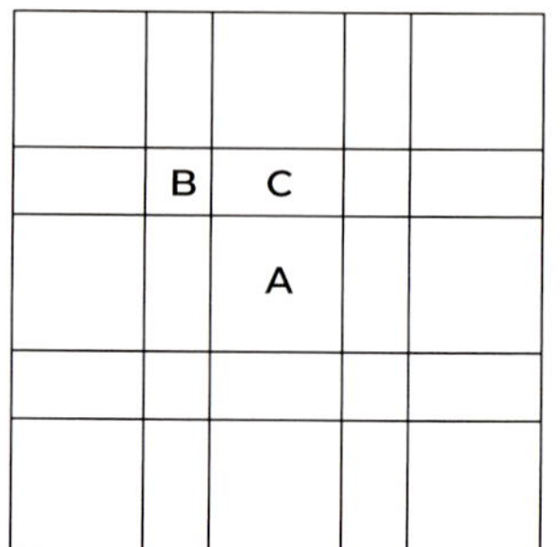

A
3½″

B
2″

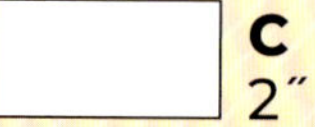

C
2″ × 3½″

february 5

CROSSED SQUARES
10″ × 10″

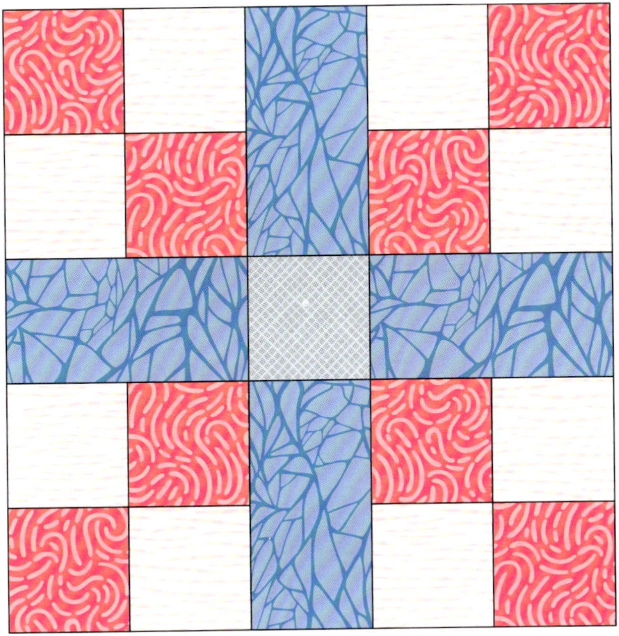

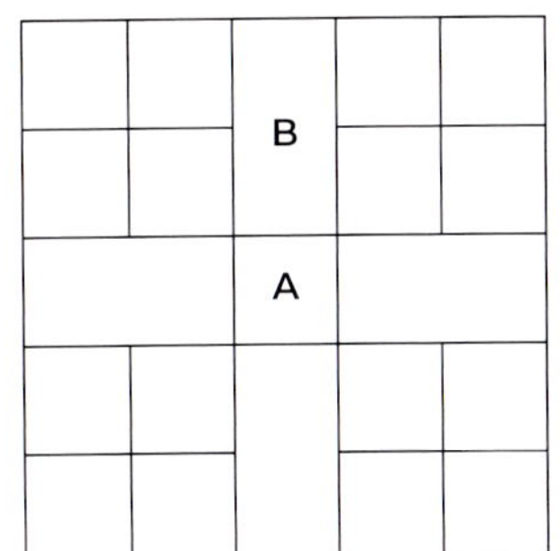

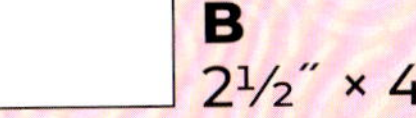

november 26

MOVING STAR

12″ × 12″

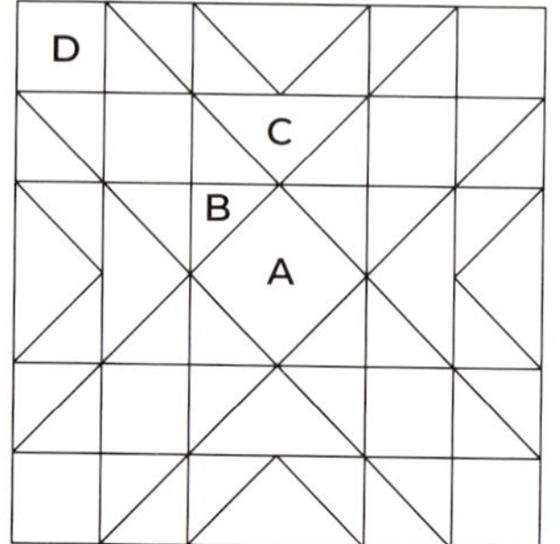

A
3⅜″

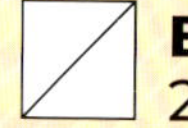

B
2⅞″

C
5¼″

D
2½″

february 6

MULTIPLE SQUARES
10″ × 10″

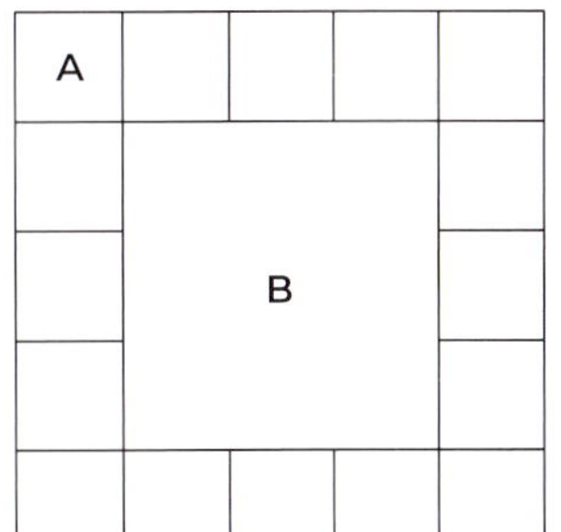

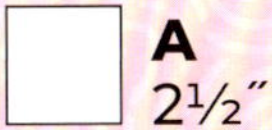

A
2½″

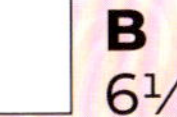

B
6½″

november 25

STEPPING STAR

18″ × 18″

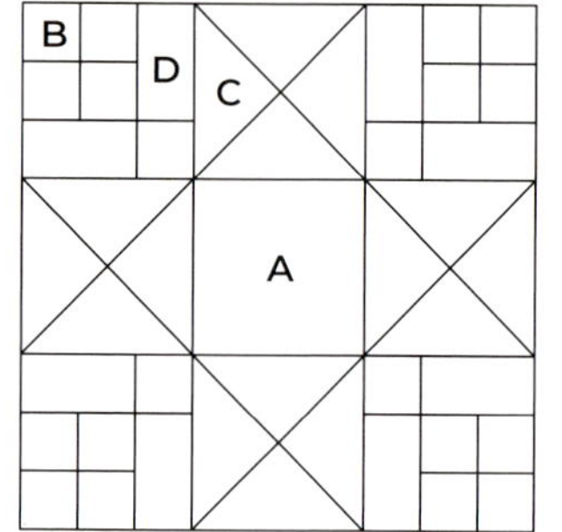

A 6½″

B 2½″

C 7¼″

D 2½″ × 4½″

february 7

4 PATCH AND RAILS

16″ × 16″

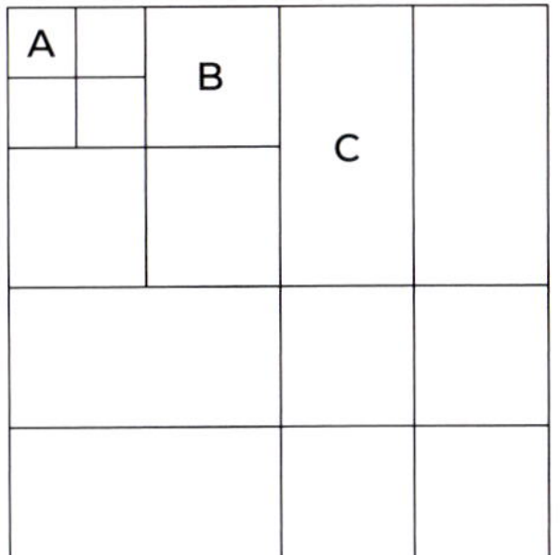

A
2½″

B
4½″

C
4½″ × 8½″

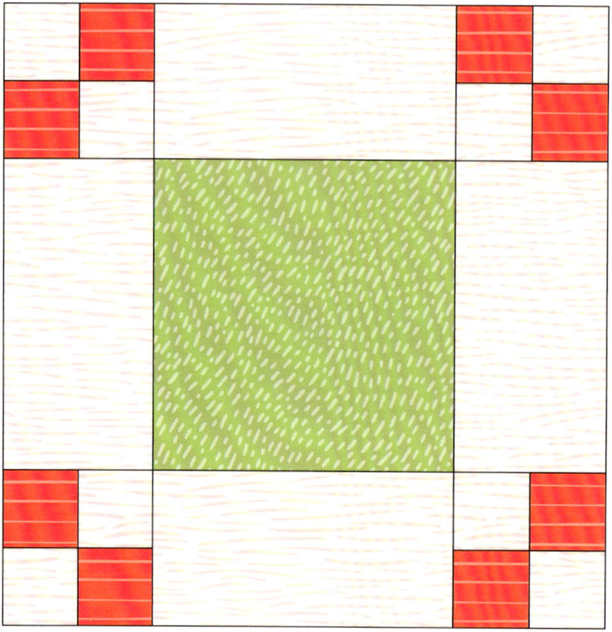

november 24

FOUR CORNERS

16″ × 16″

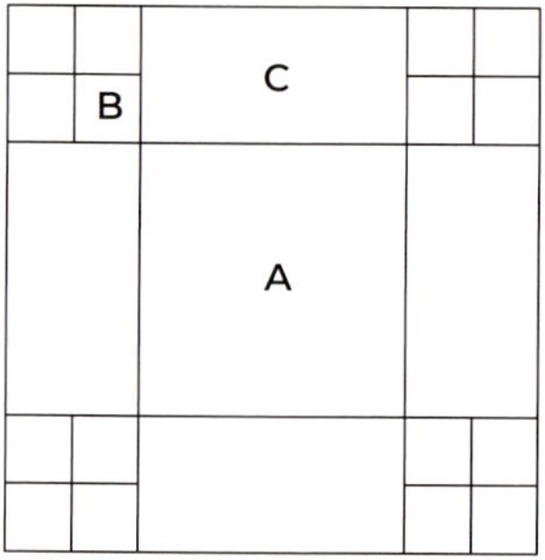

C

B

A

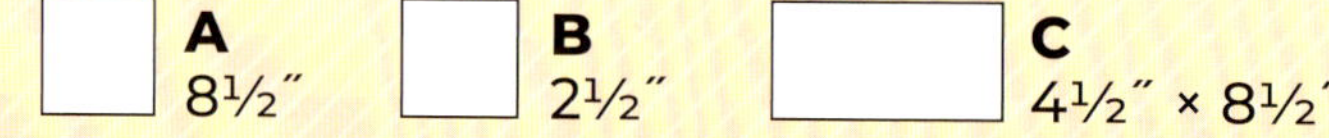

february 8

HOURGLASS VARIATION

16″ × 16″

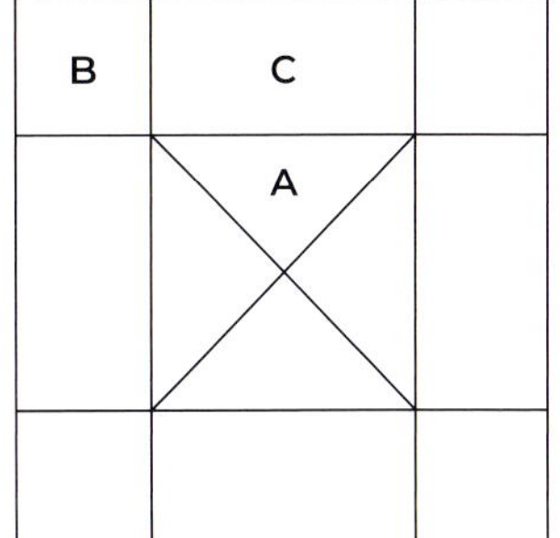

A
9¼″

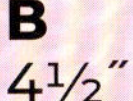

B
4½″

C
4½″ × 8½″

november 23

FLYING DUTCHMAN

12″ × 12″

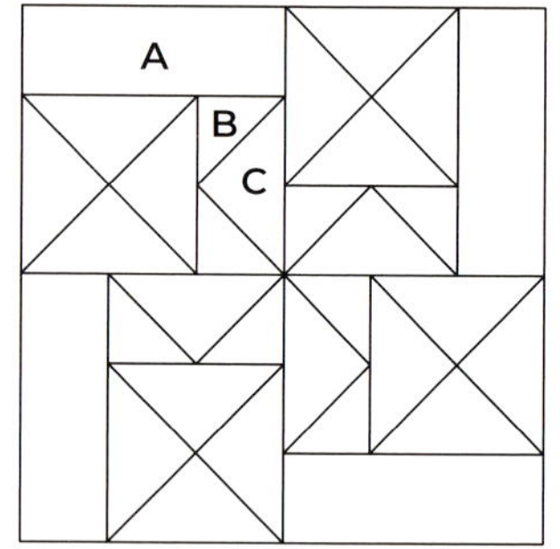

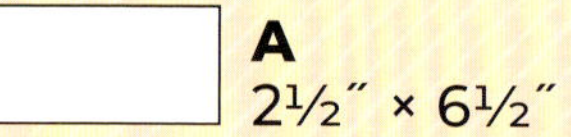

A
$2\frac{1}{2}$″ × $6\frac{1}{2}$″

B
$2\frac{7}{8}$″

C
$5\frac{1}{4}$″

february 9

LITTLE HOUSE

6″ × 6″

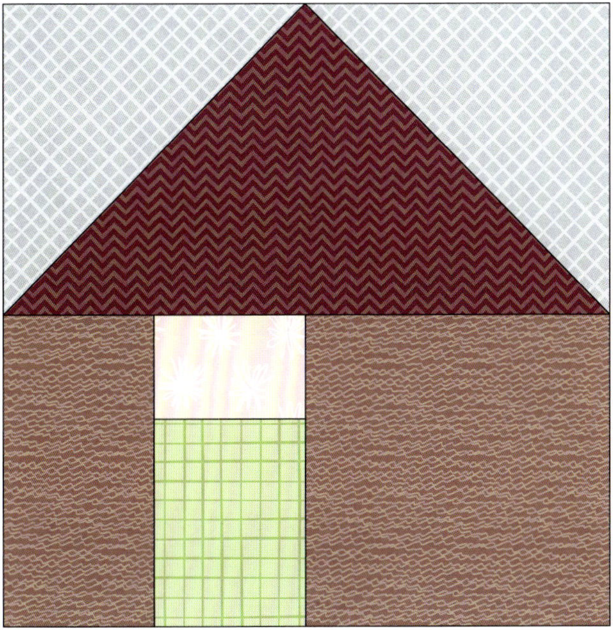

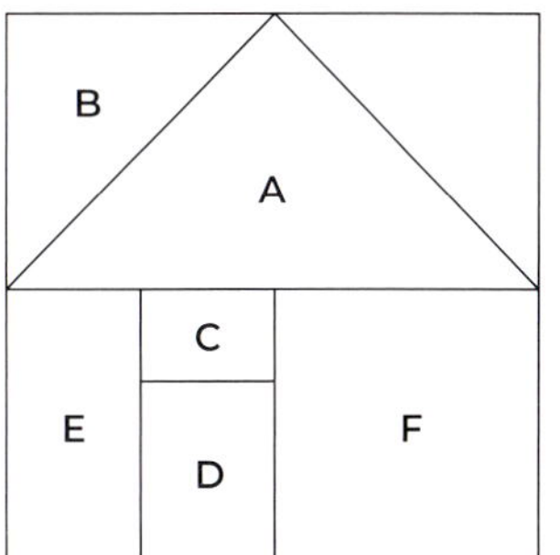

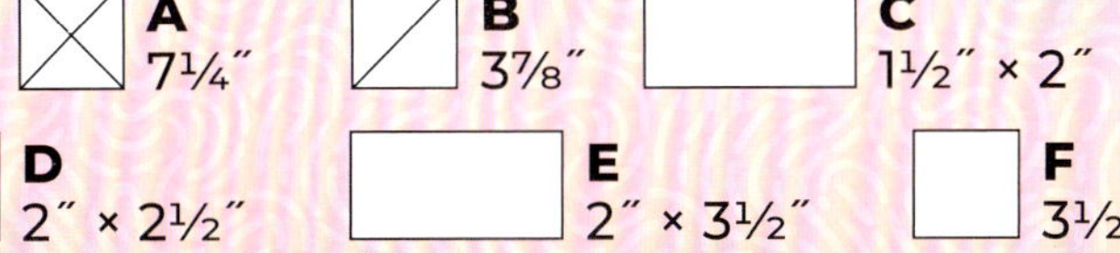

november 22

PUSS IN BOOTS

12″ × 12″

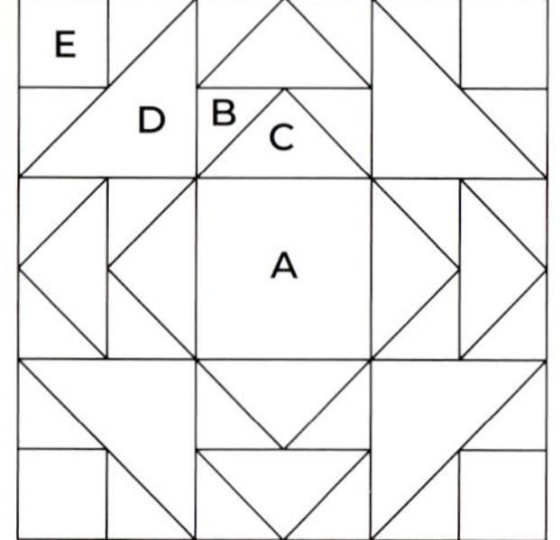

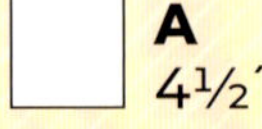

A
4½″

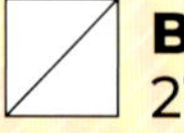

B
2⅞″

C
5¼″

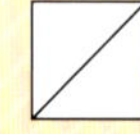

D
4⅞″

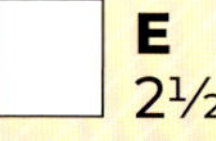

E
2½″

february 10

LONE PINE TREE

6″ × 6″

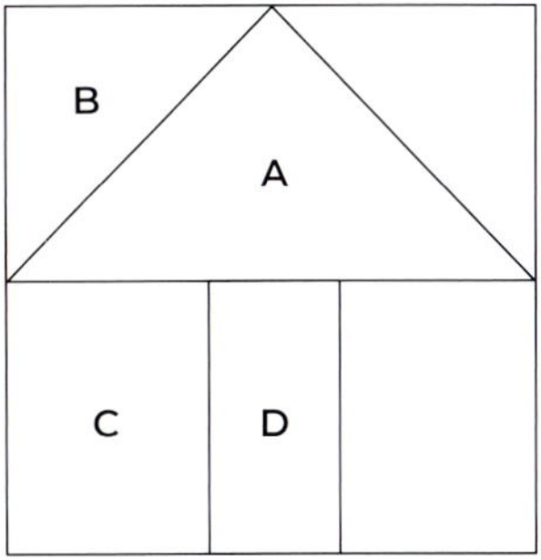

B

A

C

D

A
7¼″

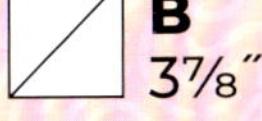

B
3⅞″

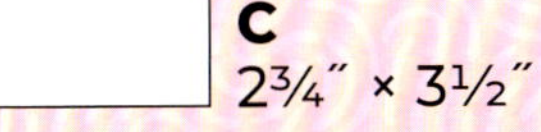

C
2¾″ × 3½″

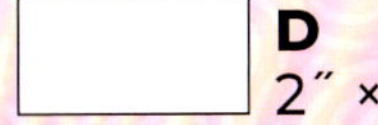

D
2″ × 3½″

november 21

DIAGONAL STAR

24″ × 24″

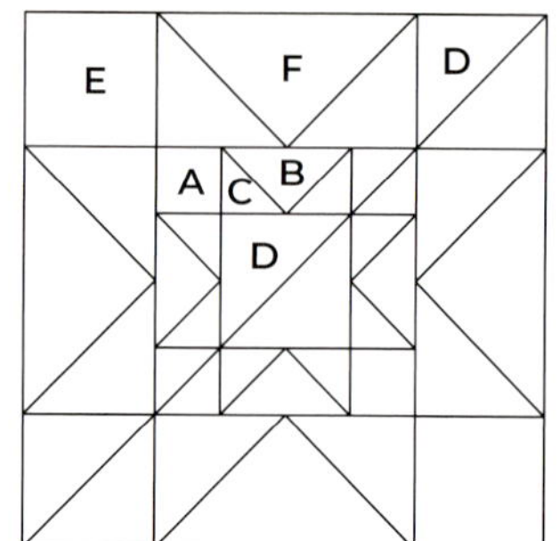

A	3½″
B	7¼″
C	3⅞″
D	6⅞″
E	6½″
F	13¼″

february 11

LITTLE STAR BLOCK

6″ × 6″

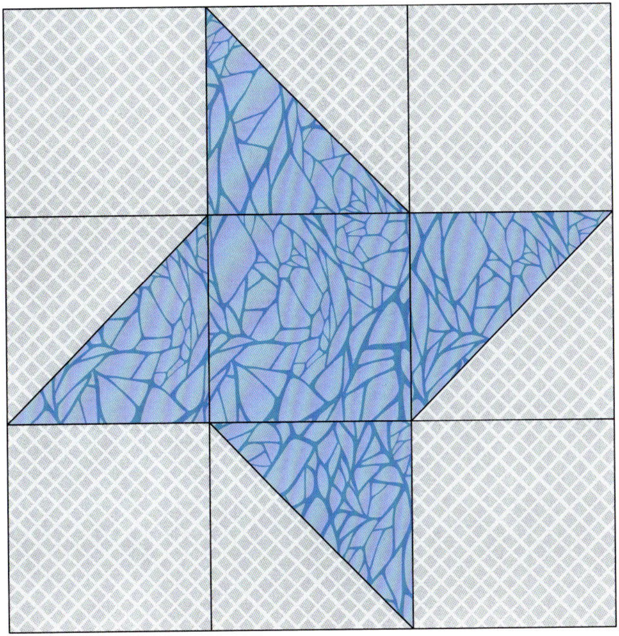

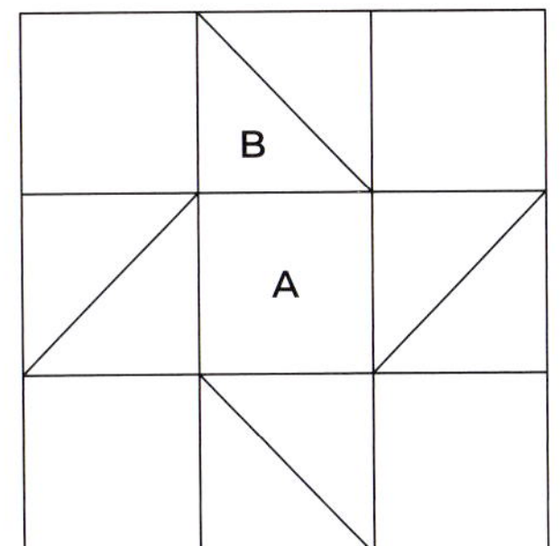

A
2½″

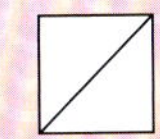

B
2⅞″

november 20

SQUASH BLOSSOM

12″ × 12″

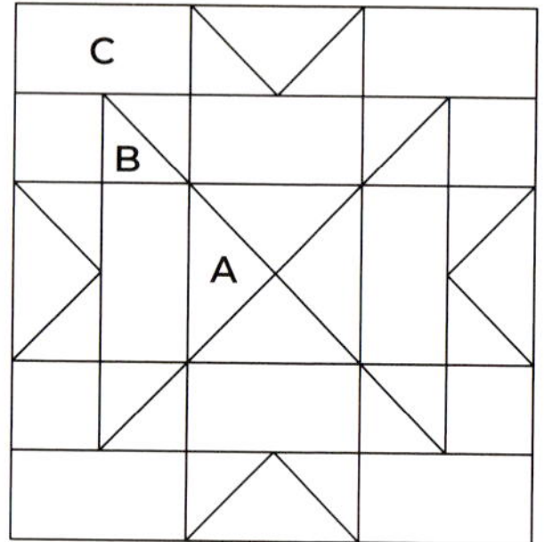

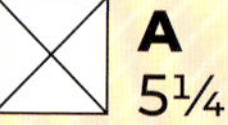

A
5¼″

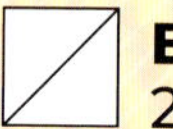

B
2⅞″

C
2½″ × 4½″

february 12

LINCOLN'S PLATFORM

14″ × 14″

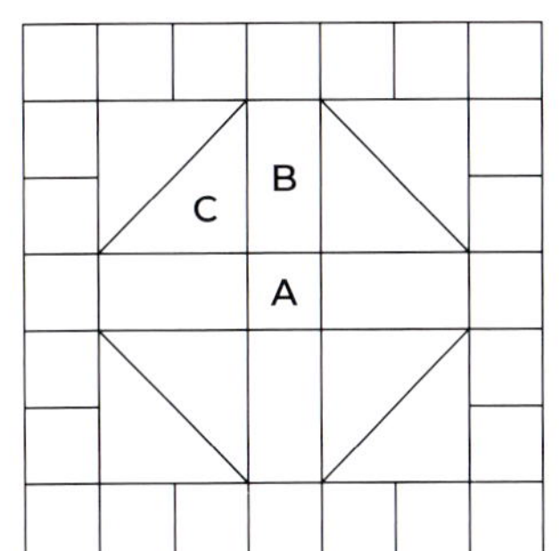

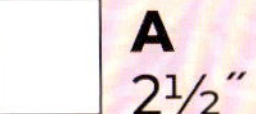

A
2½″

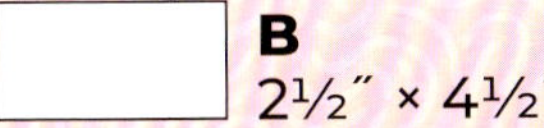

B
2½″ × 4½″

C
4⅞″

november 19

CHECKERS

12″ × 12″

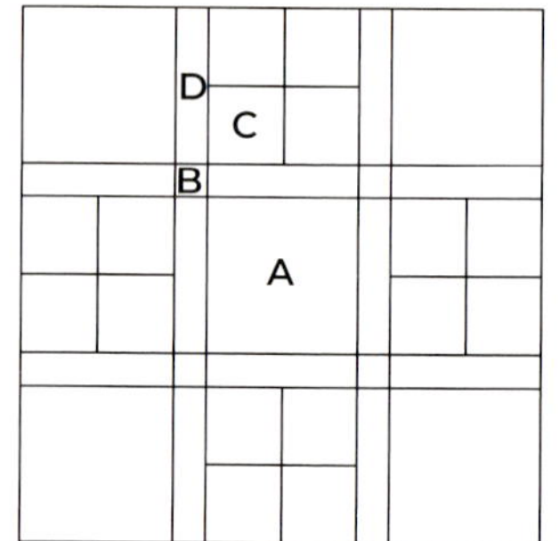

A 4″

B 1¼″

C 2¼″

D 1¼″ × 4″

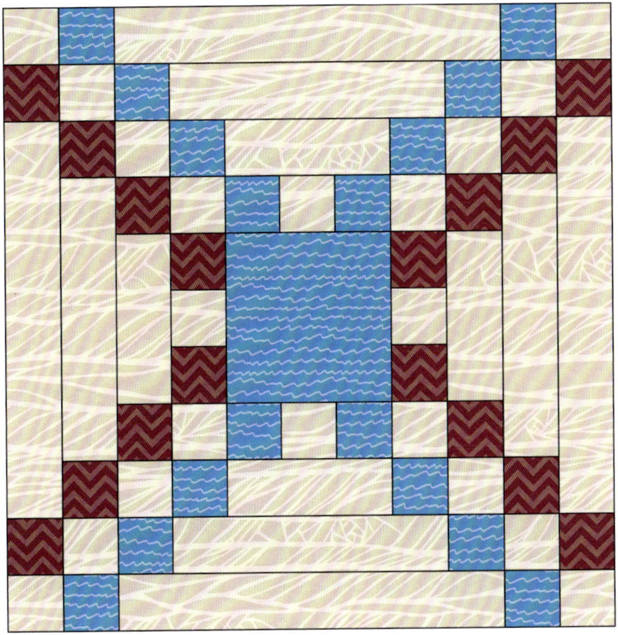

february 13

WHITEHOUSE STEPS

22″ × 22″

A 6½″

B 2½″

C 2½″ × 6½″

D 2½″ × 10½″

E 2½″ × 14½″

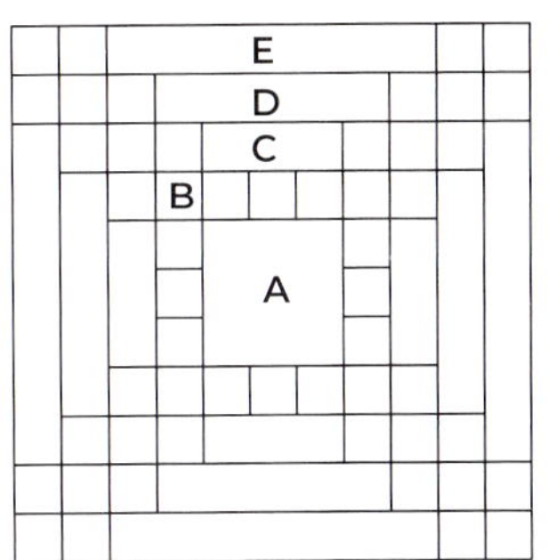

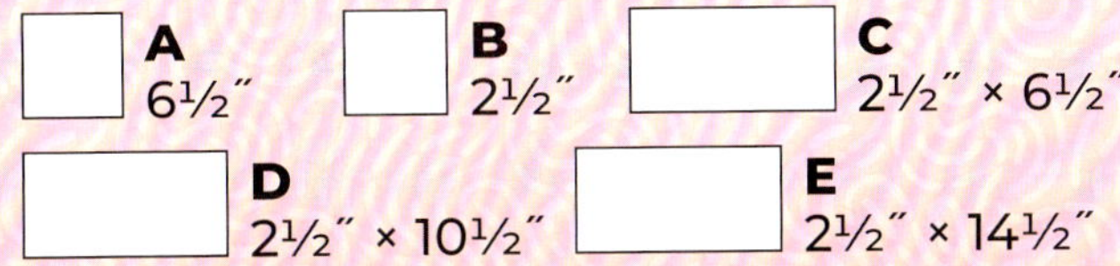

november 18

DOMINO CHAIN

10″ × 10″

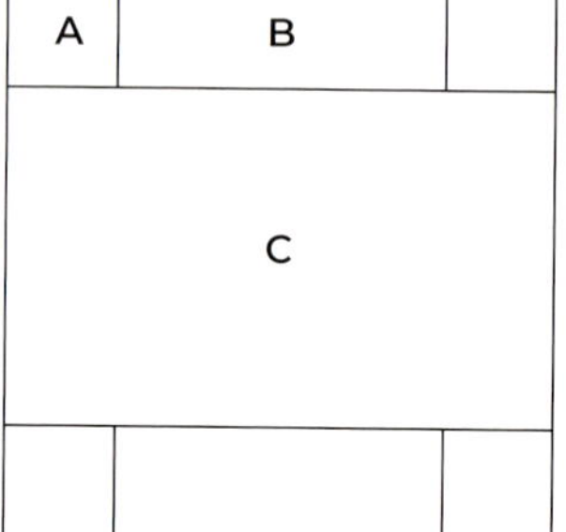

A
2½″

B
2½″ × 6½″

C
6½″ × 10½″

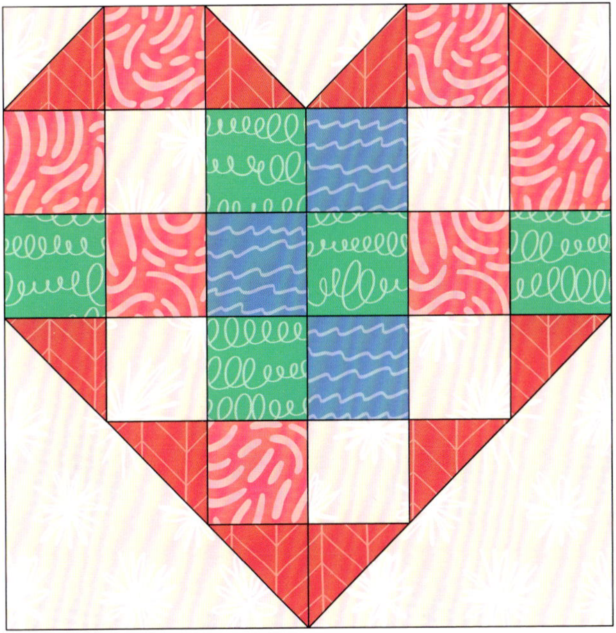

february 14

HEART BLOCK

12″ × 12″

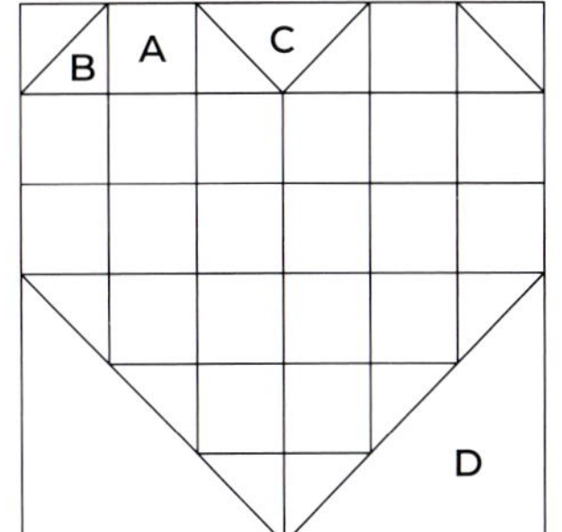

A 2½″

B 2⅞″

C 5¼″

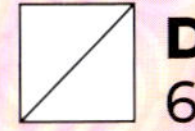

D 6⅞″

november 17

TWENTY-FIVE PATCH

10″ × 10″

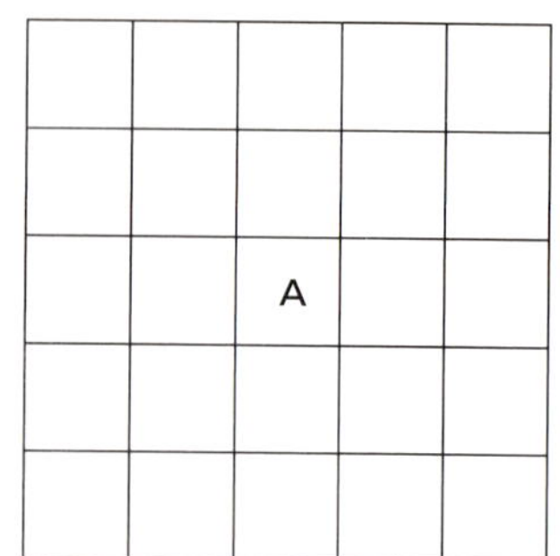

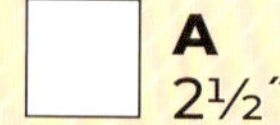

A
2½″

february 15

MEMORY STAR

18″ × 18″

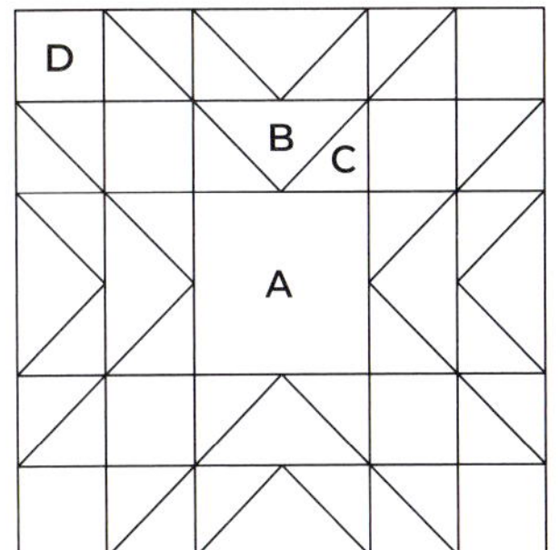

A
6½″

B
7¼″

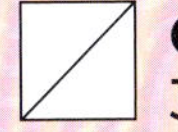

C
3⅞″

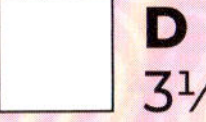

D
3½″

november 16

CROSS AND FOUR PATCH

10″ × 10″

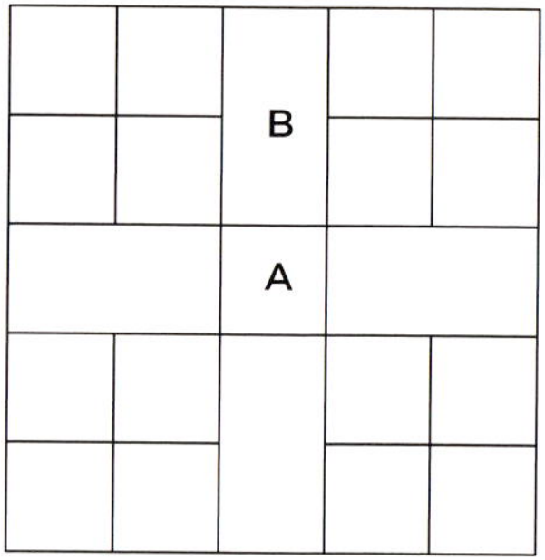

B

A

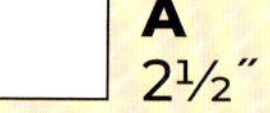

A
2½″

B
2½″ × 4½″

february 16

DOUBLE GEESE

18″ × 18″

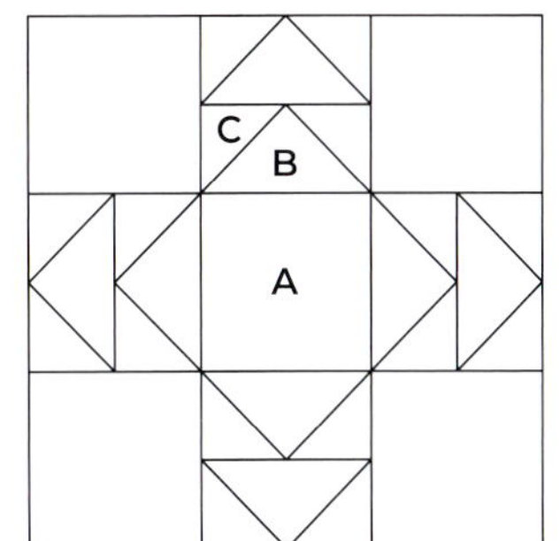

A 6½″

B 7¼″

C 3⅞″

november 15

BIG TWINKLE

18″ × 18″

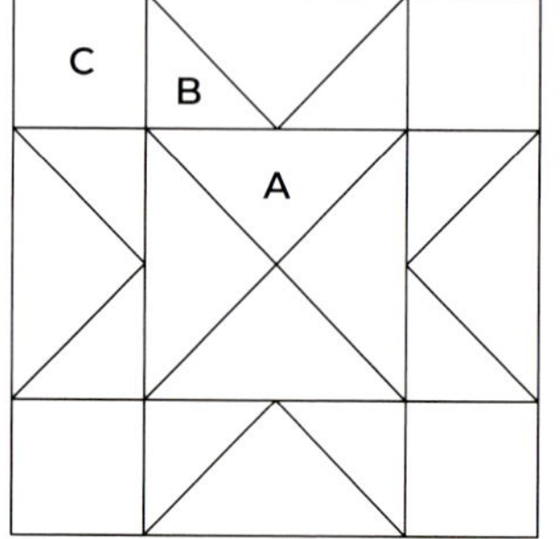

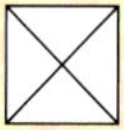

A
10¼″

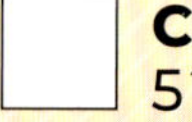

B
5⅜″

C
5″

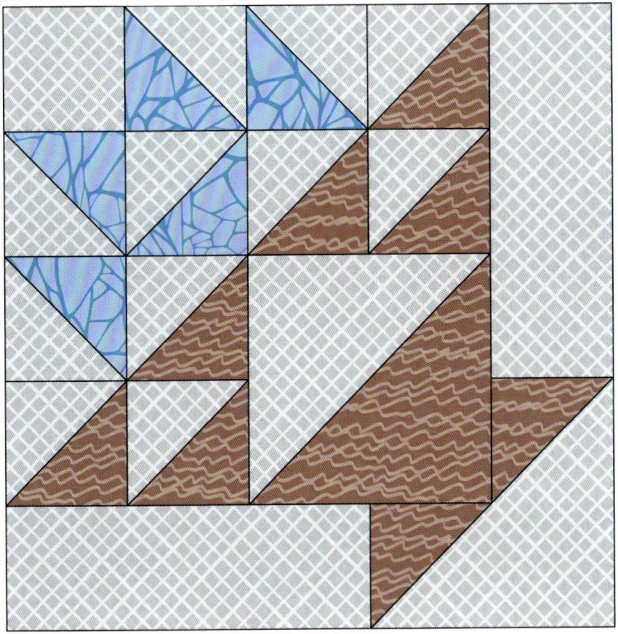

february 17

FLOWER BASKET

10″ × 10″

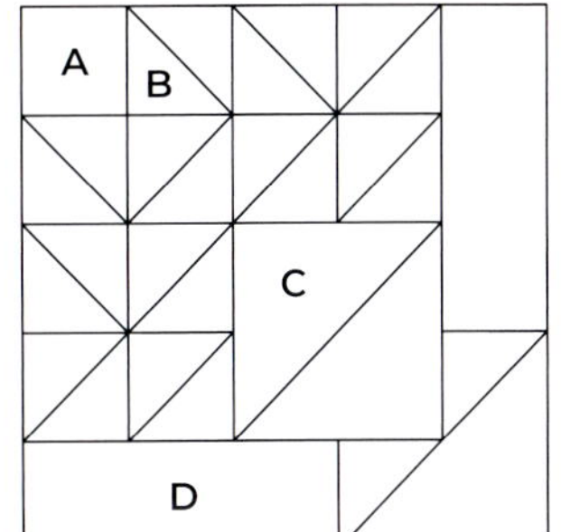

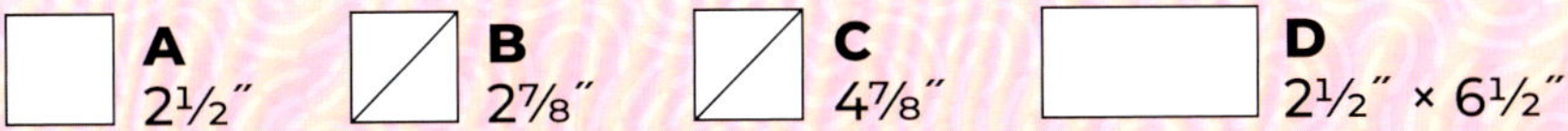

A
2½″

B
2⅞″

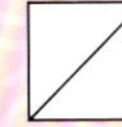

C
4⅞″

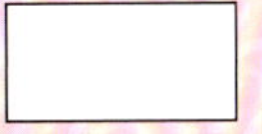

D
2½″ × 6½″

november 14

BROKEN WINDOWS

18″ × 18″

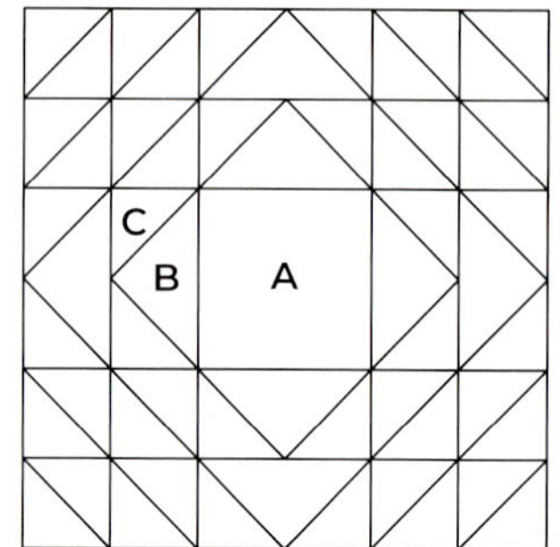

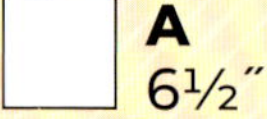

A
6½″

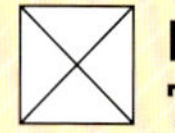

B
7¼″

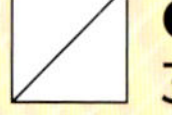

C
3⅞″

february 18

SHOOFLY

12″ × 12″

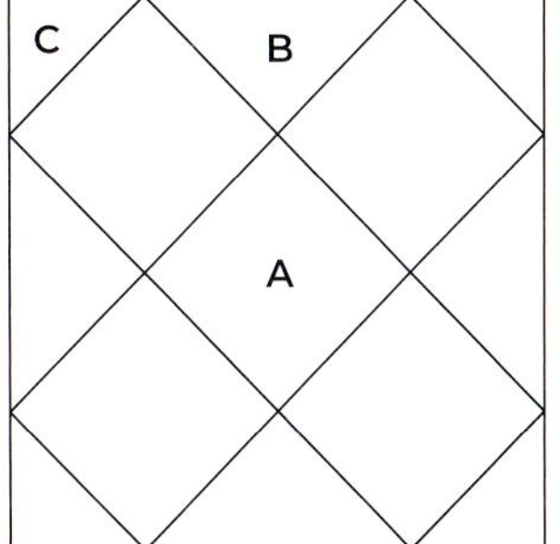

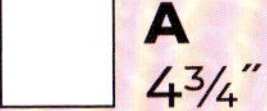

A
4¾″

B
7¼″

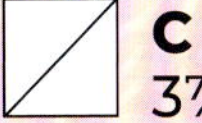

C
3⅞″

november 13

BROKEN DISH

18″ × 18″

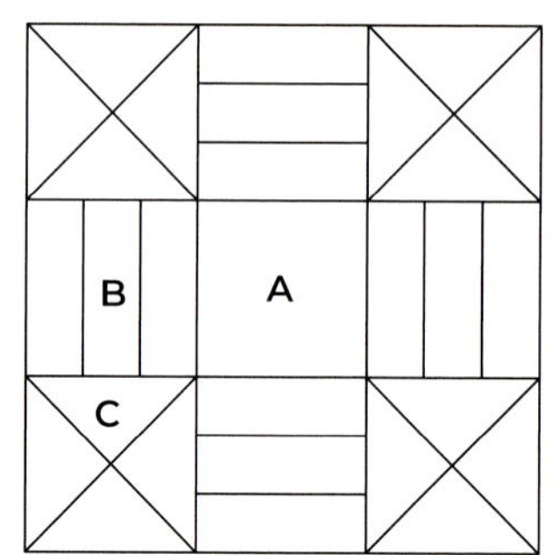

A
6½″

B
2½″ × 6½″

C
7¼″

february 19

CROW'S NEST

9″ × 9″

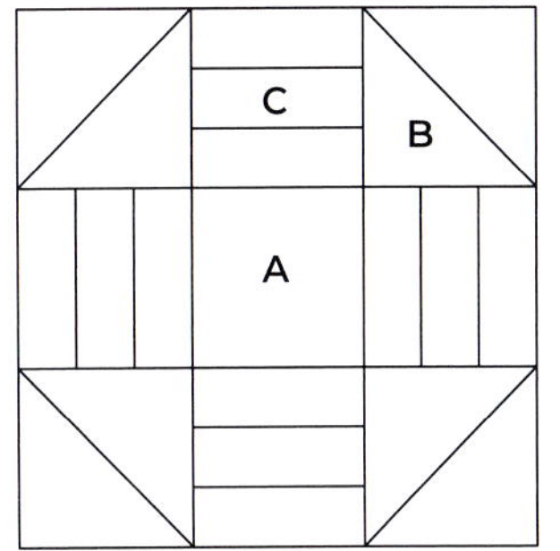

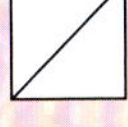

A
3½″

B
3⅞″

C
1½″ × 3½″

november 12

AZTEC JEWEL
18″ × 18″

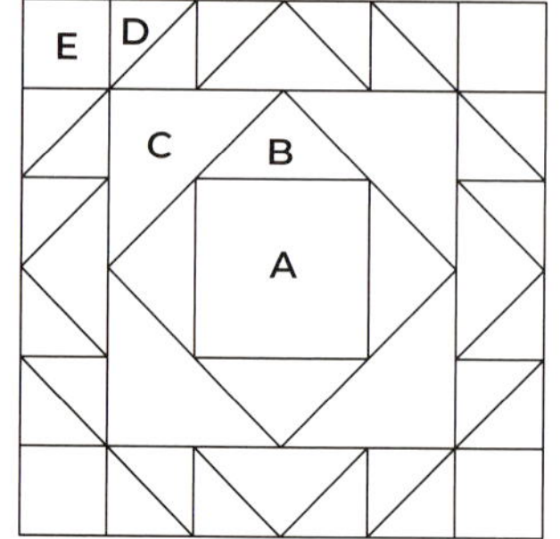

A
6½″

B
7¼″

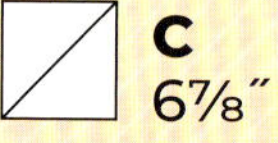

C
6⅞″

D
3⅞″

E
3½″

february 20

WILD GOOSE CHASE

10″ × 10″

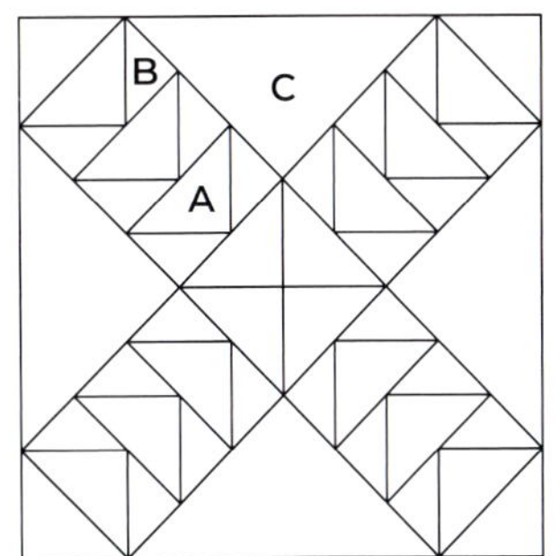

A 2 7/8″

B 3 1/4″

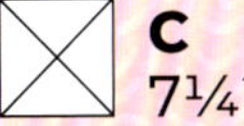

C 7 1/4″

november 11

DOUBLE STAR

12″ × 12″

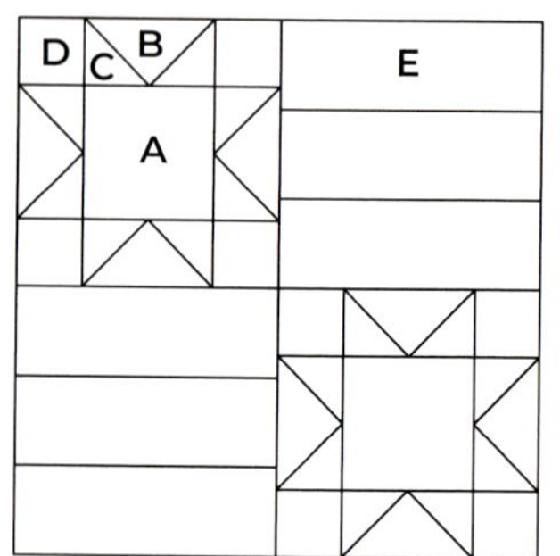

A
3½″

B
4¼″

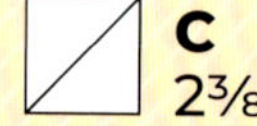

C
2⅜″

D
2″

E
2½″ × 6½″

february 21

KING'S CROWN
16″ × 16″

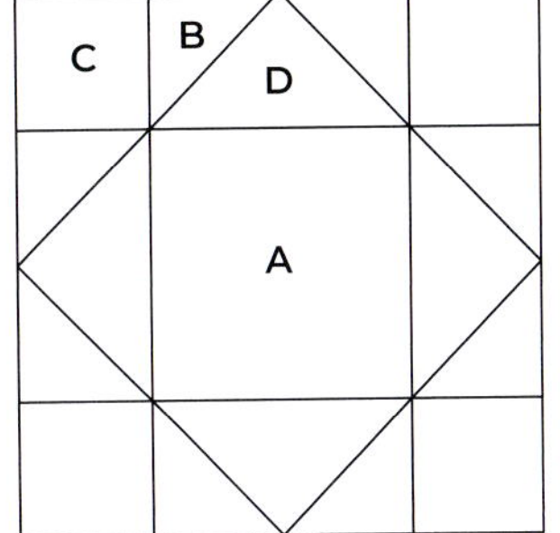

A
8½″

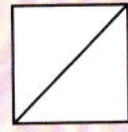

B
4⅞″

C
4½″

D
9¼″

november 10

ARBOR WINDOW

18″ × 18″

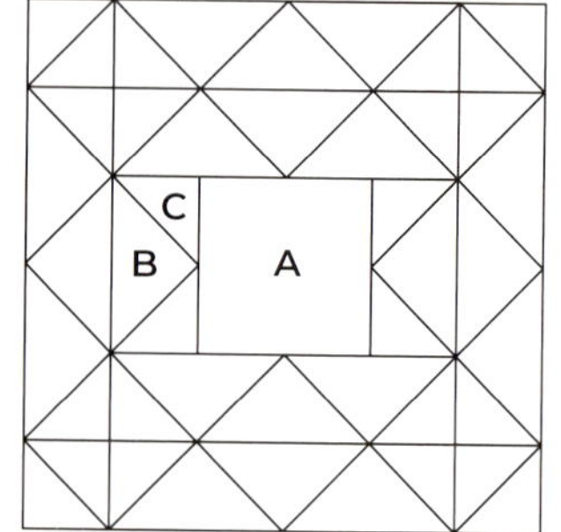

A 6½″

B 7¼″

C 3⅞″

february 22

WASHINGTON SQUARE

12″ × 12″

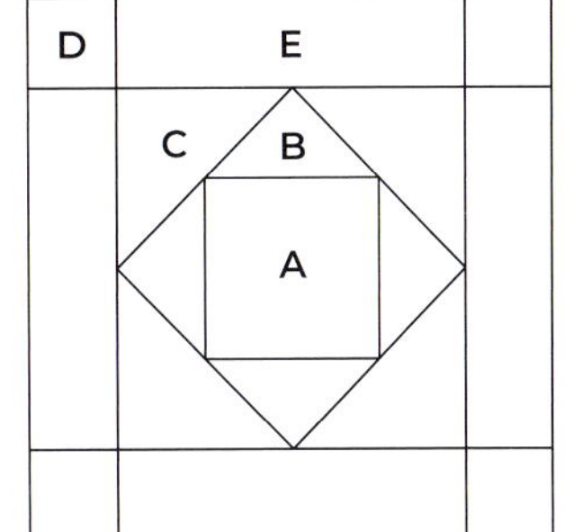

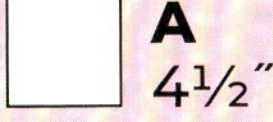

A
4½″

B
5¼″

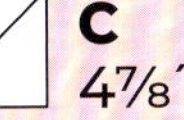

C
4⅞″

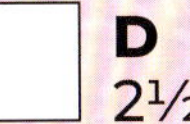

D
2½″

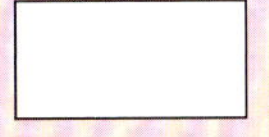

E
2½″ × 8½″

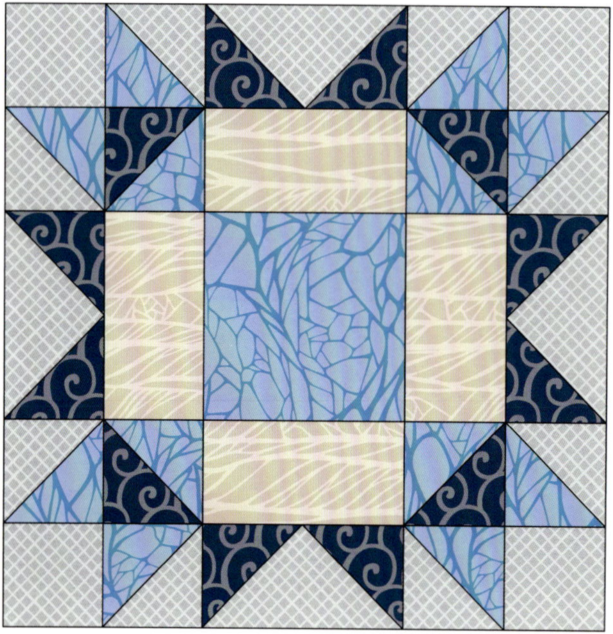

november 9

ARIZONA BLOCK

18″ × 18″

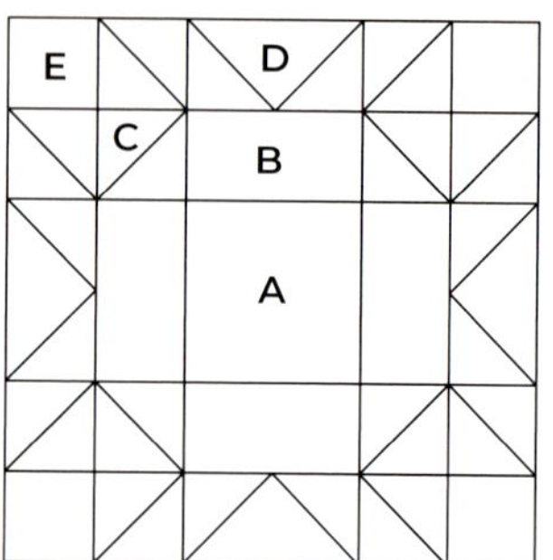

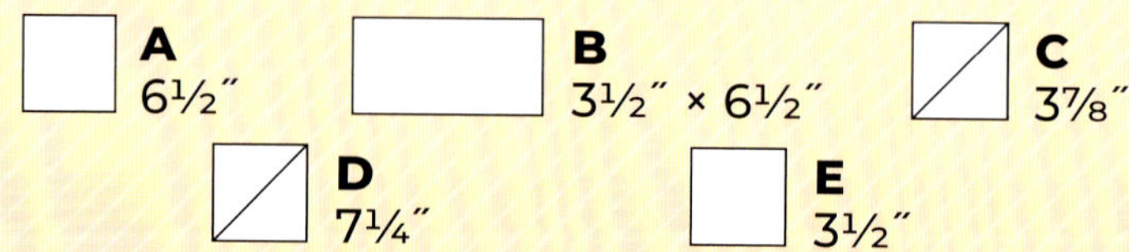

february 23

DOUBLE CENTENNIAL

16″ × 16″

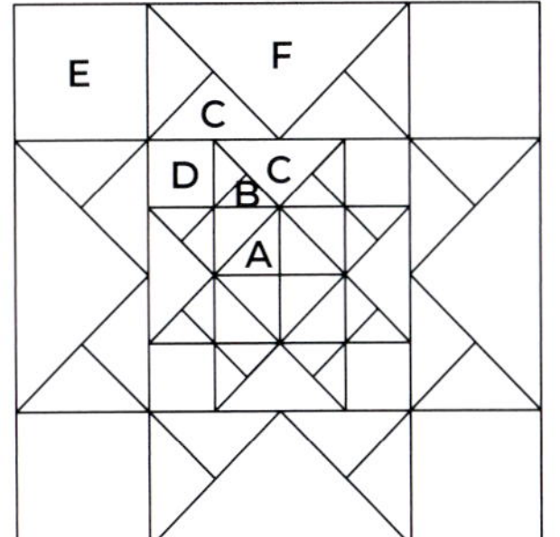

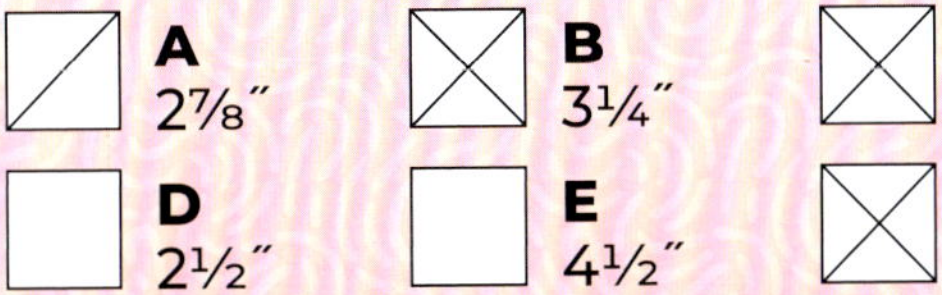

A 2⅞″

B 3¼″

C 5¼″

D 2½″

E 4½″

F 9¼″

november 8

SOUVENIR VARIATION

15″ × 15″

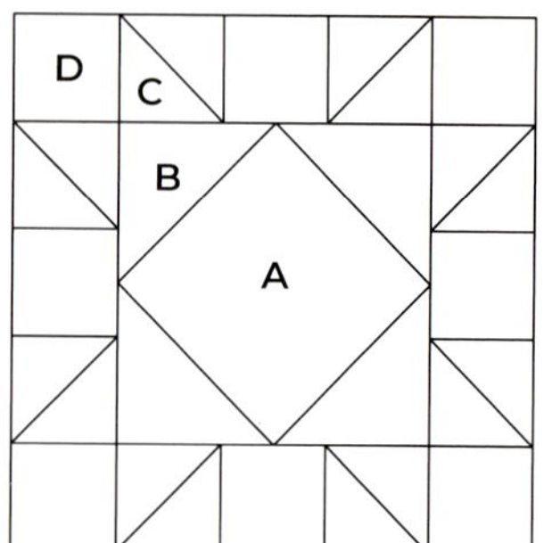

A
6⅞″

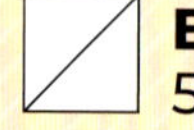

B
5⅜″

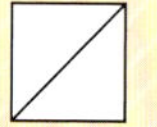

C
3⅞″

D
3½″

february 24

SAGE BUD

12″ × 12″

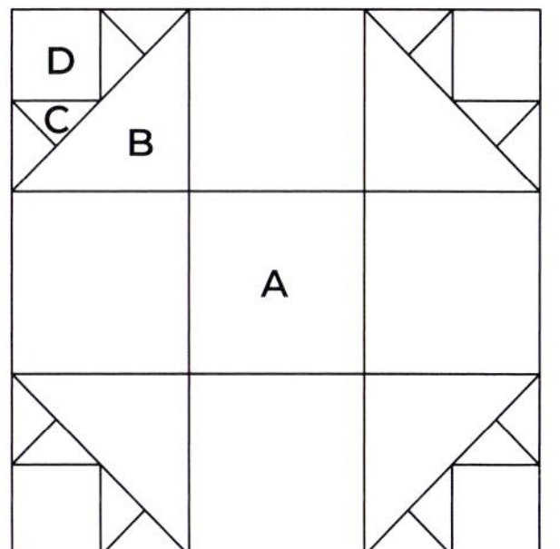

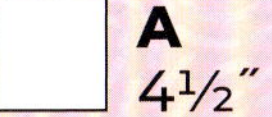

A
4½″

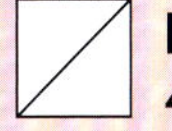

B
4⅞″

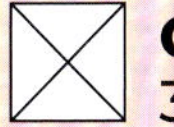

C
3¼″

D
2½″

november 7

CHURN DASHER

15″ × 15″

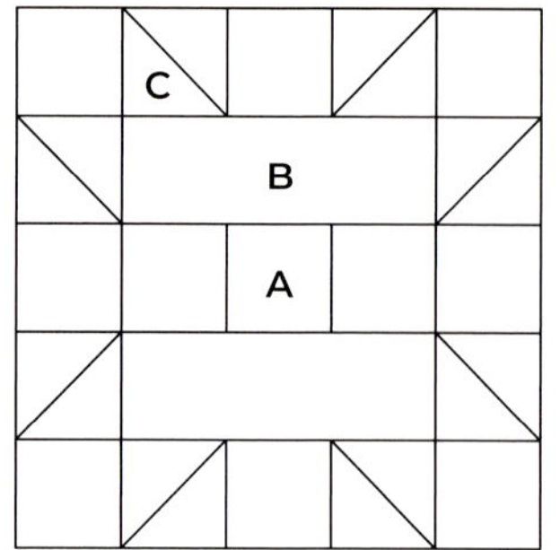

A
3½″

B
3½″ × 9½″

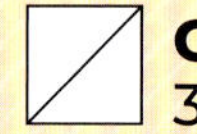

C
3⅞″

february 25

DIAMOND FACETS

15″ × 15″

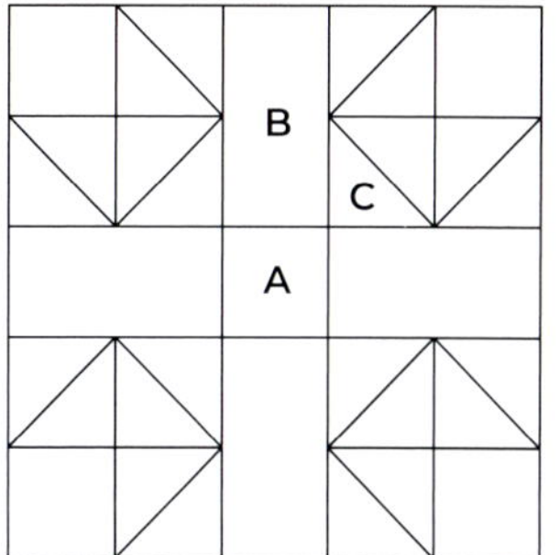

A
3½″

B
3½″ × 6½″

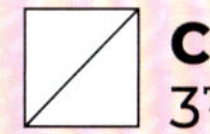

C
3⅞″

november 6

GENTLEMAN'S FANCY

12″ × 12″

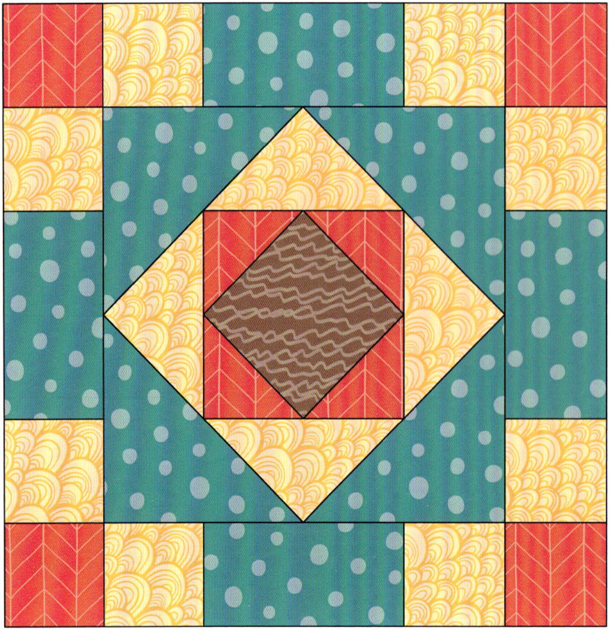

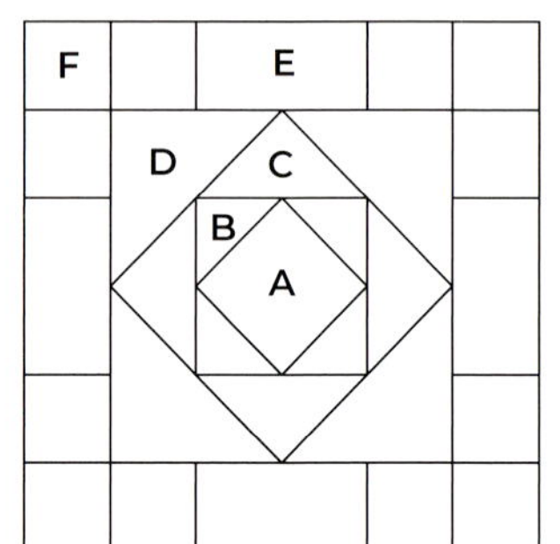

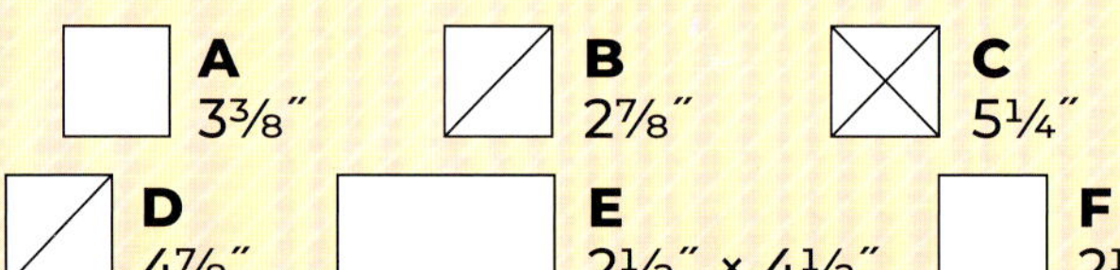

february 26

CRISS CROSS BLOCK
15″ × 15″

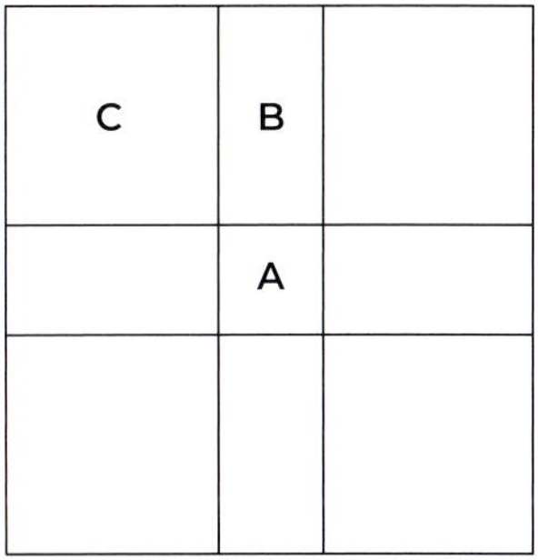

C	B	
	A	

A
3½″

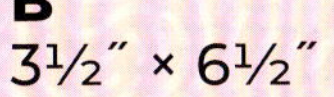

B
3½″ × 6½″

C
6½″

november 5

WOVEN STAR

24″ × 24″

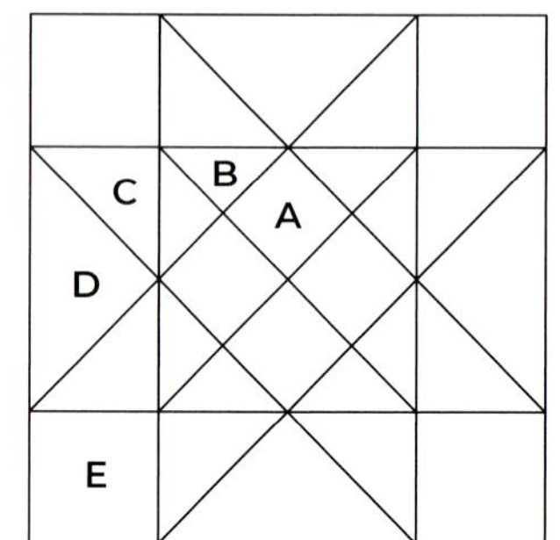

A 4¾″

B 7¼″

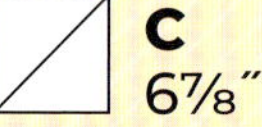

C 6⅞″

D 13¼″

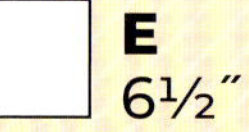

E 6½″

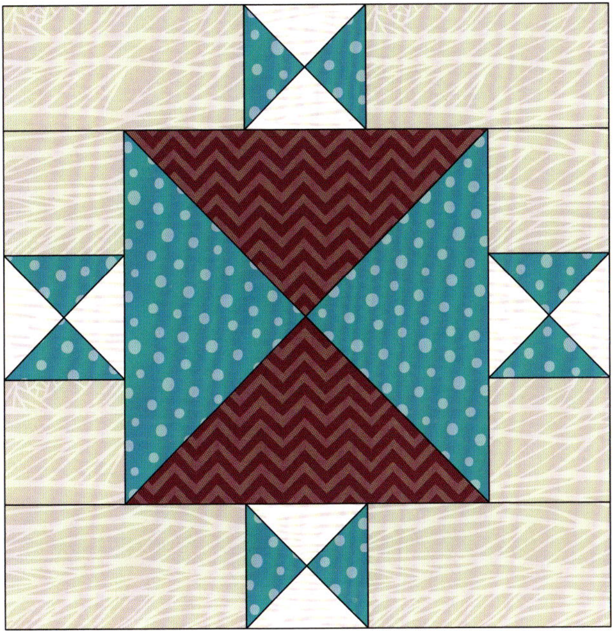

february 27

DOUBLE HOURGLASS BLOCK

15″ × 15″

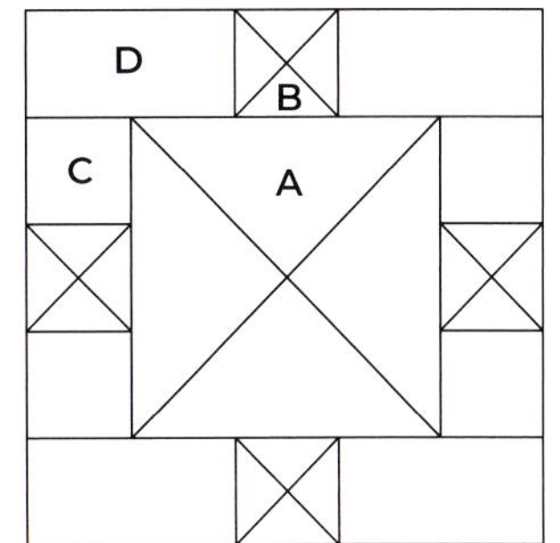

A
10¼″

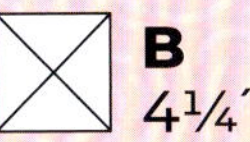

B
4¼″

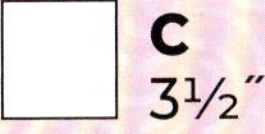

C
3½″

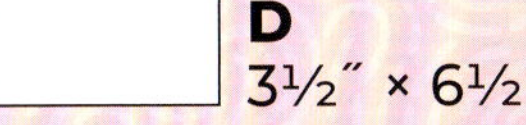

D
3½″ × 6½″

november 4

FOUR PATCH AND BARS

18″ × 18″

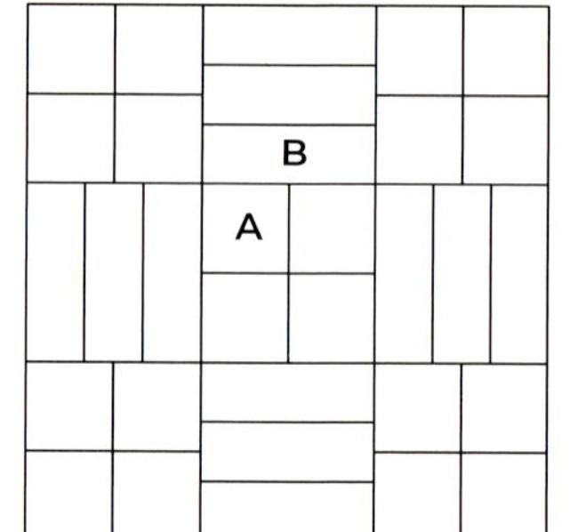

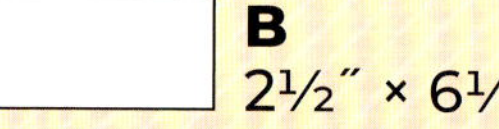

A 3½″

B 2½″ × 6½″

february 28

GEMS BLOCK

15″ × 15″

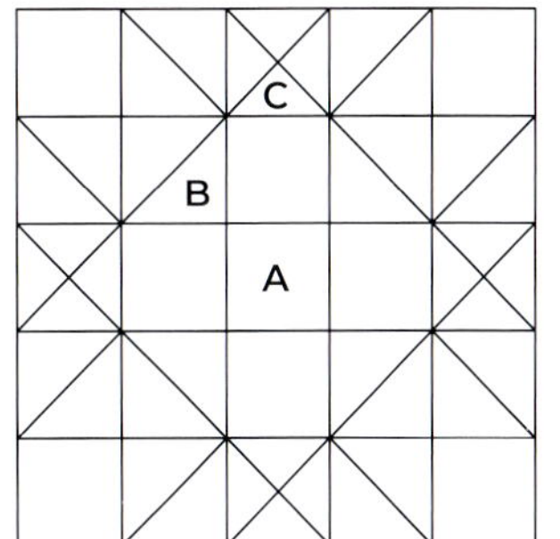

A 3½″

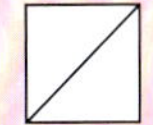

B 3⅞″

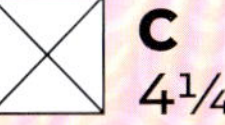

C 4¼″

november 3

TRIPLE BARS AND SQUARES

18″ × 18″

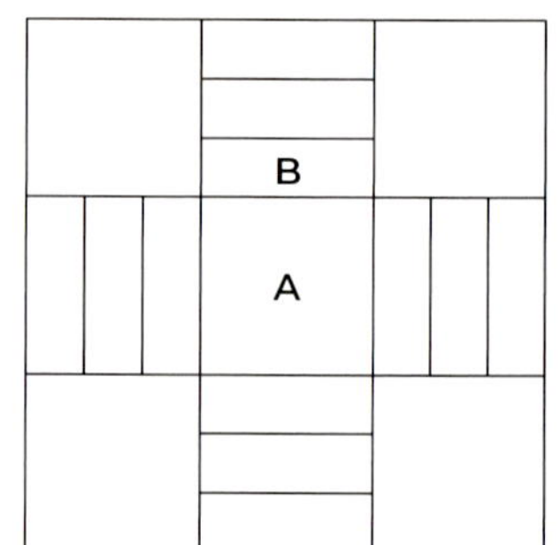

A
6½″

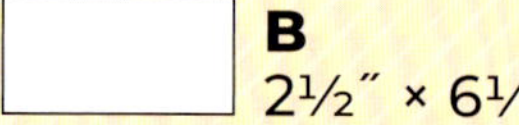

B
2½″ × 6½″

february 29

CHICAGO GEESE

12″ × 12″

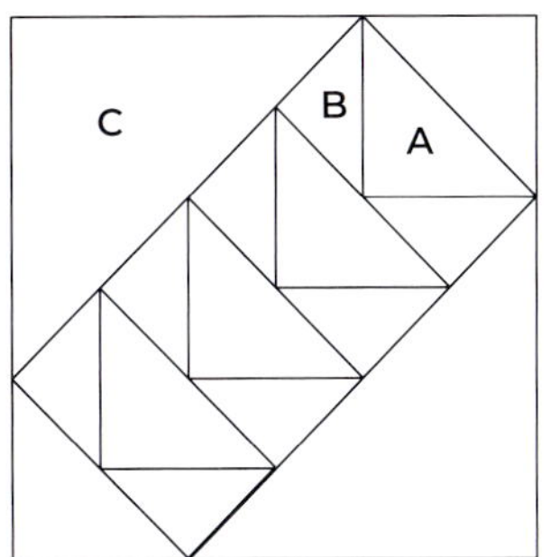

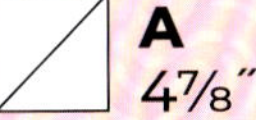

A
4⅞″

B
5¼″

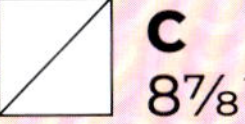

C
8⅞″

november 2

BARS AND TRIANGLES

18″ × 18″

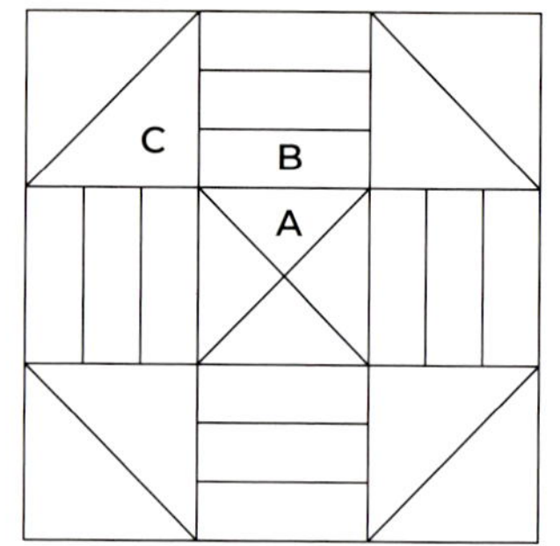

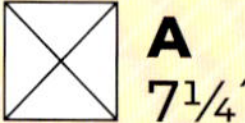

A
7¼″

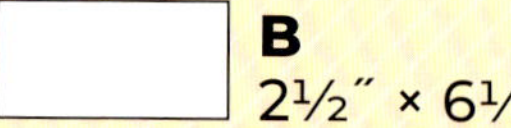

B
2½″ × 6½″

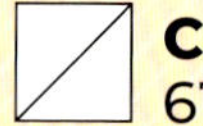

C
6⅞″

march 1

T BLOCK

12″ × 12″

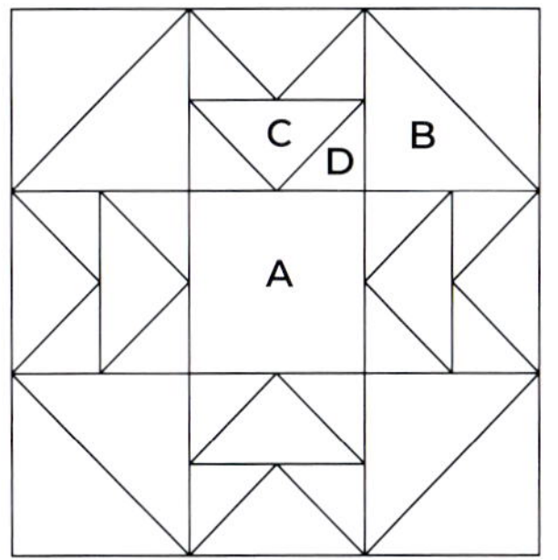

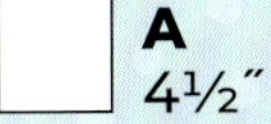

A
4½″

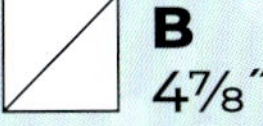

B
4⅞″

C
5¼″

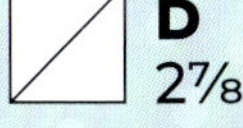

D
2⅞″

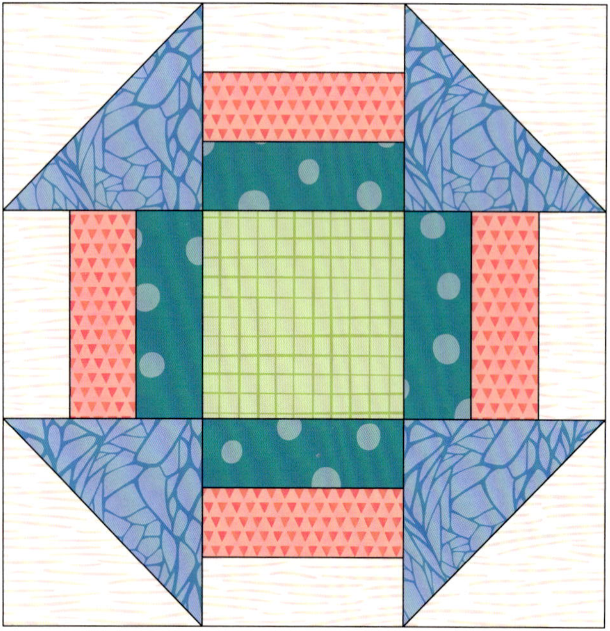

november 1

TRIPLE BAR

18″ × 18″

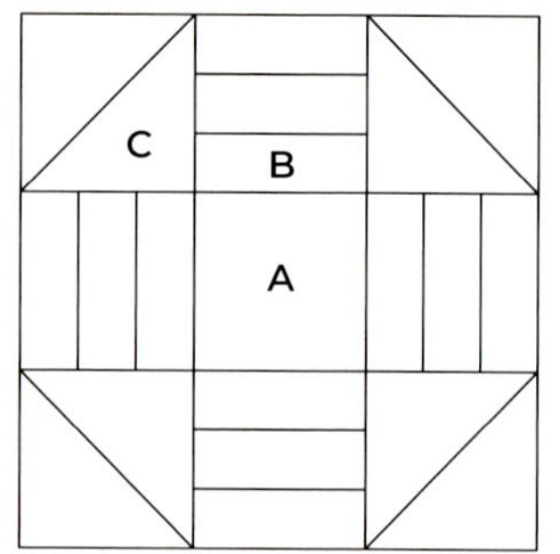

A
6½″

B
2½″ × 6½″

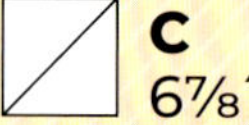

C
6⅞″

march 2

HOLE IN THE BARN DOOR

12″ × 12″

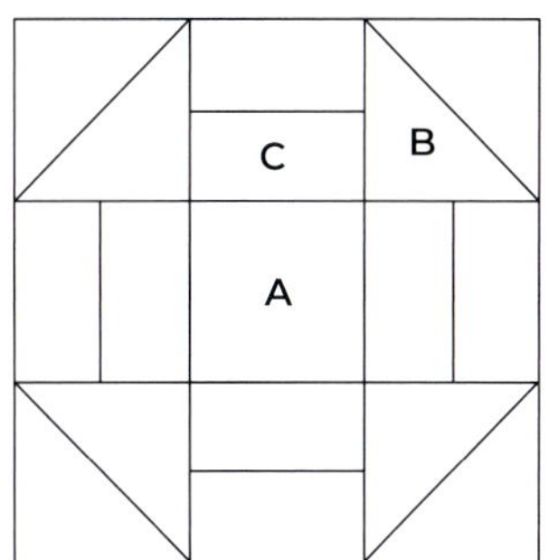

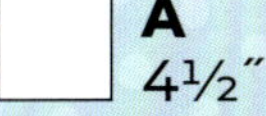

A
4½″

B
4⅞″

C
2½″ × 4½″

october 31

PUMPKIN PATCH

12″ × 12″

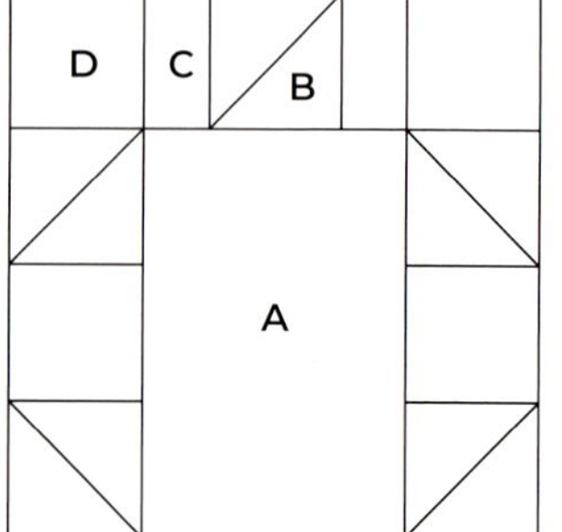

A
6½″ × 9½″

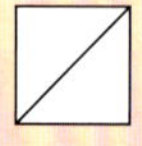

B
3⅞″

C
2″ × 3½″

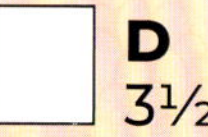

D
3½″

march 3

CIRCLING HEARTS

12″ × 12″

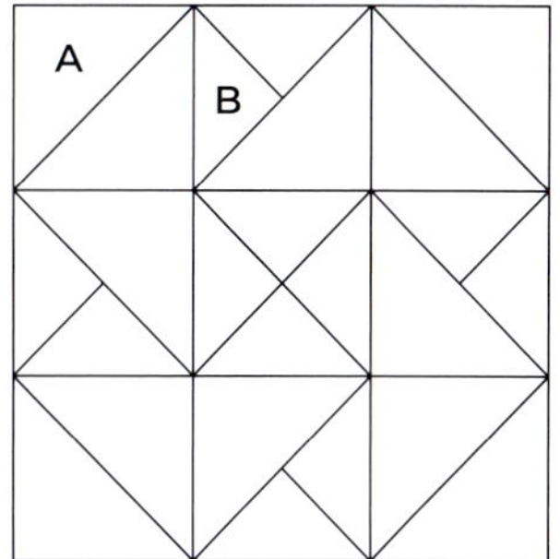

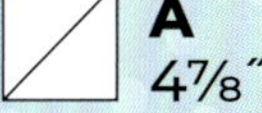

A
4⅞″

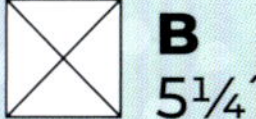

B
5¼″

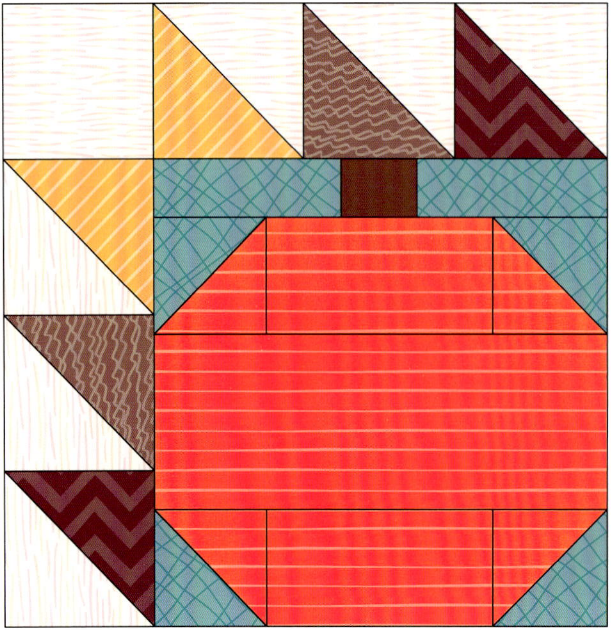

october 30

SPIKY PUMPKIN

8″ × 8″

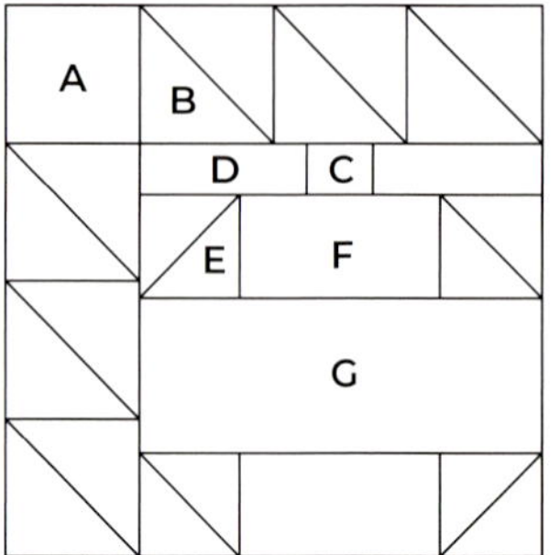

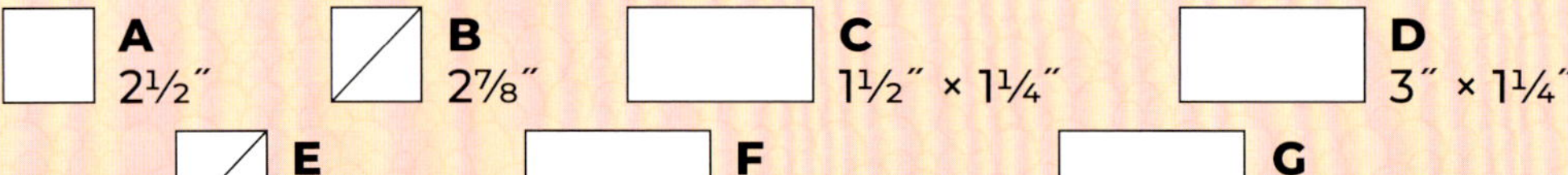

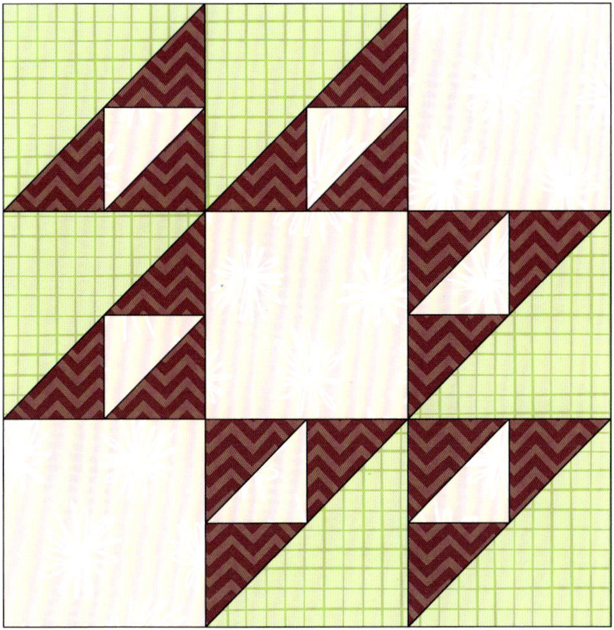

march 4

DOUBLE PYRAMIDS

12″ × 12″

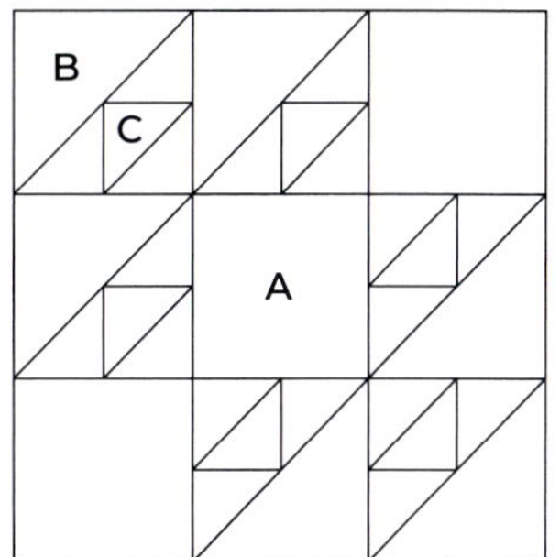

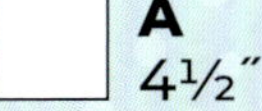
A
4½″

B
4⅞″

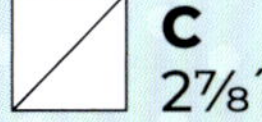
C
2⅞″

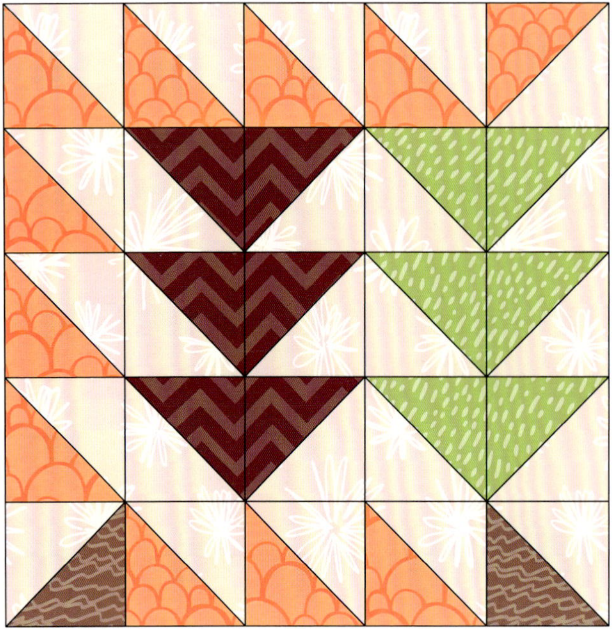

october 29

INDIAN TRAILS

15″ × 15″

A
3⅞″

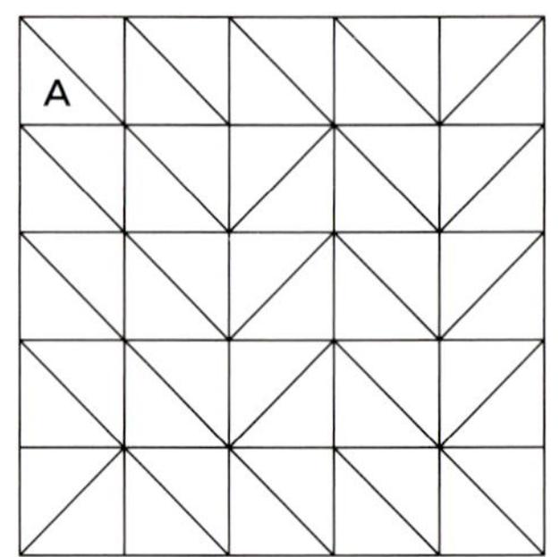

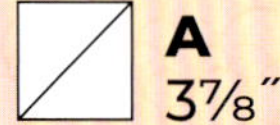

march 5

CLAY'S CHOICE

12″ × 12″

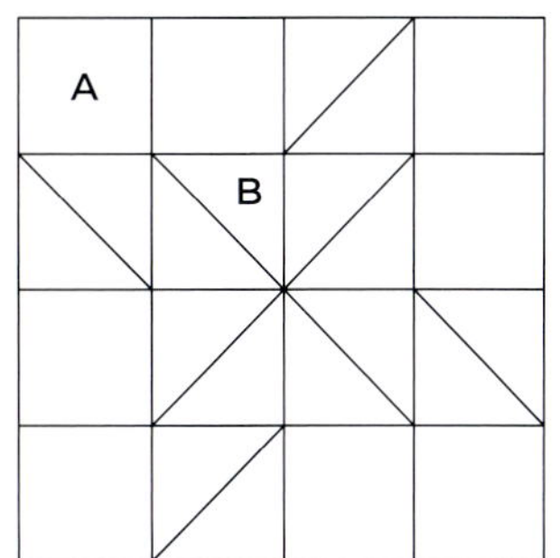

A
3½″

B
3⅞″

october 28

WILD GOOSE CHASE

12″ × 12″

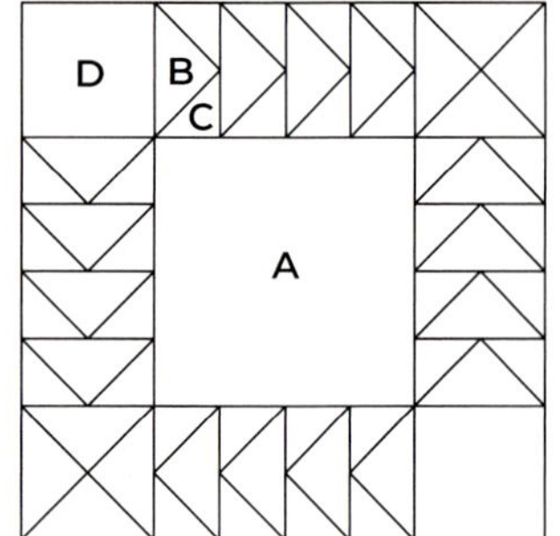

A
6½″

B
4¼″

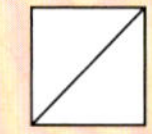

C
2⅜″

D
3½″

march 6

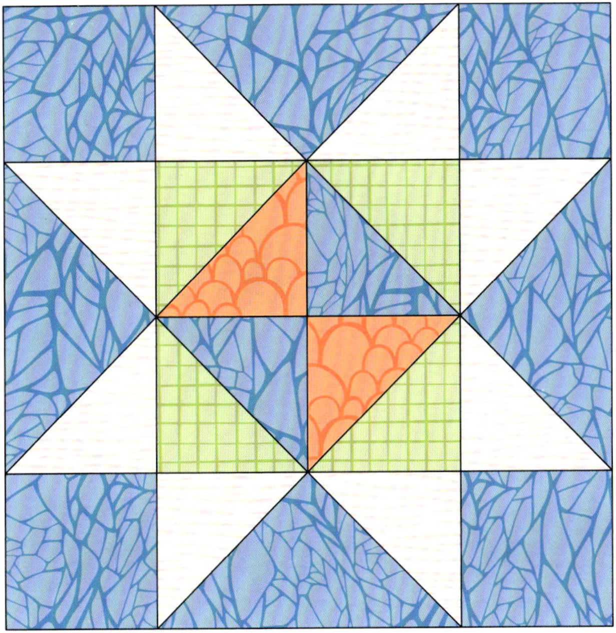

MARTHA WASHINGTON STAR

12″ × 12″

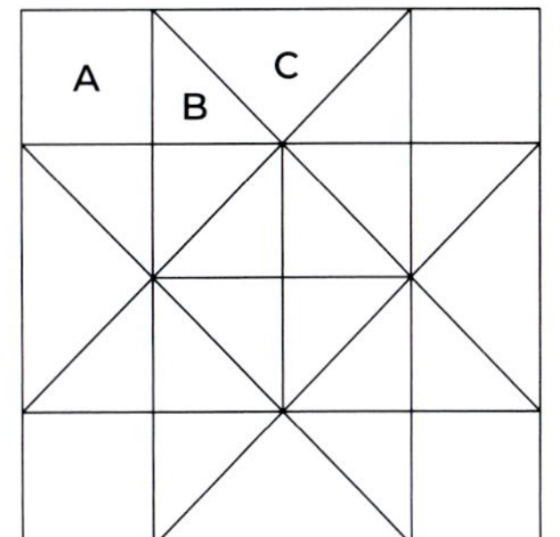

A
3½″

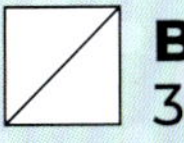

B
3⅞″

C
7¼″

october 27

THREE LITTLE GEESE

12″ × 12″

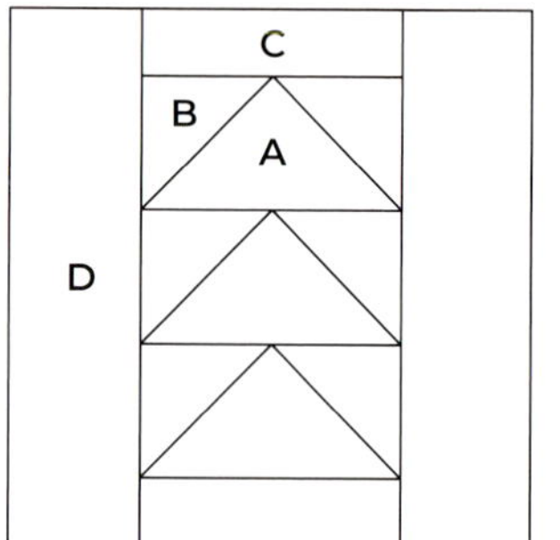

A
7¼″

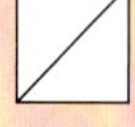

B
3⅞″

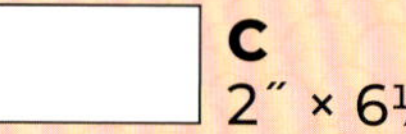

C
2″ × 6½″

D
3½″ × 12½″

FOX AND GEESE

12″ × 12″

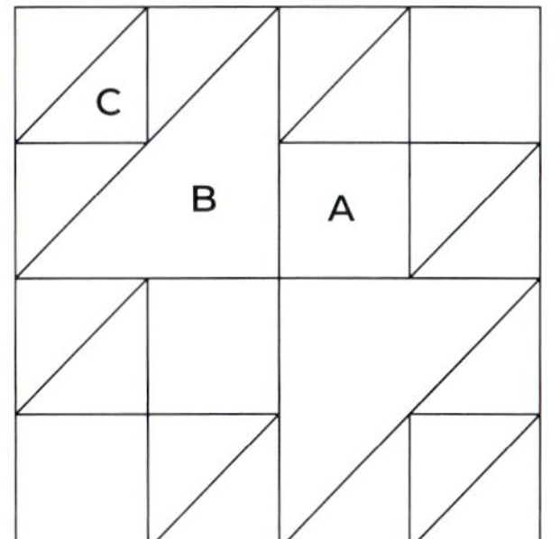

A
3½″

B
6⅞″

C
3⅞″

october 26

RAILROAD CROSSING

12″ × 12″

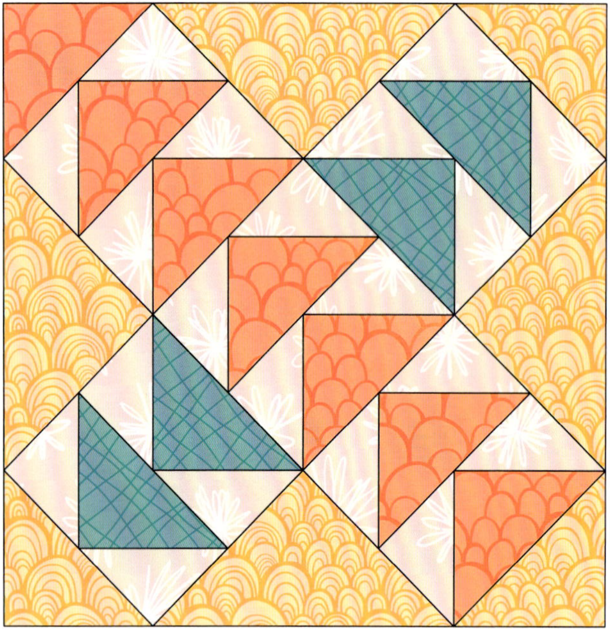

A
3⅞″

B
4¼″

C
7¼″

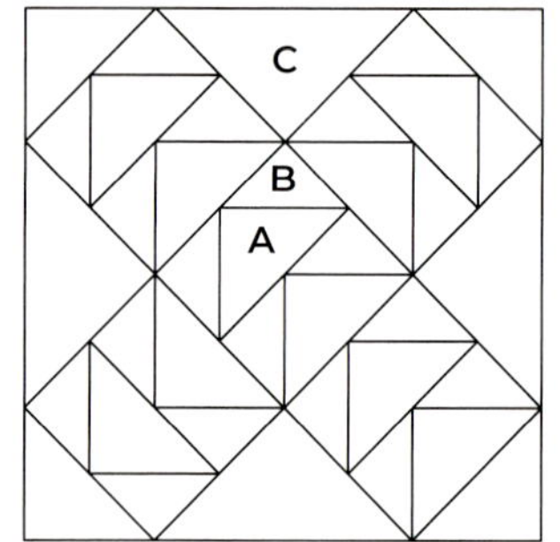

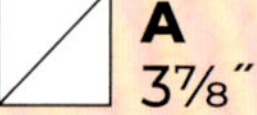

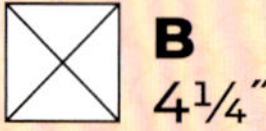

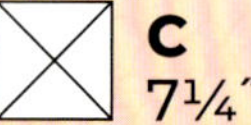

march 8

VARIABLE STAR

12″ × 12″

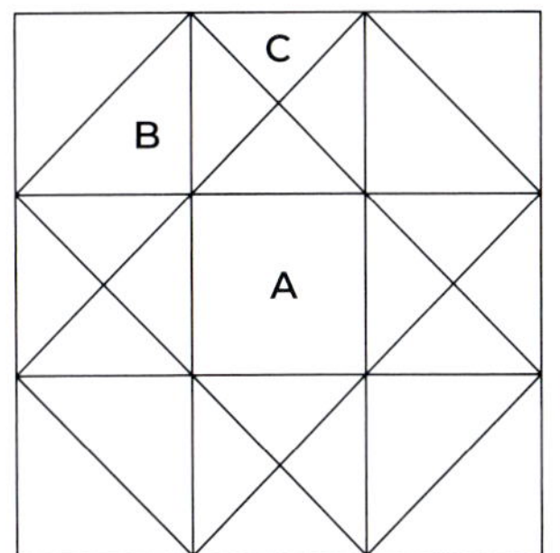

A
4½″

B
4⅞″

C
5¼″

october 25

PINWHEEL GEESE

12″ × 12″

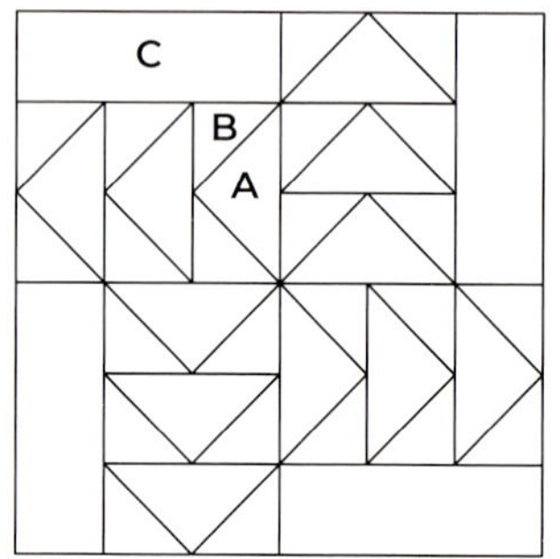

A
5¼″

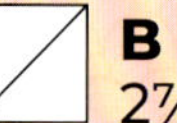

B
2⅞″

C
2½″ × 6½″

march 9

OHIO STAR

12″ × 12″

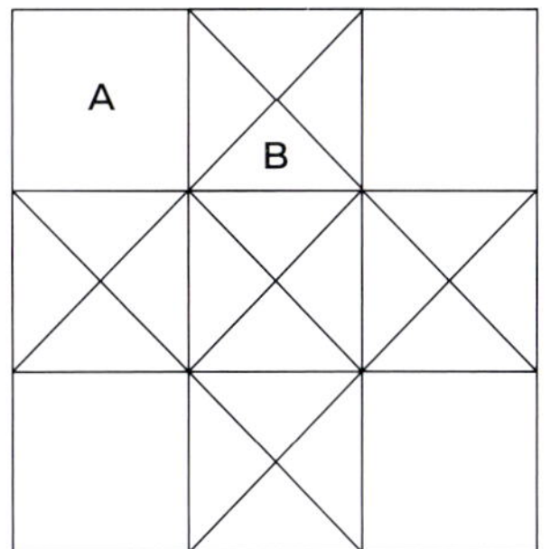

A
4½″

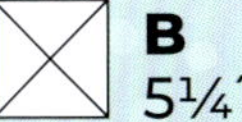

B
5¼″

october 24

GOSLING GO ROUND

12″ × 12″

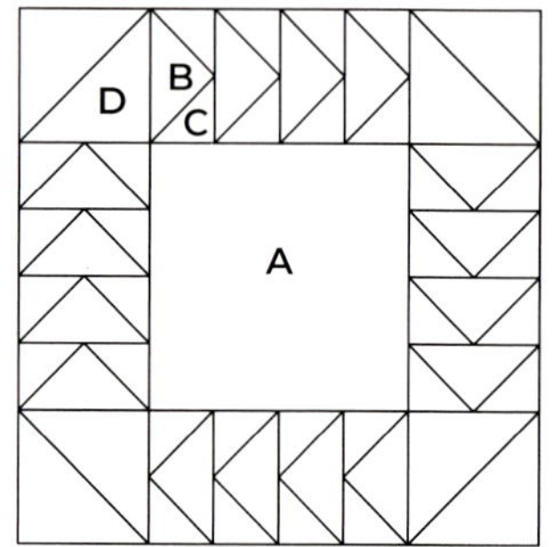

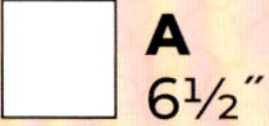

A
6½″

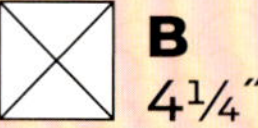

B
4¼″

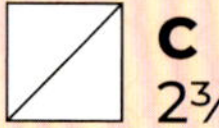

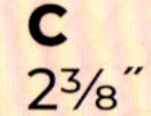

C
2⅜″

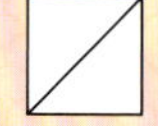

D
3⅞″

march 10

OLD MAID'S PUZZLE

12″ × 12″

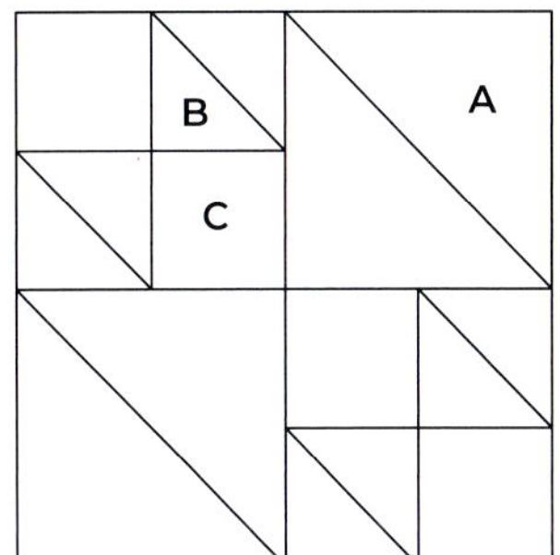

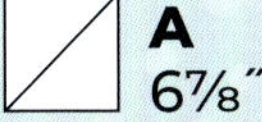

A
6⅞″

B
3⅞″

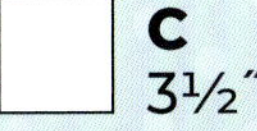

C
3½″

october 23

GEESE ON THE MOVE

12″ × 12″

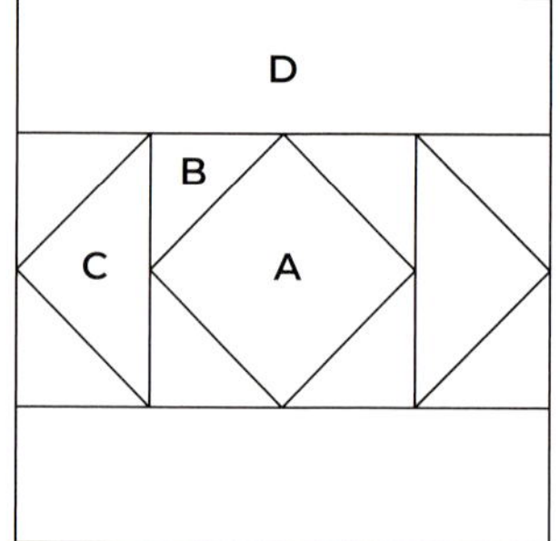

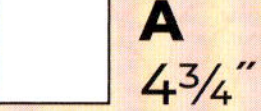

A
4¾″

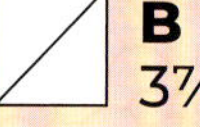

B
3⅞″

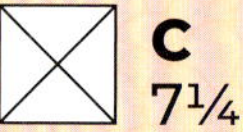

C
7¼″

D
3½″ × 12½″

march 11

HILARY'S GARDEN

15″ × 15″

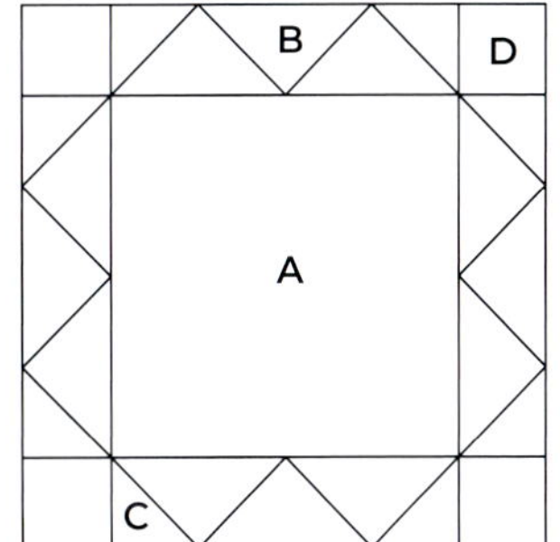

A
10½″

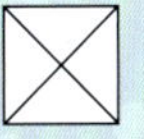

B
6¼″

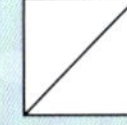

C
3⅜″

D
3″

october 22

GEESE MIGRATION

12″ × 12″

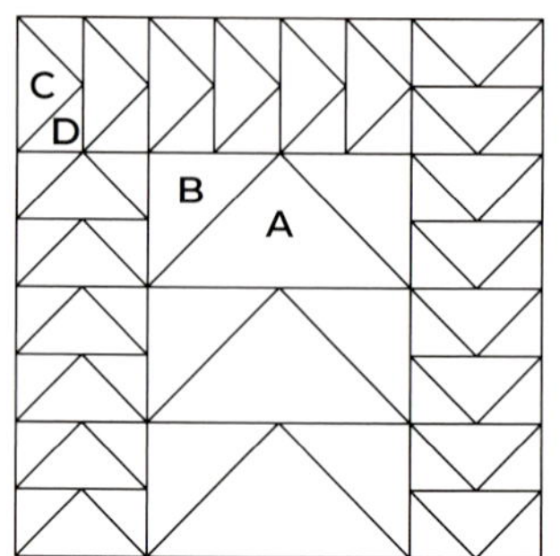

A
7¼″

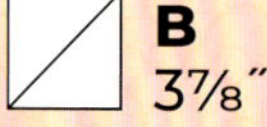
B
3⅞″

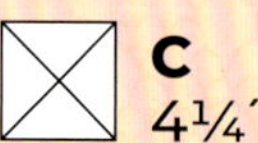
C
4¼″

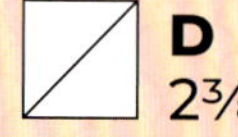
D
2⅜″

march 12

FOUR PATCH GARDEN

15″ × 15″

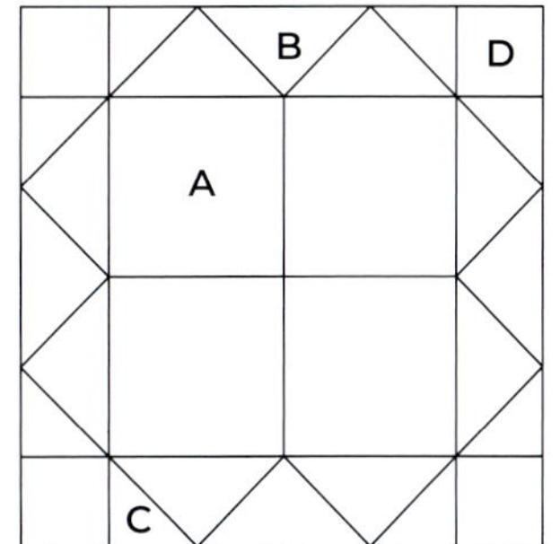

A
5½″

B
6¼″

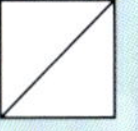

C
3⅜″

D
3″

october 21

GEESE IN THE TREES

12″ × 12″

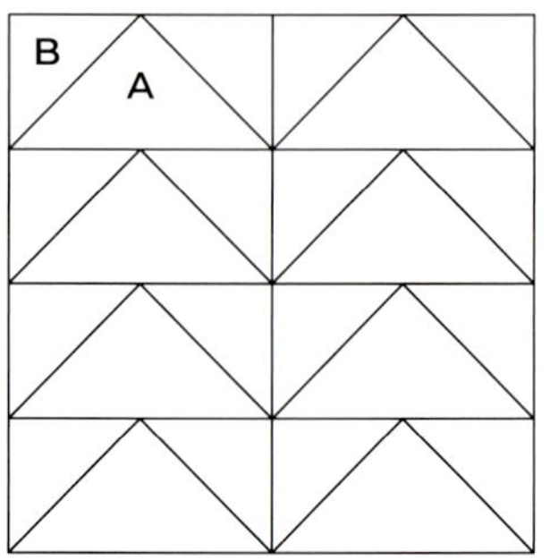

A
7¼″

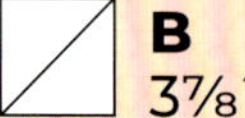

B
3⅞″

march 13

THE COMFORT BLOCK

12″ × 12″

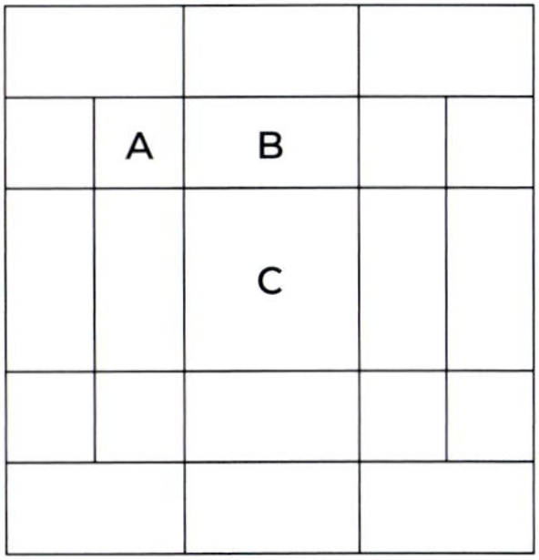

A

B

C

A
2½″

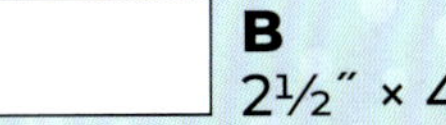

B
2½″ × 4½″

C
4½″

october 20

GEESE IN FORMATION

12″ × 12″

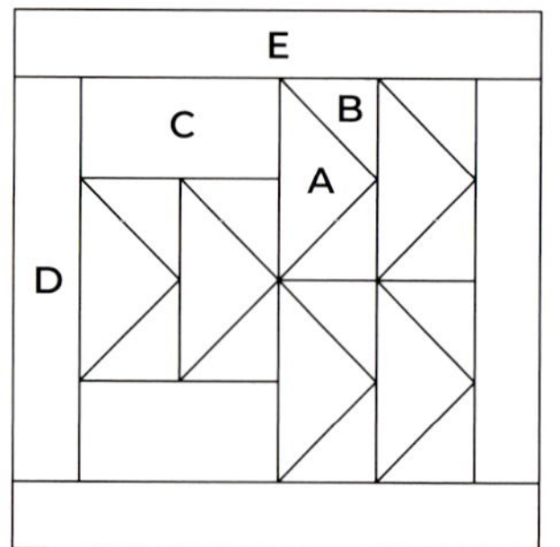

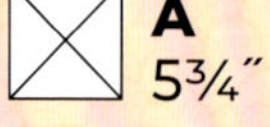

A
5¾″

B
3⅛″

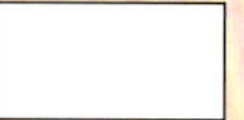

C
2¾″ × 5″

D
2″ × 9½″

E
2″ × 12½″

march 14

CROWN OF THORNS

12″ × 12″

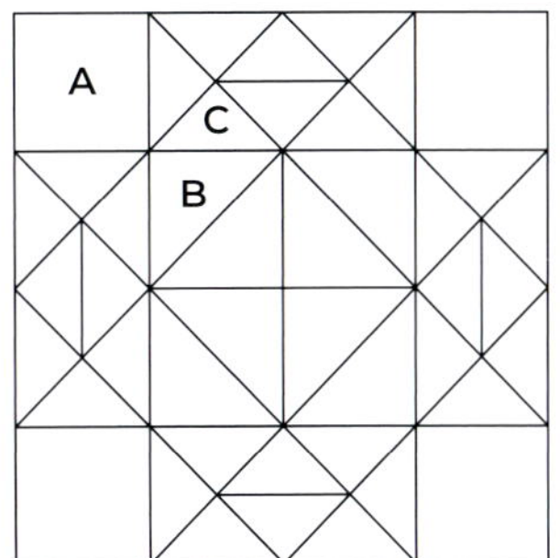

A
3½″

B
3⅞″

C
4¼″

october 19

DAY AND NIGHT GEESE

12″ × 12″

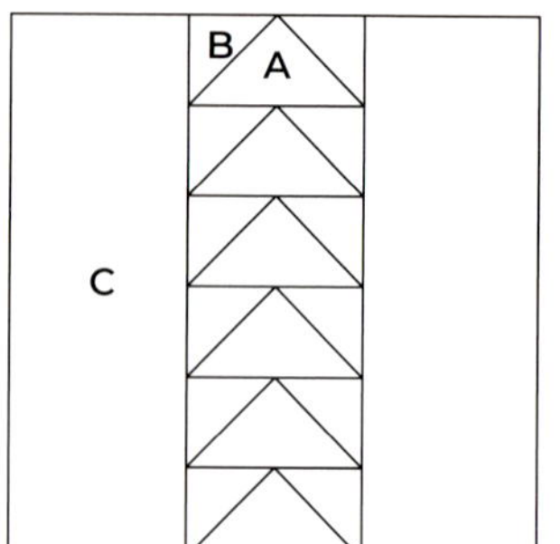

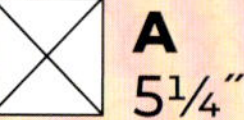

A
5¼″

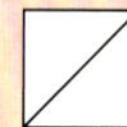

B
2⅞″

C
4½″ × 12½″

march 15

JACOB'S LADDER

12″ × 12″

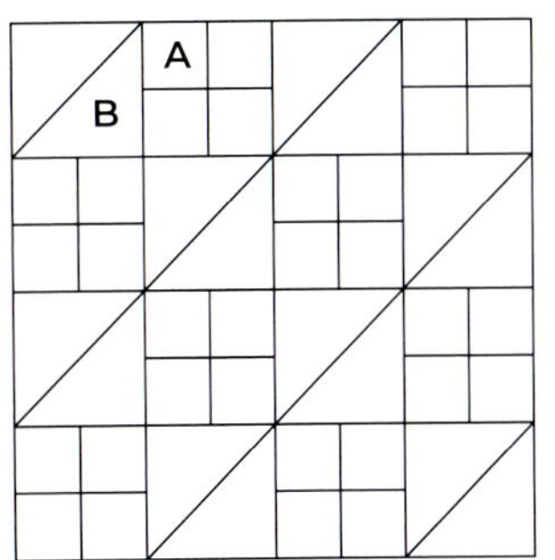

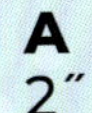

A
2″

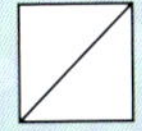

B
3⅞″

october 18

FOLLOW THE LEADER

12″ × 12″

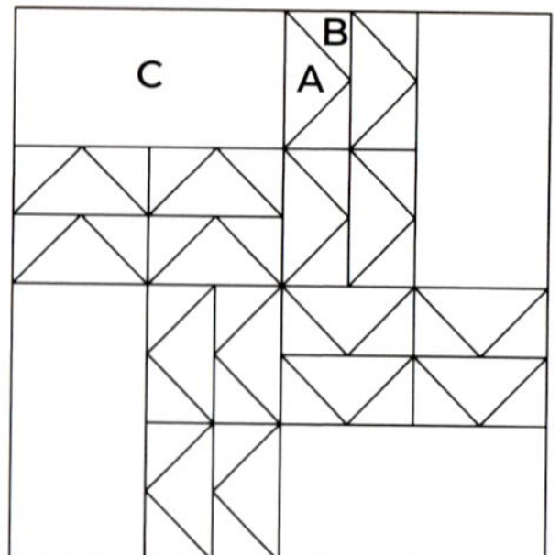

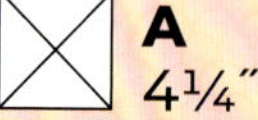

A
4¼″

B
2⅜″

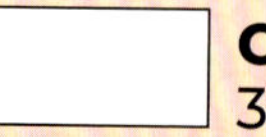

C
3½″ × 6½″

march 16

SPINNING WHEEL
12″ × 12″

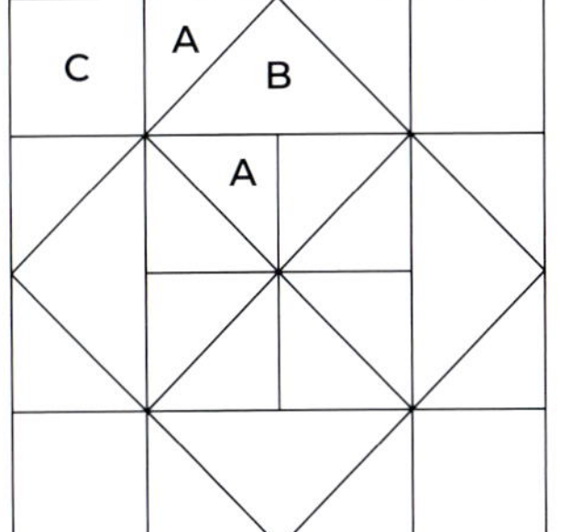

A 3⅞″

B 7¼″

C 3½″

october 17

COMING AND GOING GEESE

12″ × 12″

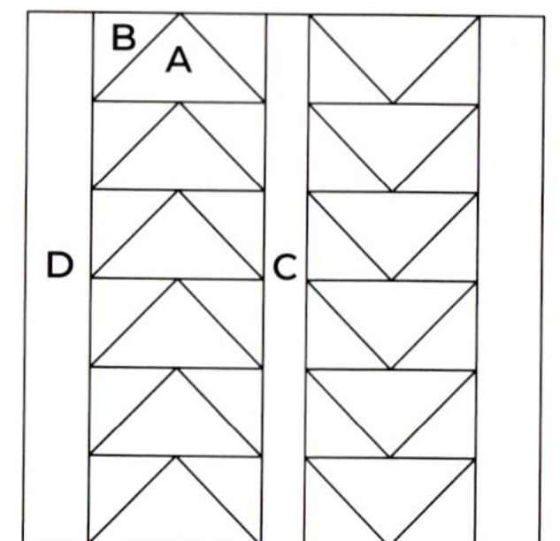

A
5¼″

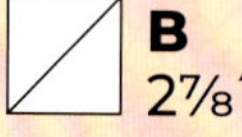

B
2⅞″

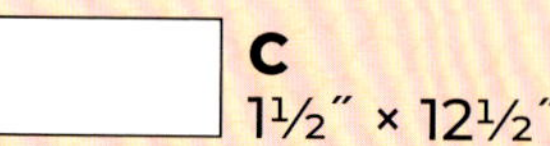

C
1½″ × 12½″

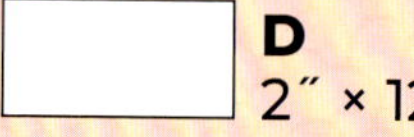

D
2″ × 12½″

march 17

LUCKY IRISH BLOCK

14″ × 14″

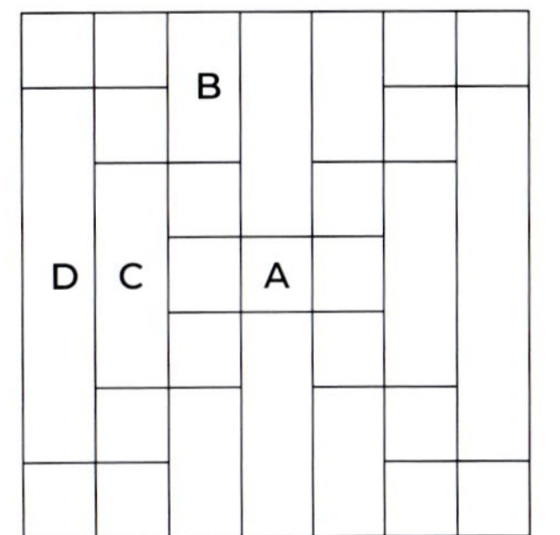

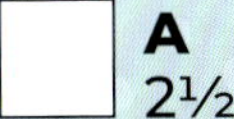

A
2½″

B
2½″ × 4½″

C
2½″ × 6½″

D
2½″ × 10½″

october 16

BIG AND LITTLE GEESE

12″ × 12″

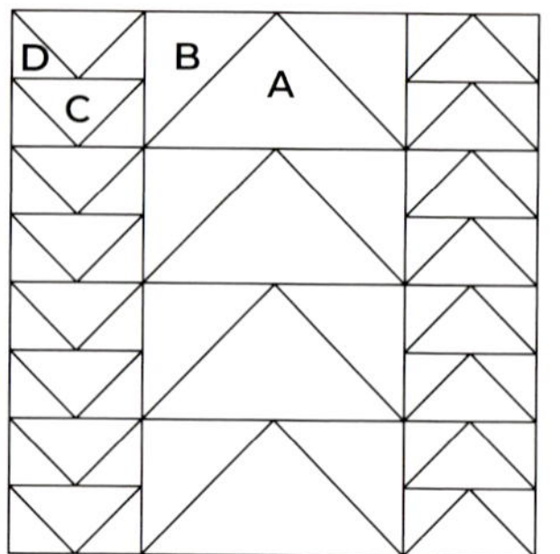

A
7¼″

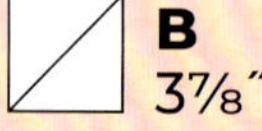

B
3⅞″

C
4¼″

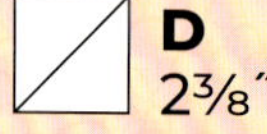

D
2⅜″

march 18

COBBLESTONES

14″ × 14″

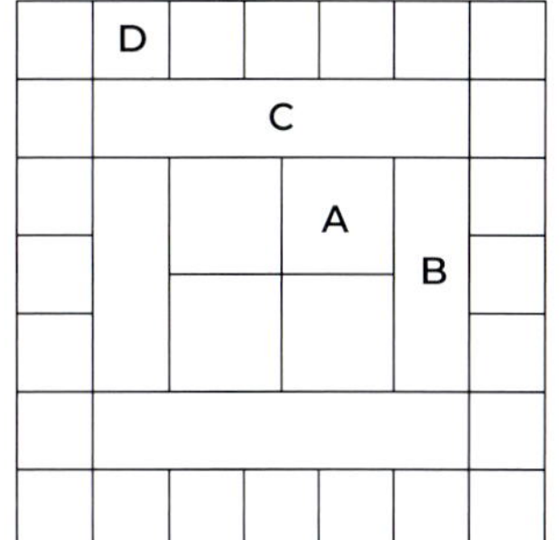

A
3½″

B
2½″ × 6½″

C
2½″ × 10½″

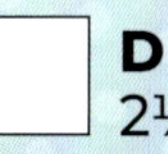

D
2½″

october 15

FOX AND GEESE SQUARED

16″ × 16″

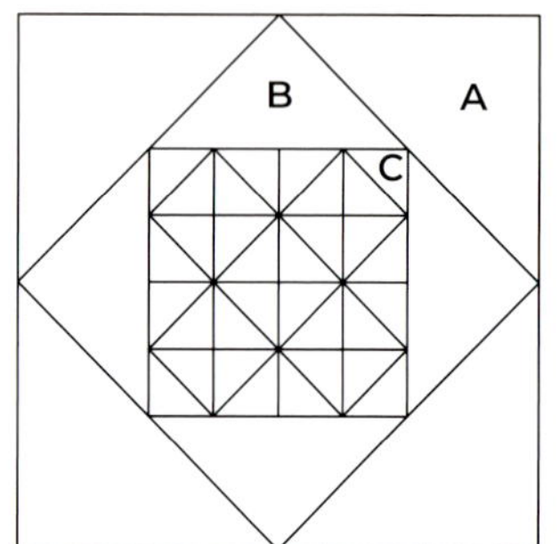

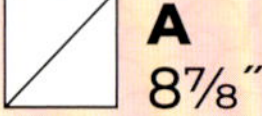

A
8⅞″

B
9¼″

C
2⅞″

march 19

STEPPING STONES
16″ × 16″

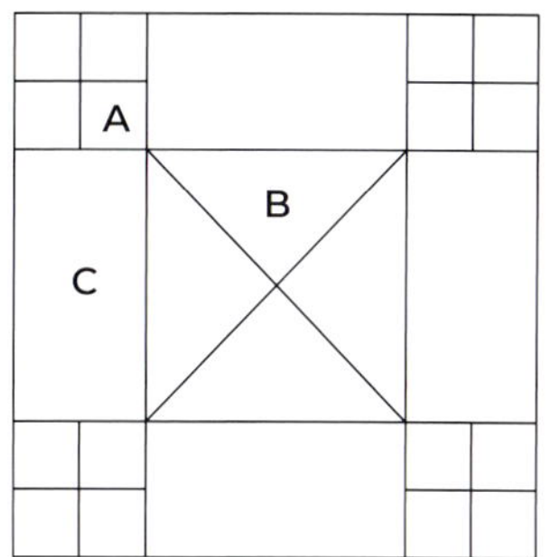

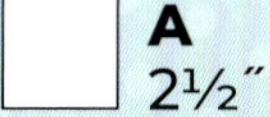
A
2½″

B
9¼″

C
4½″ × 8½″

october 14

TREE OF TEMPTATION

24″ × 24″

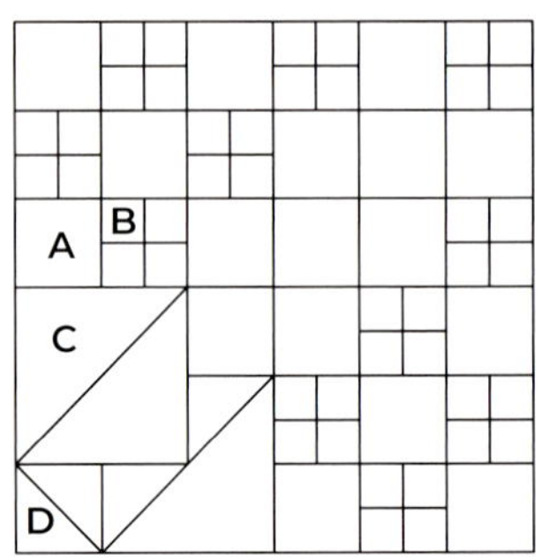

A
4½″

B
2½″

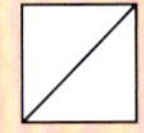

C
8⅞″

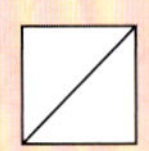

D
4⅞″

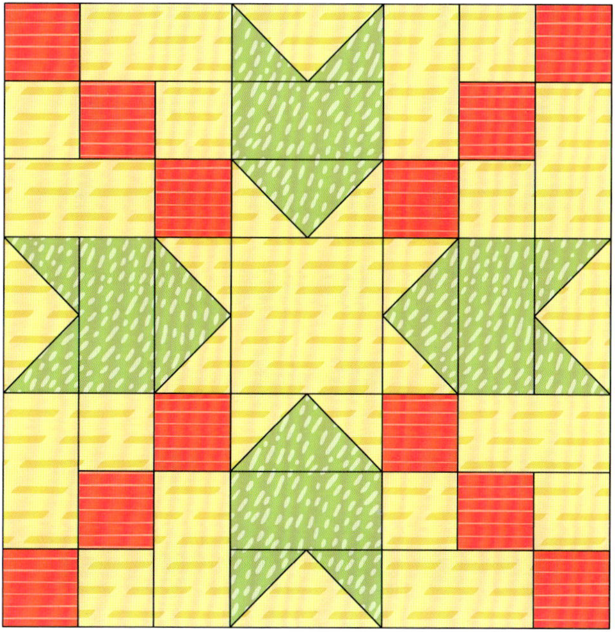

march 20

BLACKFORD'S BEAUTY

16″ × 16″

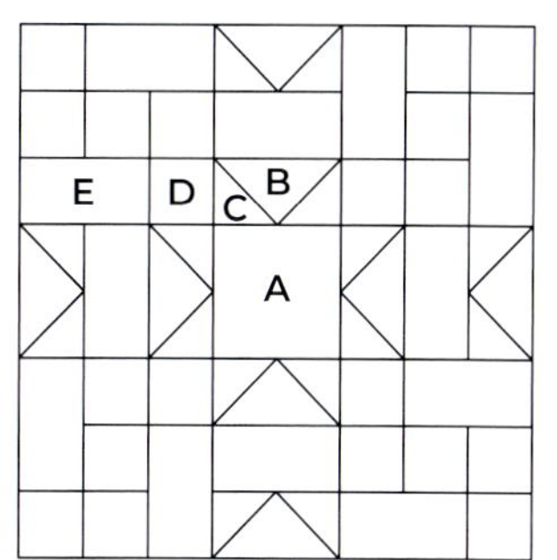

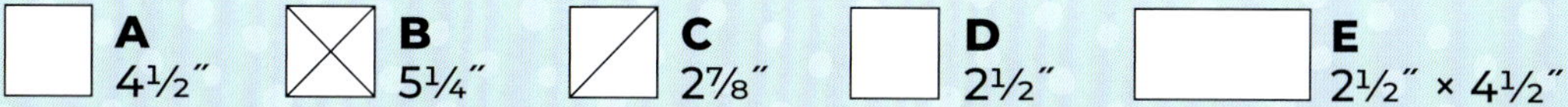

A 4½″

B 5¼″

C 2⅞″

D 2½″

E 2½″ × 4½″

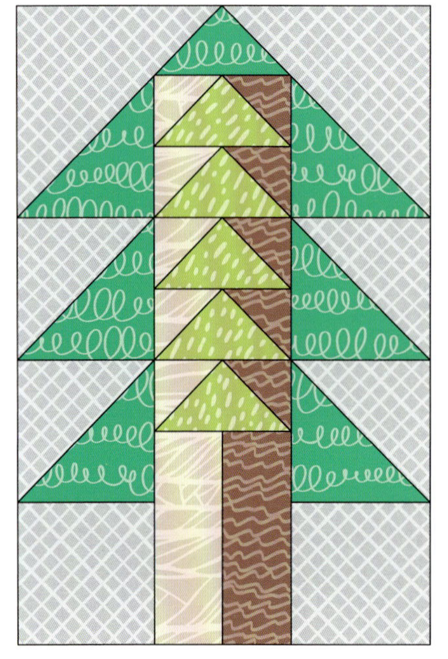

october 13

PINE TREE

12″ × 18″

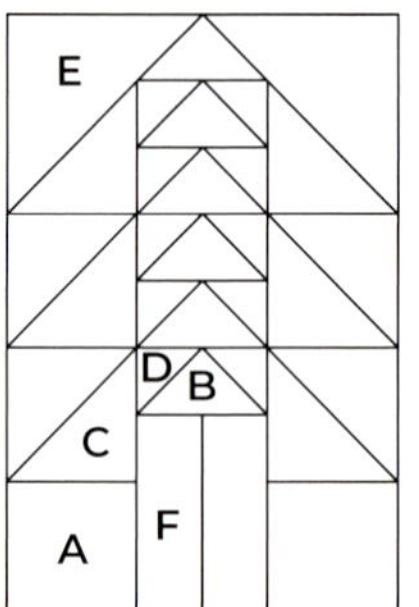

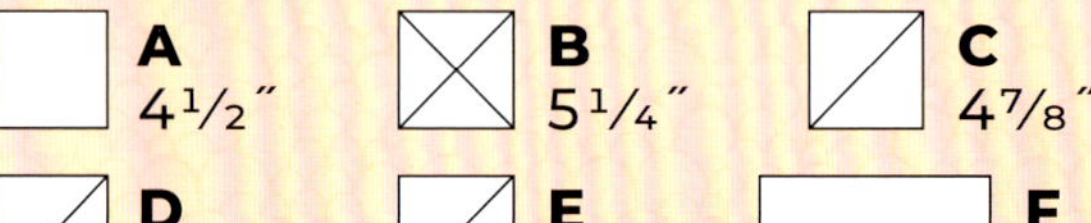

march 21

QUEEN'S CROWN
16″ × 16″

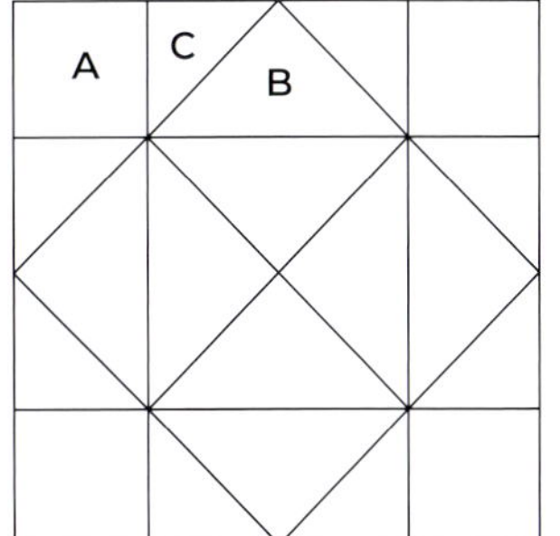

A
4½″

B
9¼″

C
4⅞″

october 12

SANTA MARIA

12″ × 12″

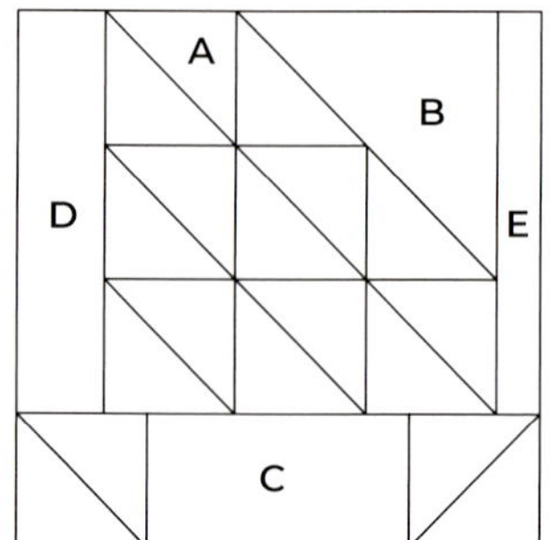

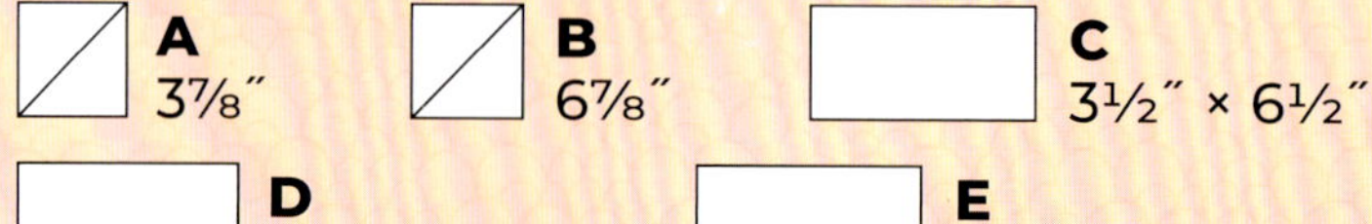

march 22

ALBUM BLOCK

8″ × 8″

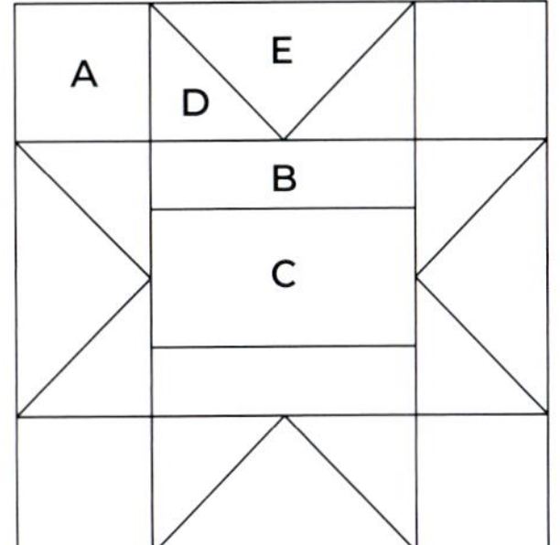

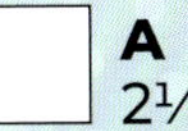

A
2½″

B
1½″ × 4½″

C
2½″ × 4½″

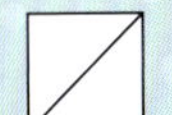

D
2⅞″

E
5¼″

october 11

PINTA

12″ × 12″

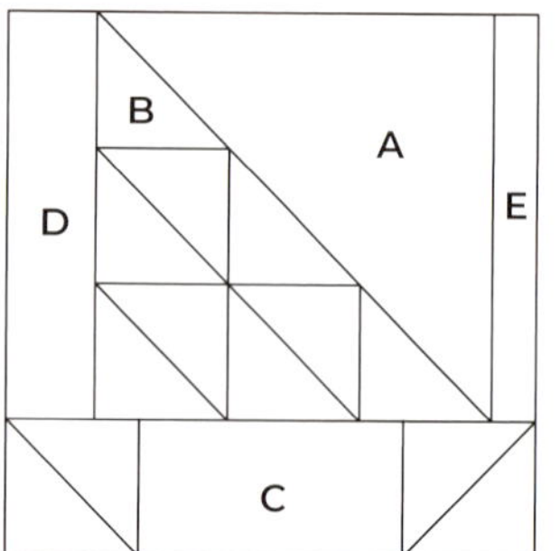

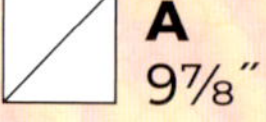

A
9⅞″

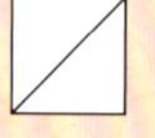

B
3⅞″

C
3½″ × 6½″

D
2½″ × 9½″

E
1½″ × 9½″

march 23

DANCING BETTY

8″ × 8″

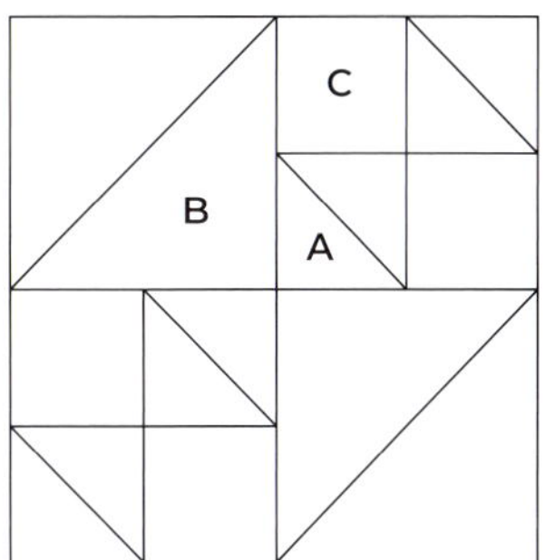

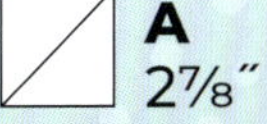

A
2⅞″

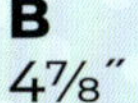

B
4⅞″

C
2½″

october 10

NIÑA
12″ × 12″

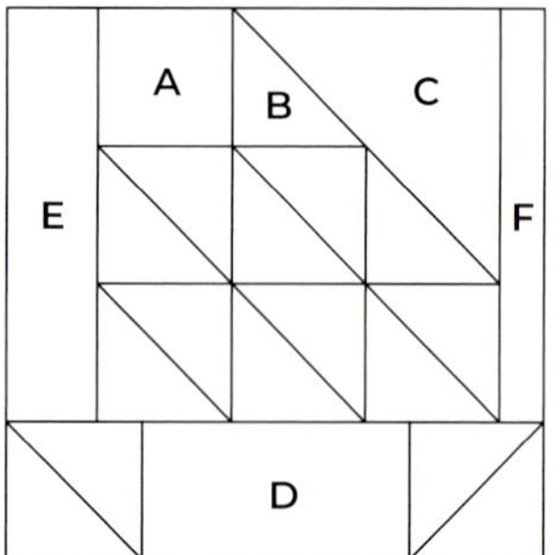

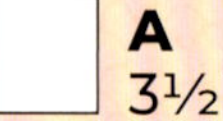

A
3½″

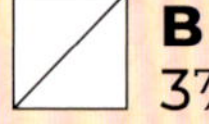

B
3⅞″

C
6⅞″

D
3½″ × 6½″

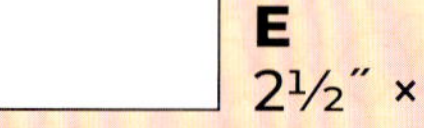

E
2½″ × 9½″

F
1½″ × 9½″

march 24

SARAH'S CHOICE

8″ × 8″

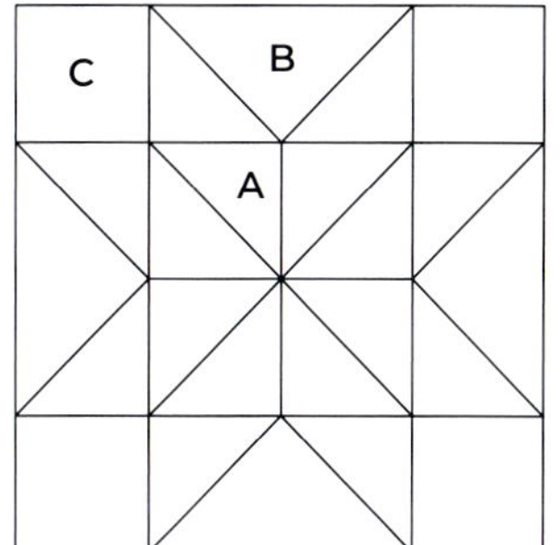

A
2⅞″

B
5¼″

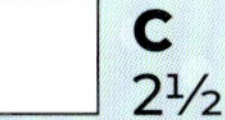

C
2½″

october 9

OCEAN WAVES VARIATION

12″ × 12″

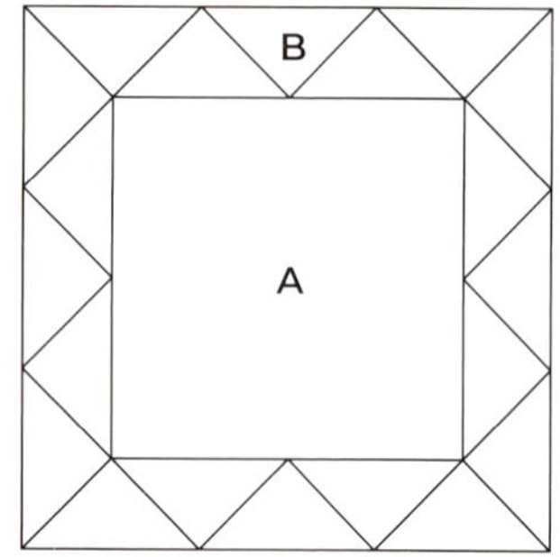

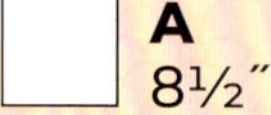

A
8½″

B
5¼″

march 25

FOUR PATCH VARIATION

8″ × 8″

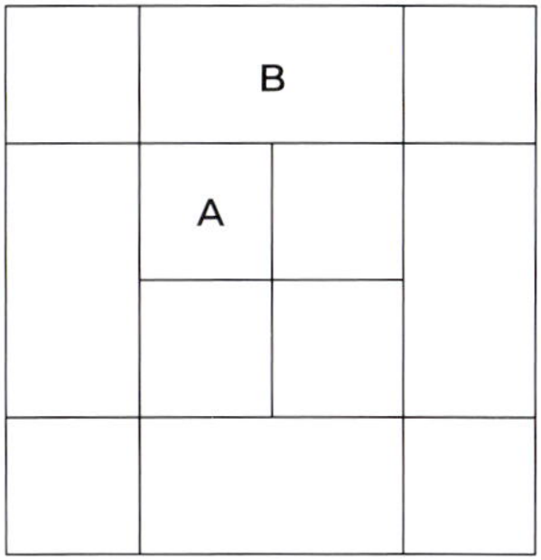

B

A

A
2½″

B
2½″ × 4½″

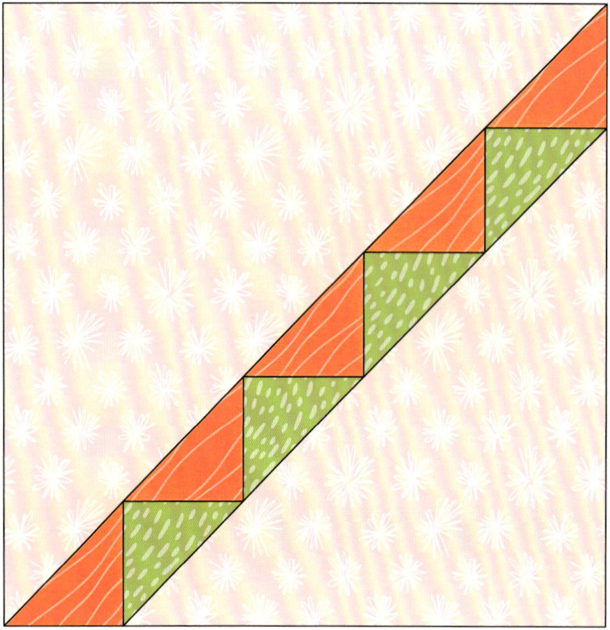

october 8

VINES AT THE WINDOW

12″ × 12″

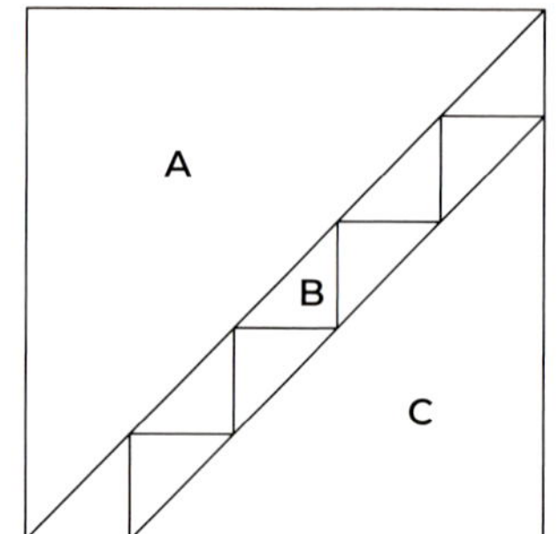

A
12⅞″

B
2⅞″

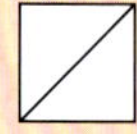

C
10⅞″

march 26

CAKE STAND

16″ × 16″

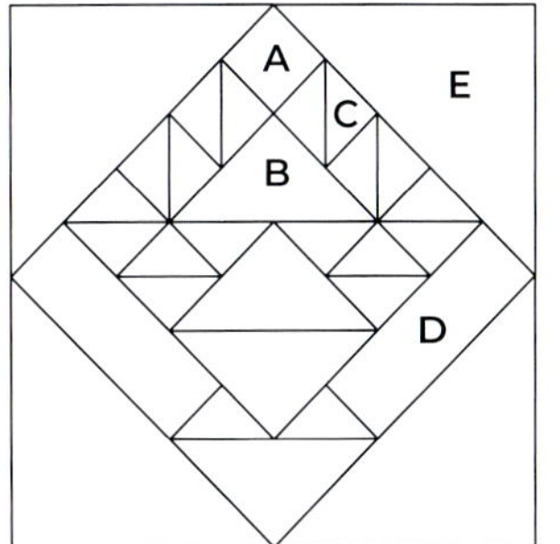

A 2¾″

B 5⅜″

C 3⅛″

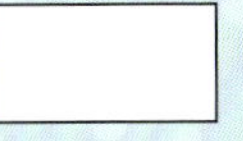

D 2¾″ × 7¼″

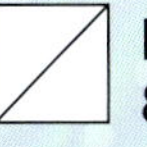

E 8⅞″

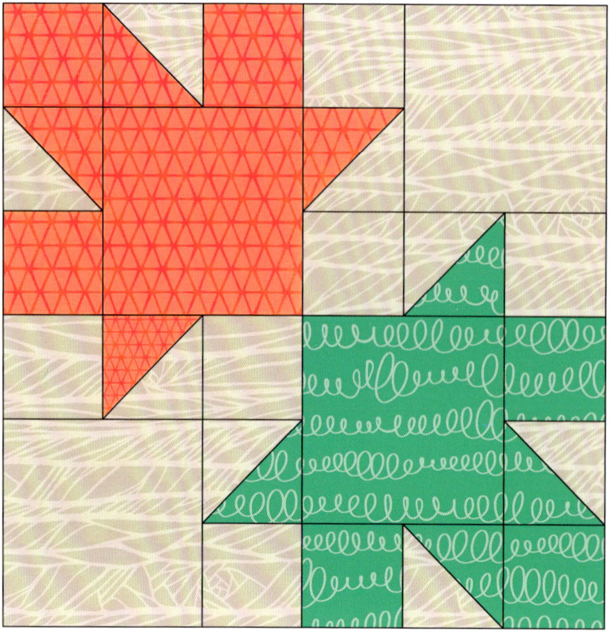

october 7

OZARK MAPLE LEAF

12″ × 12″

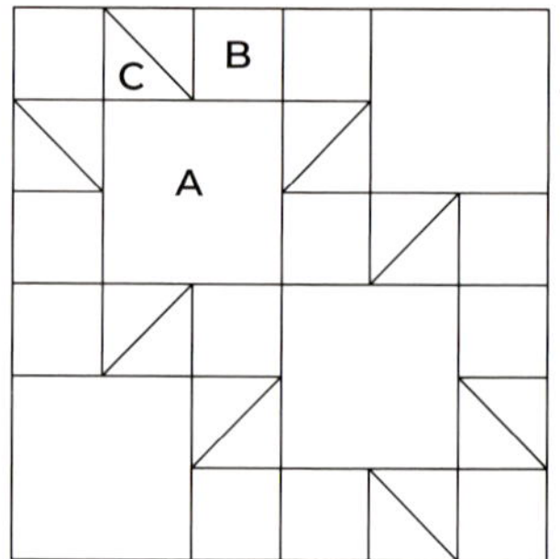

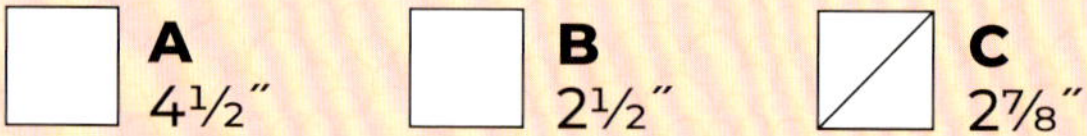

A 4½″

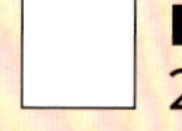

B 2½″

C 2⅞″

march 27

DOUBLE PINWHEEL

12″ × 12″

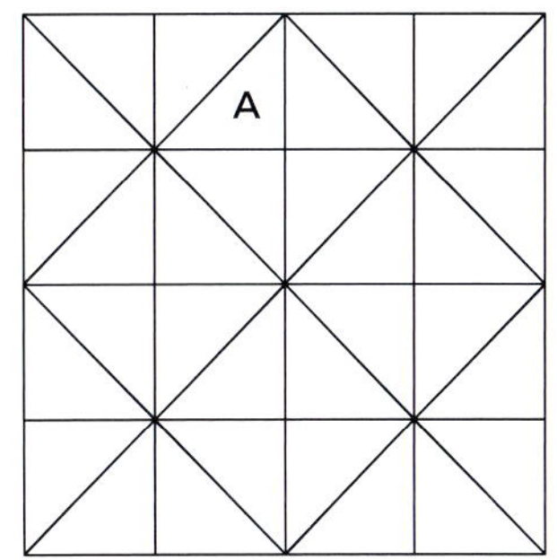

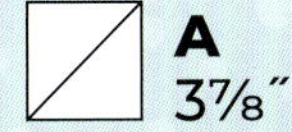

A
3⅞″

october 6

DOUBLE Z

12″ × 12″

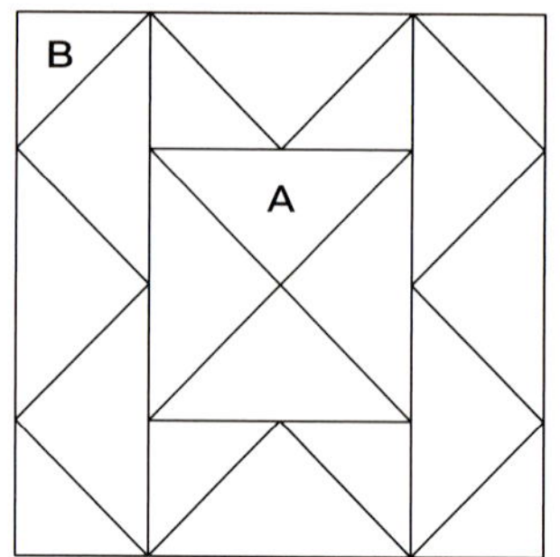

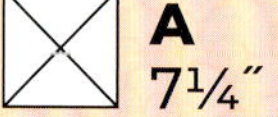

A
$7\frac{1}{4}$″

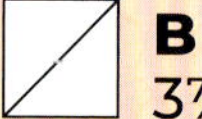

B
$3\frac{7}{8}$″

march 28

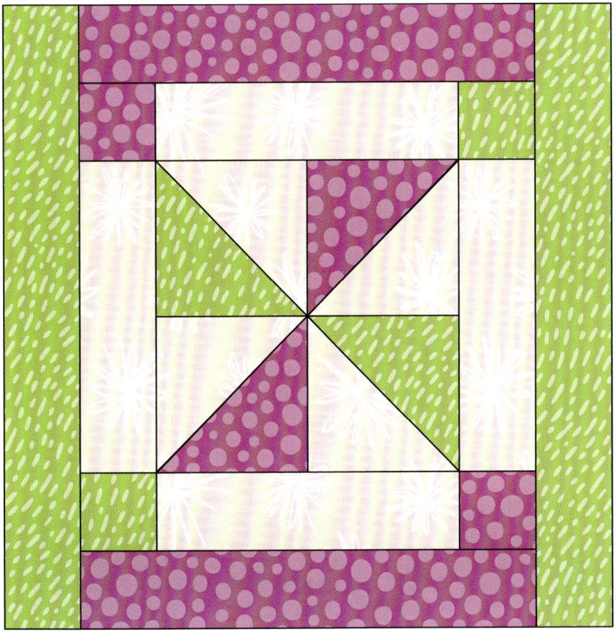

PINWHEEL VARIATION

12″ × 12″

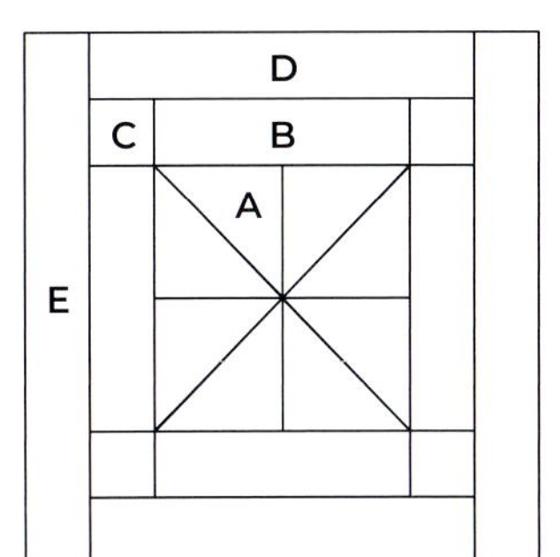

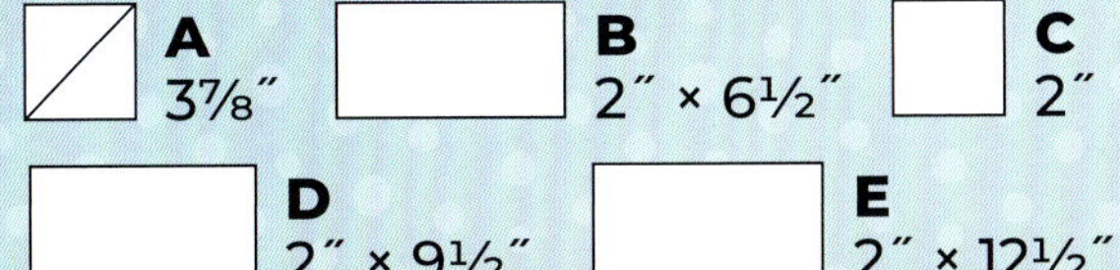

october 5

JACK IN THE BOX

12″ × 12″

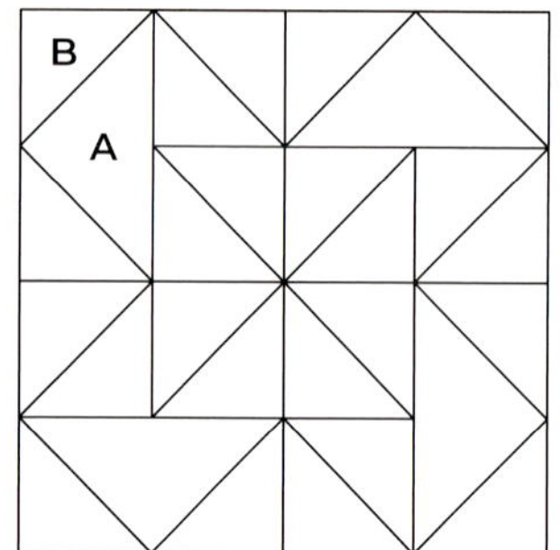

A
7¼″

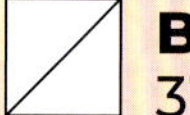

B
3⅞″

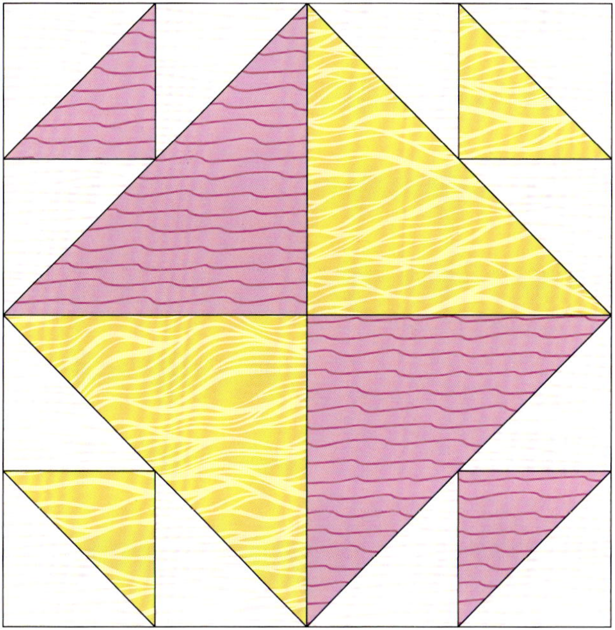

march 29

TRIANGLE X

12″ × 12″

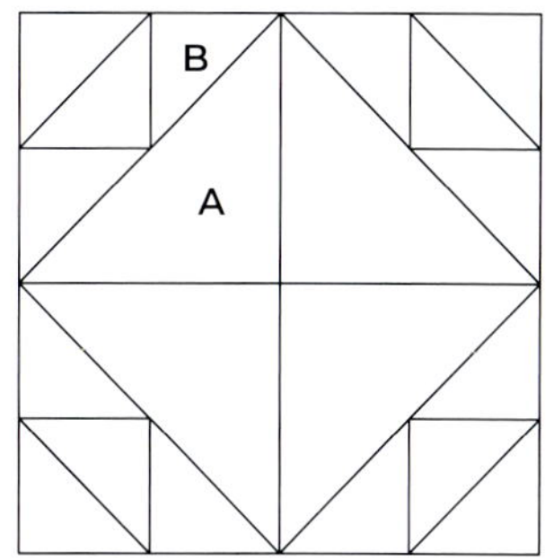

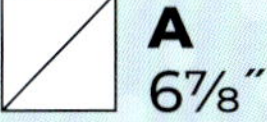

A
6⅞″

B
3⅞″

october 4

KATIE'S CHOICE

10″ × 10″

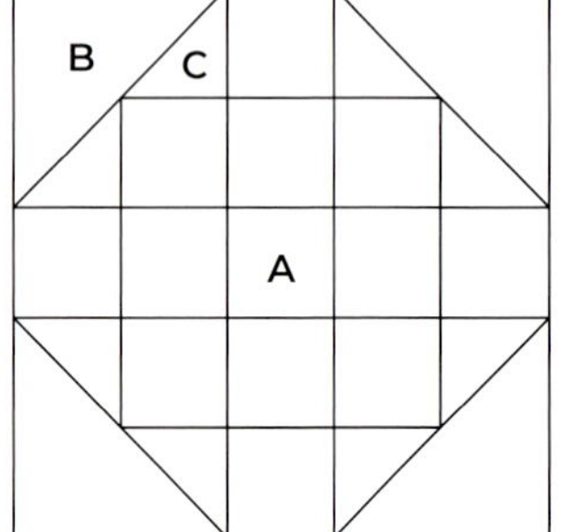

A 2½″

B 4⅞″

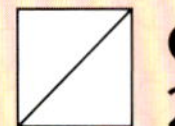
C 2⅞″

march 30

PICNIC PATCH

12″ × 12″

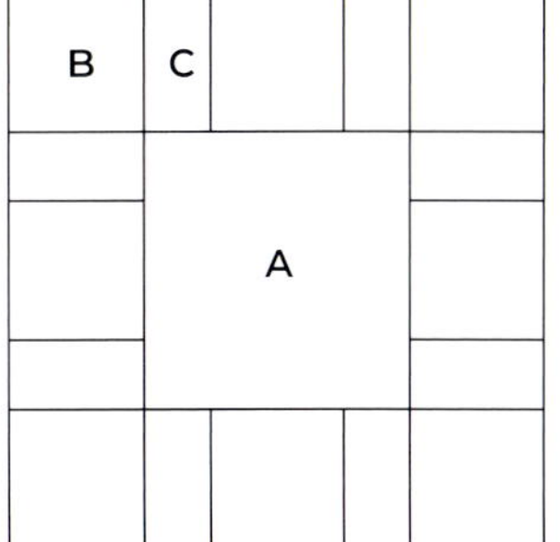

A
6½″

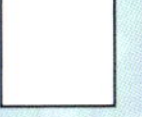

B
3½″

C
2″ × 3½″

october 3

CHURN DASH

10″ × 10″

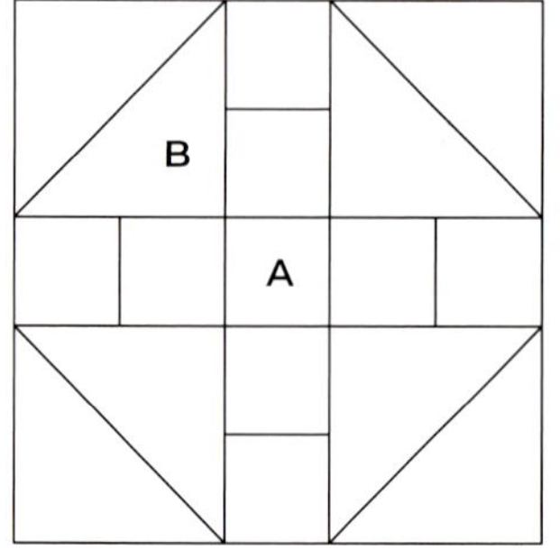

A
2½″

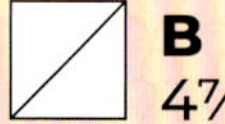

B
4⅞″

march 31

ROSEBUD BLOCK

18″ × 18″

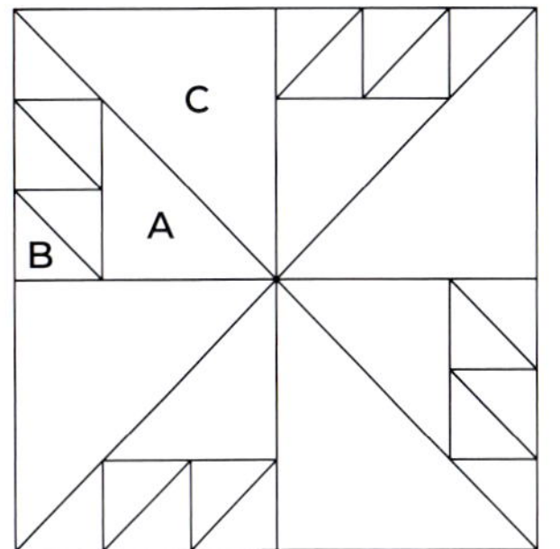

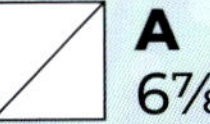
A
6⅞″

B
3⅞″

C
9⅞″

october 2

COMFORT BLOCK

20″ × 20″

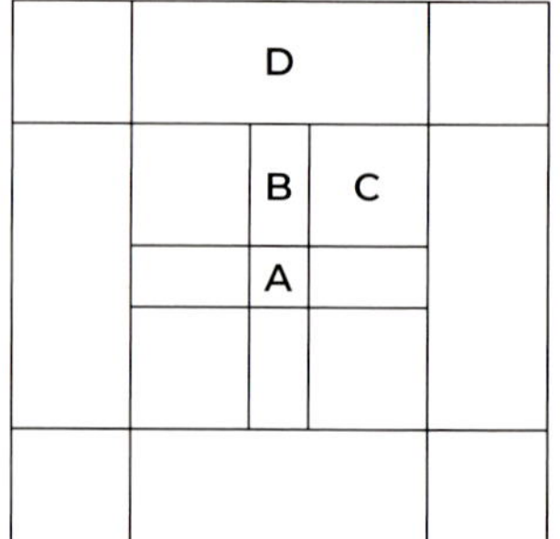

A
2½″

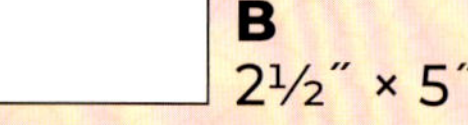

B
2½″ × 5″

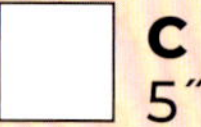

C
5″

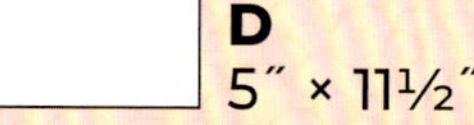

D
5″ × 11½″

april 1

ALABAMA

18″ × 18″

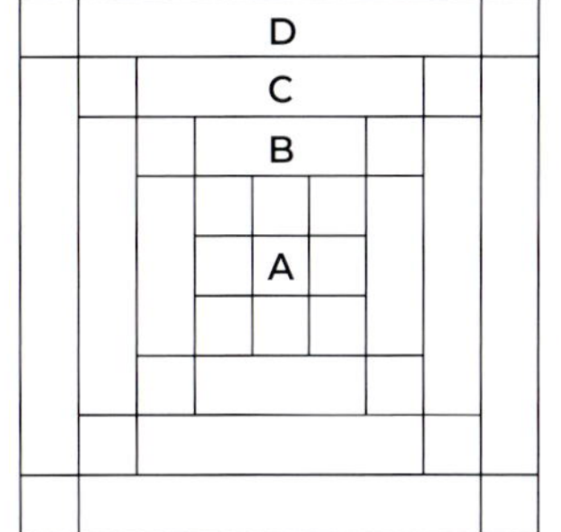

A
2½″

B
2½″ × 6½″

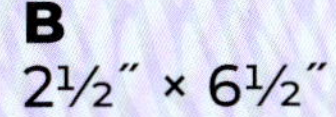

C
2½″ × 10½″

D
2½″ × 14½″

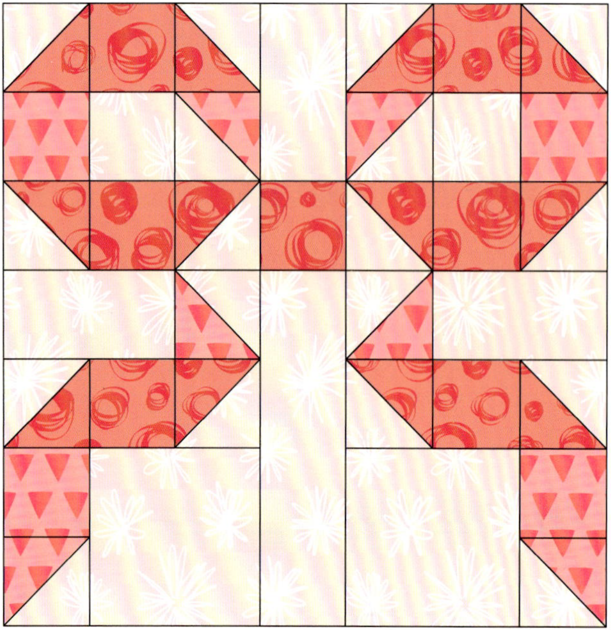

october 1

PIECED RIBBON

14″ × 14″

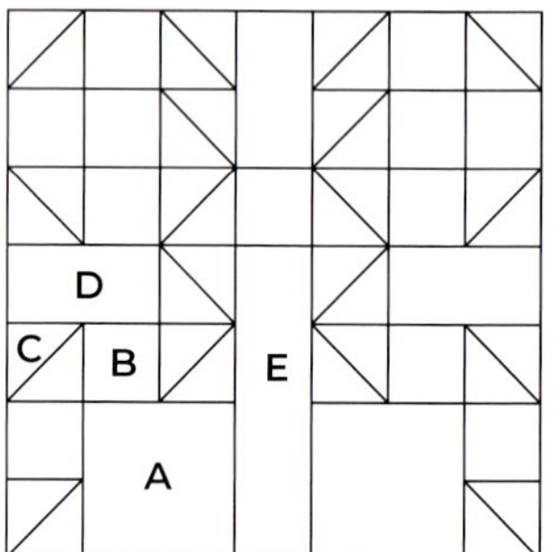

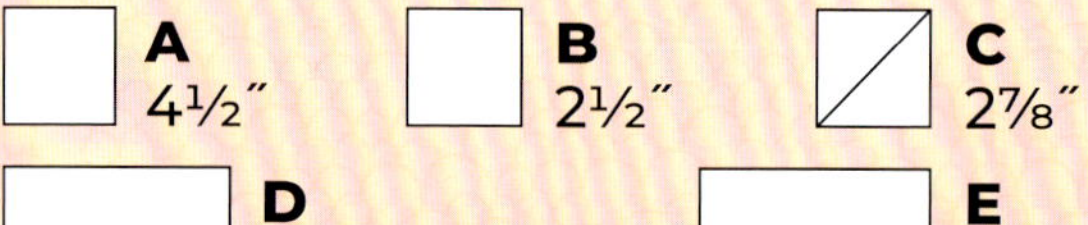

april 2

ANTIQUE TILE

18″ × 18″

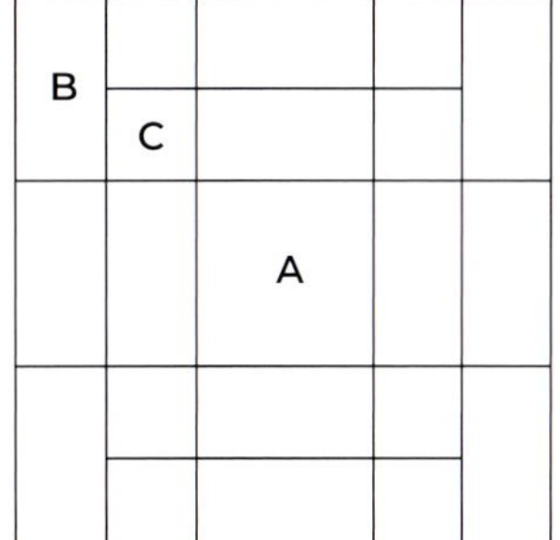

A
6½″

B
3½″ × 6½″

C
3½″

september 30

BEAR'S PAW PATCHES

14″ × 14″

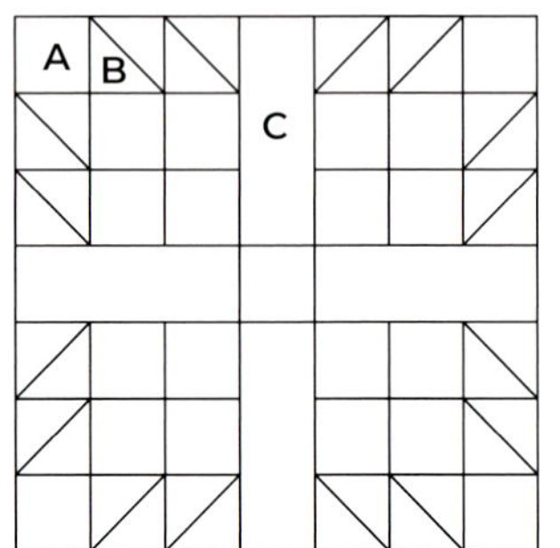

A
2½″

B
2⅞″

C
2½″ × 6½″

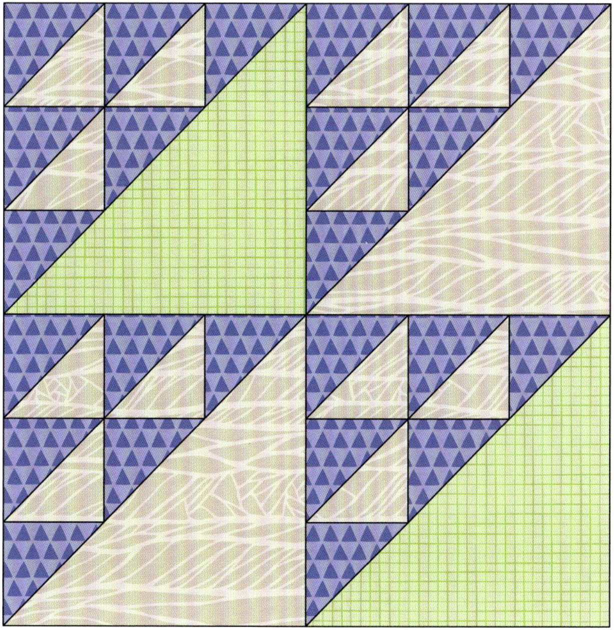

april 3

FLOCK OF BIRDS

18″ × 18″

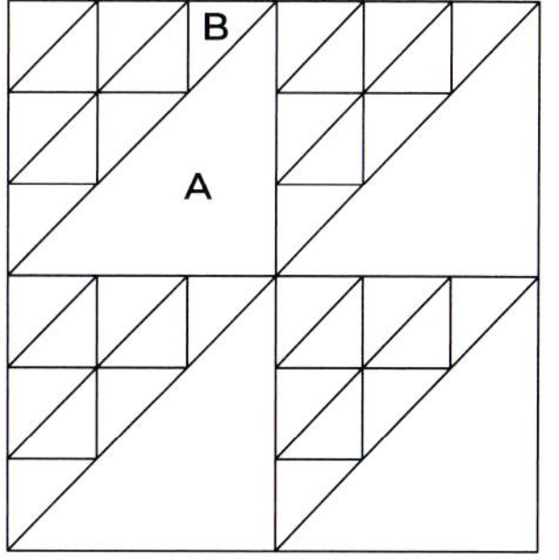

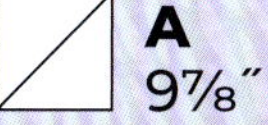

A
9⅞″

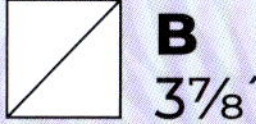

B
3⅞″

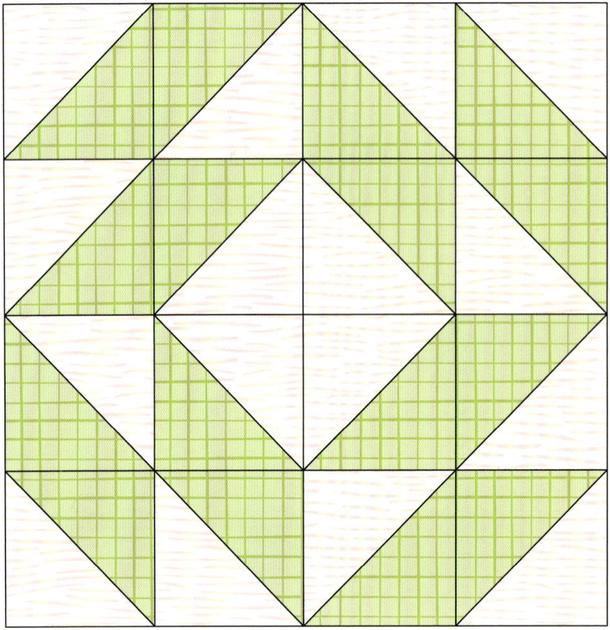

september 29

MOSAIC TRIANGLES

14″ × 14″

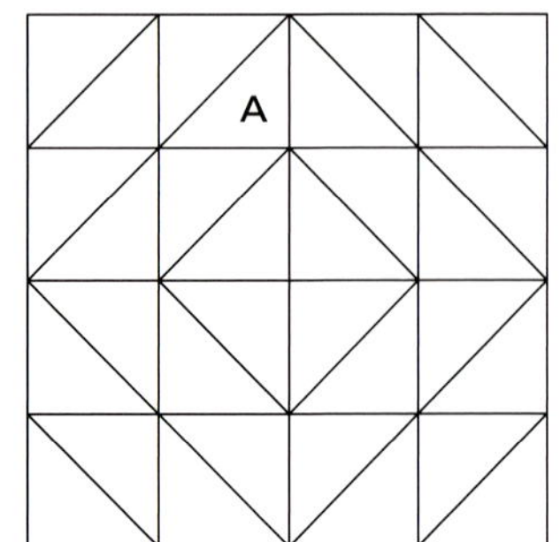

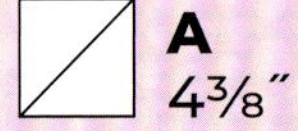

A
4⅜″

april 4

SUNSHINE

18″ × 18″

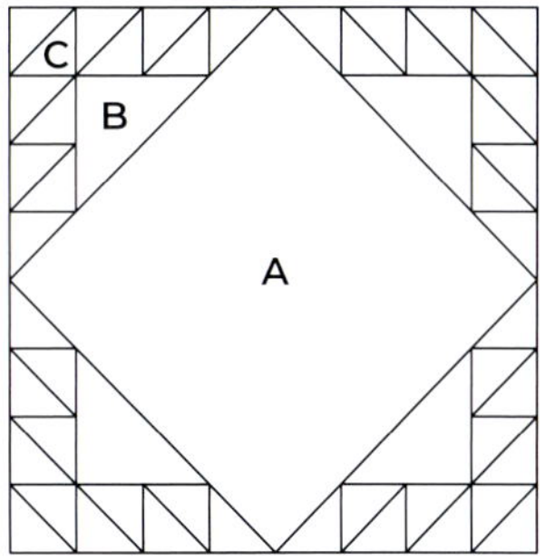

A
13¼″

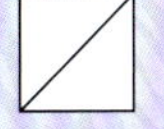

B
5⅜″

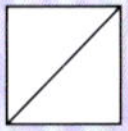

C
3⅛″

september 28

GRIZZLY BLOCK

14″ × 14″

A 2⅞″

B 2½″

C 4½″

D 2½″ × 6½″

april 5

SQUARES AND TRIANGLES

18″ × 18″

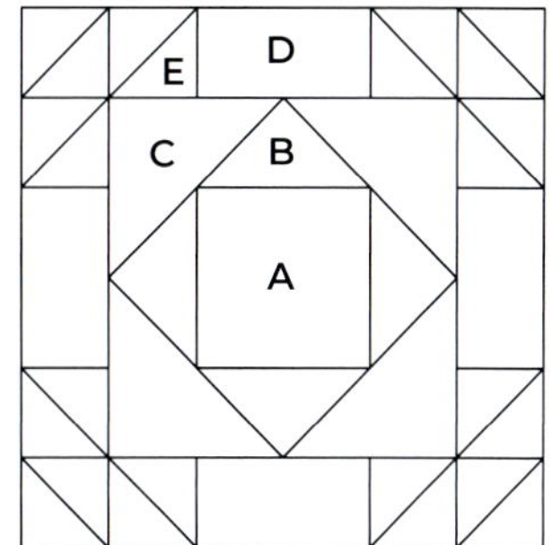

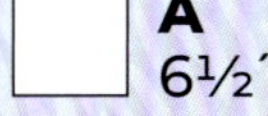

A
6½″

B
7¼″

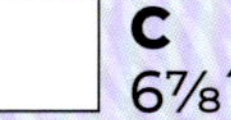

C
6⅞″

D
3½″ × 6½″

E
3⅞″

september 27

MOTHER'S FANCY

14″ × 14″

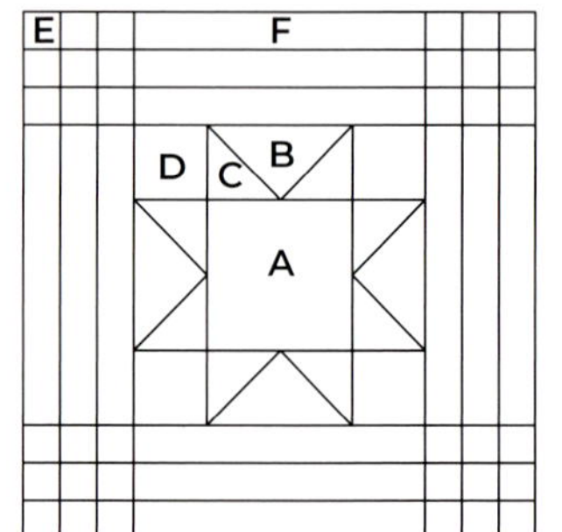

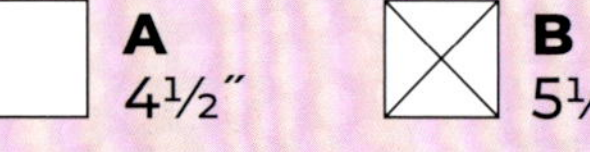

A 4½″

B 5¼″

C 2⅞″

D 2½″

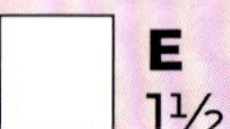

E 1½″

F 1½″ × 8½″

april 6

DOUBLE 9 PATCH
18″ × 18″

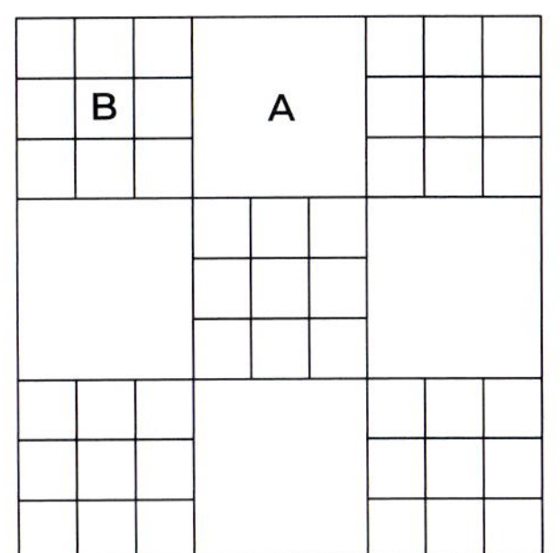

A
6½″

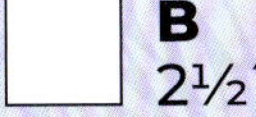

B
2½″

september 26

PRICKLY PEAR

14″ × 14″

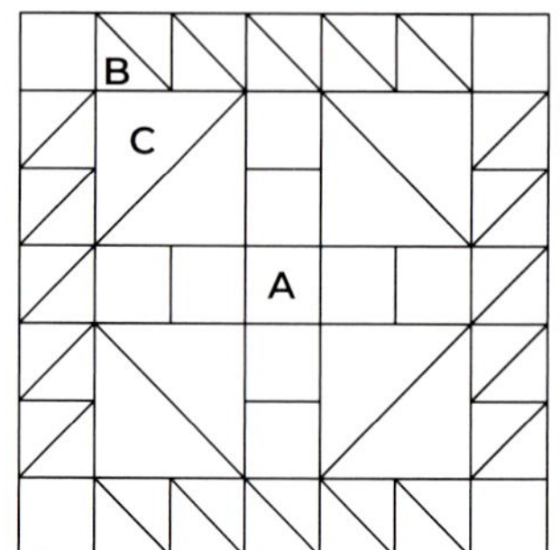

A
2½″

B
2⅞″

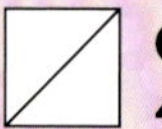

C
4⅞″

april 7

LONDON ROADS

18″ × 18″

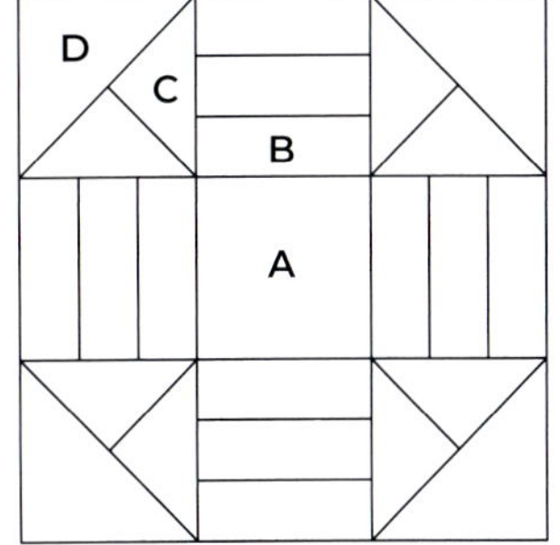

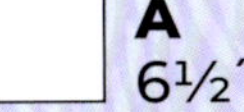

A
6½″

B
2½″ × 6½″

C
7¼″

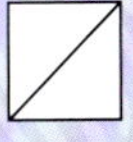

D
6⅞″

september 25

MILLSTONE

12″ × 12″

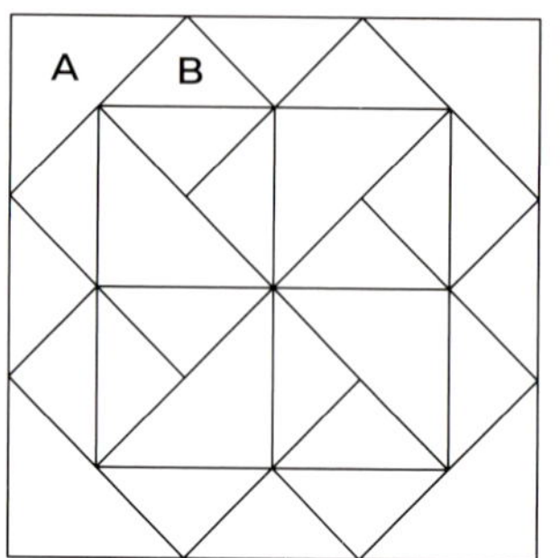

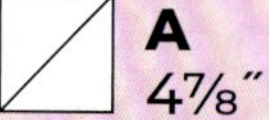

A
4⅞″

B
5¼″

april 8

ROLLING GEARS

18″ × 18″

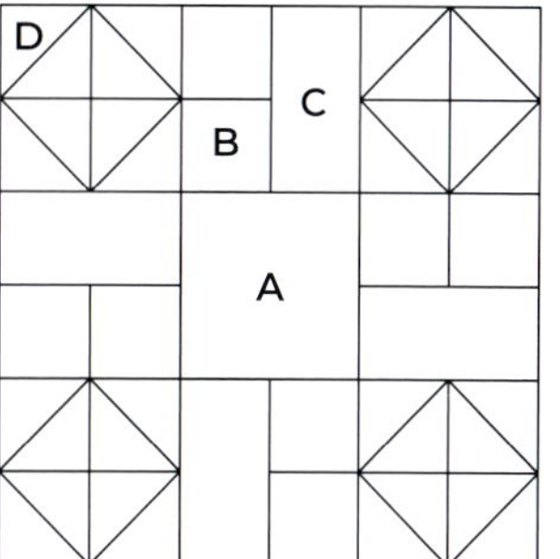

A
6½″

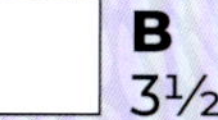

B
3½″

C
3½″ × 6½″

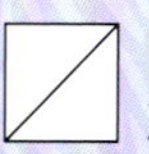

D
3⅞″

september 24

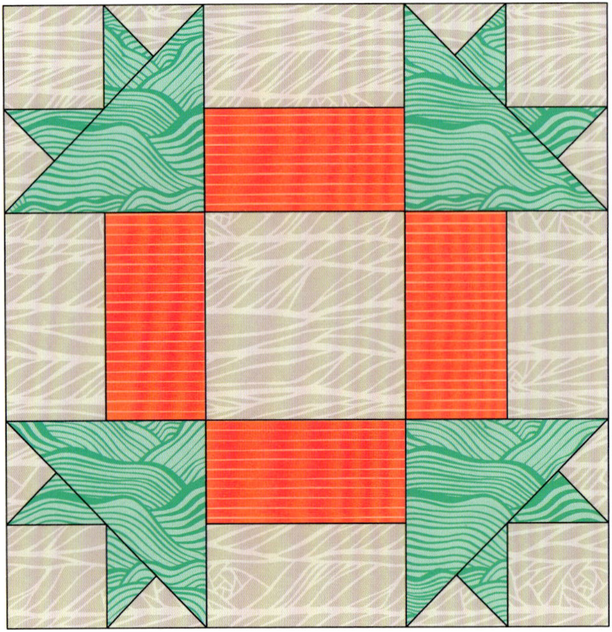

SAGE BUD VARIATION

12″ × 12″

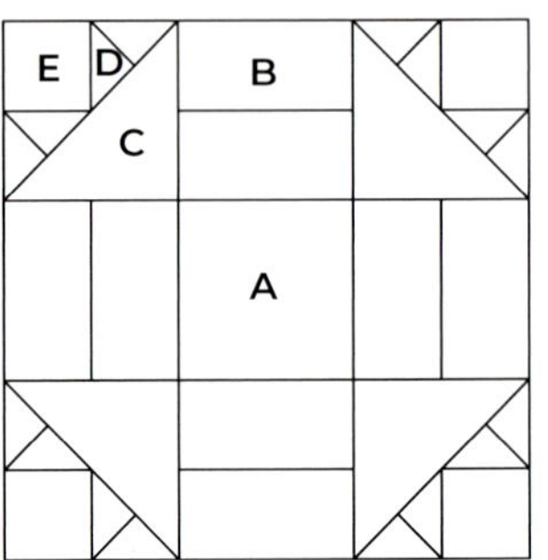

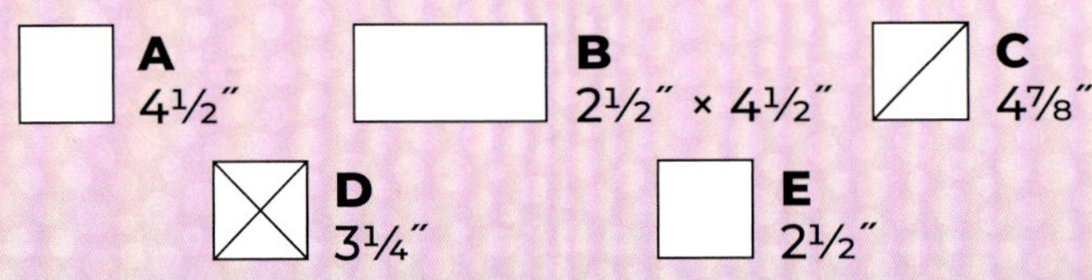

april 9

FOUR PATCH ON POINT

9″ × 9″

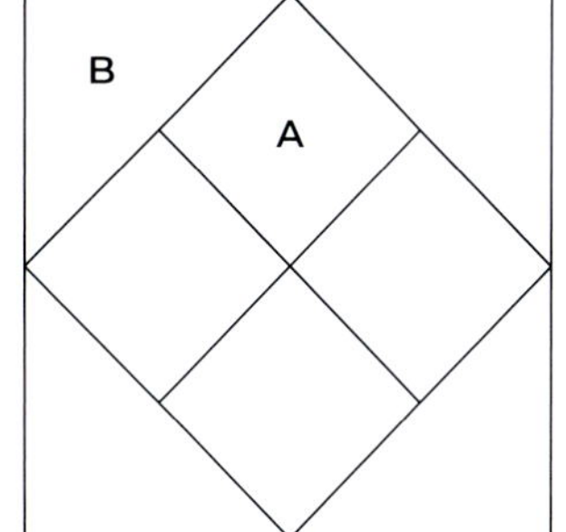

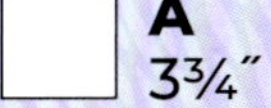

A
3¾″

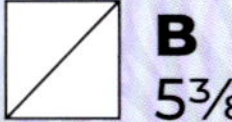

B
5⅜″

september 23

BLIND MAN'S FANCY

12″ × 12″

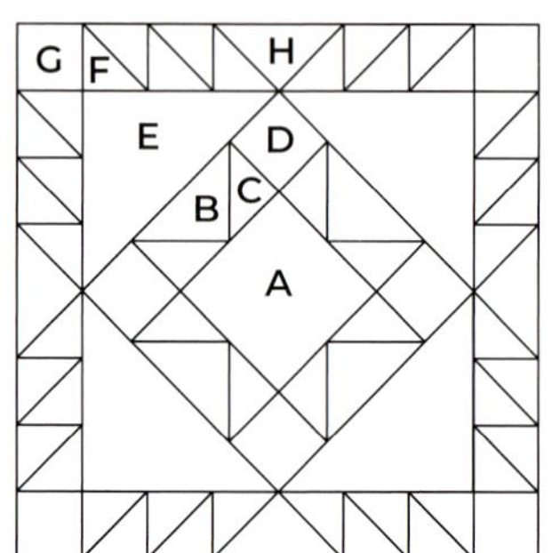

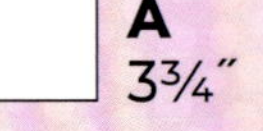

A
3¾″

B
4½″

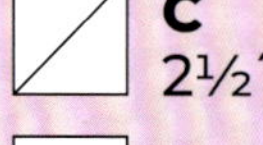

C
2½″

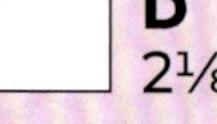

D
2⅛″

E
5⅜″

F
2⅜″

G
2″

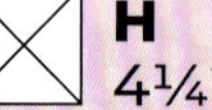

H
4¼″

april 10

NINE PATCH VARIATION

9″ × 9″

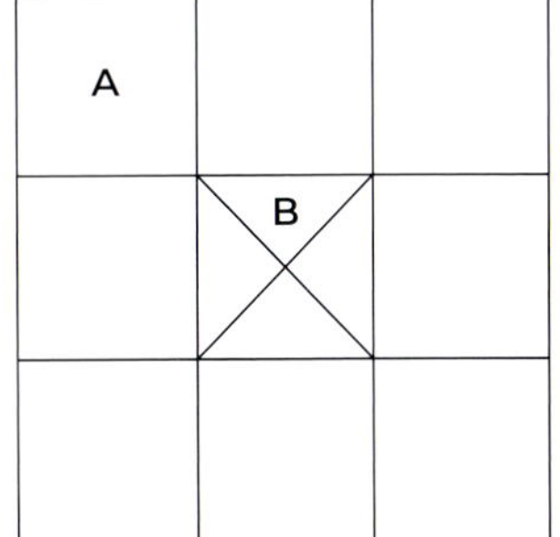

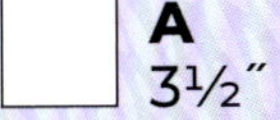

A
3½″

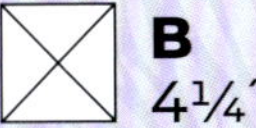

B
4¼″

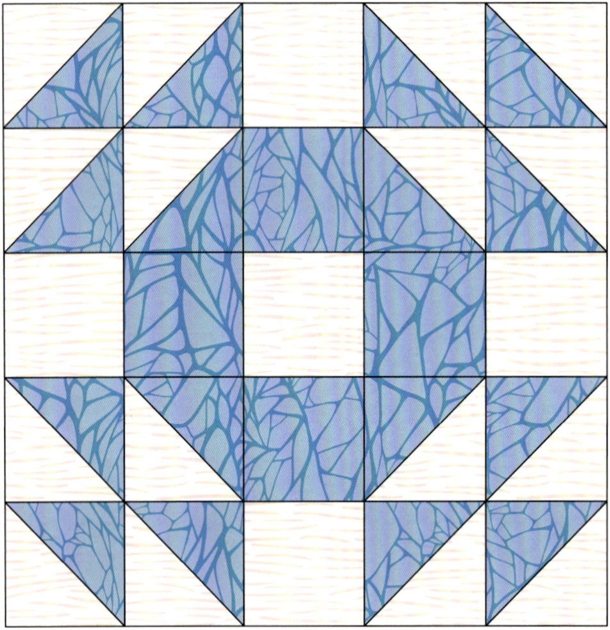

september 22

GEORGETOWN CIRCLE
10″ × 10″

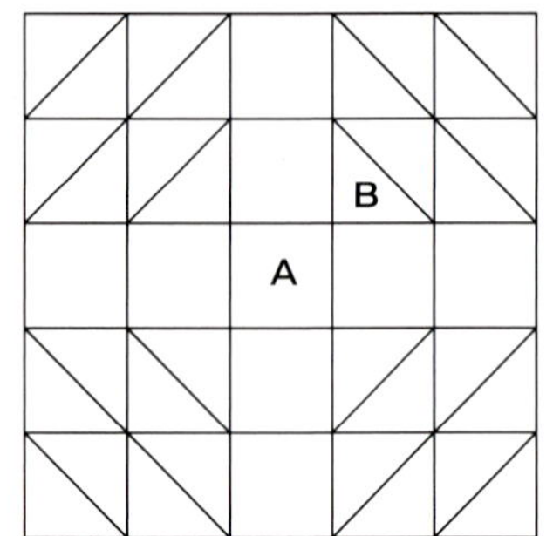

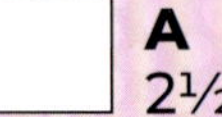
A
$2\frac{1}{2}$″

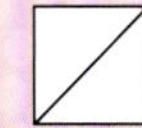
B
$2\frac{7}{8}$″

april 11

PINWHEEL ON POINT

9″ × 9″

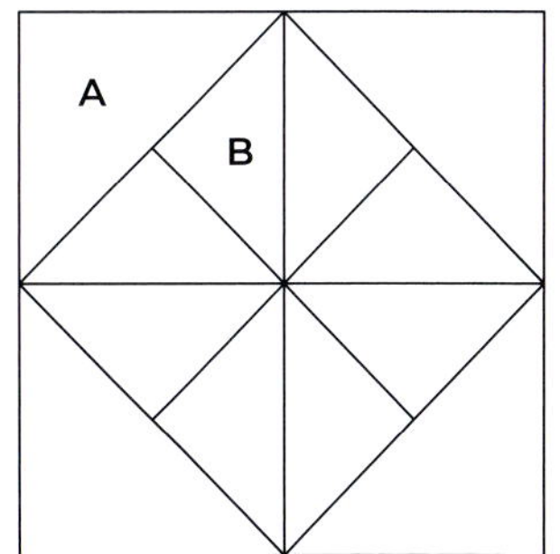

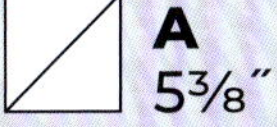

A
5⅜″

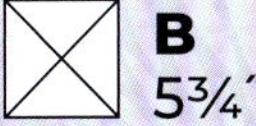

B
5¾″

september 21

MEMORY STAR VARIATION

12″ × 12″

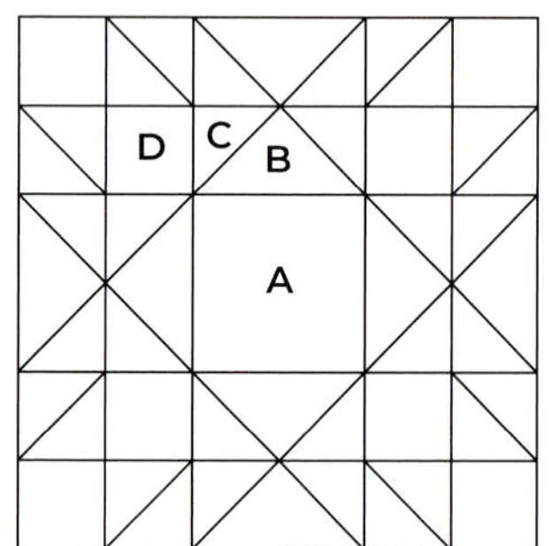

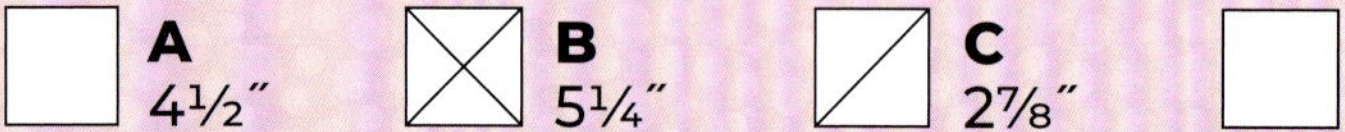

A
4½″

B
5¼″

C
2⅞″

D
2½″

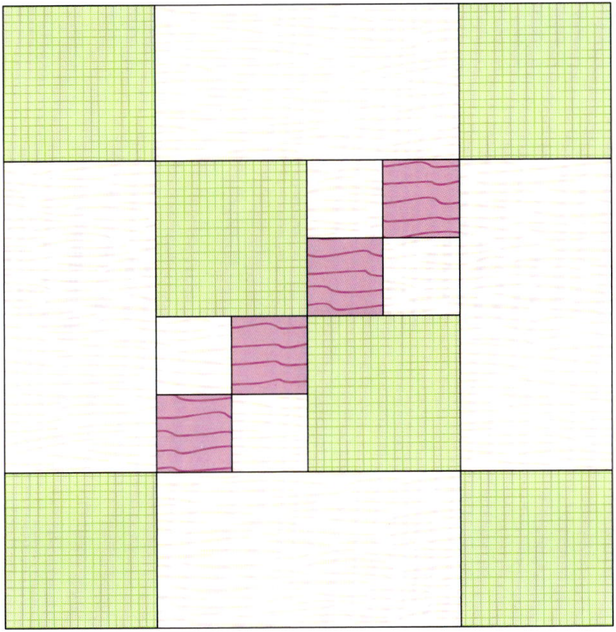

april 12

DOUBLE 4 PATCH
16″ × 16″

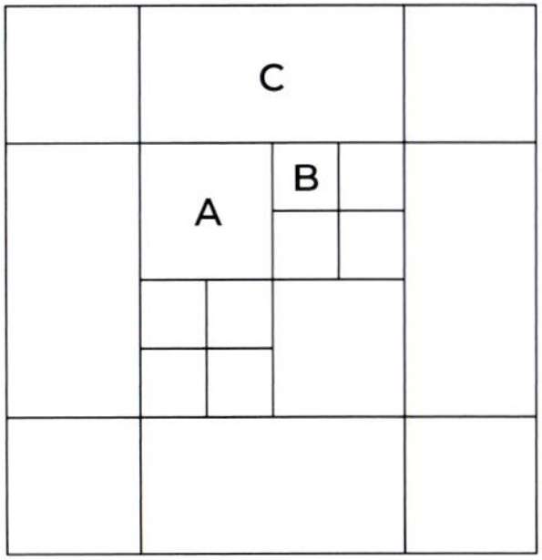

C

B

A

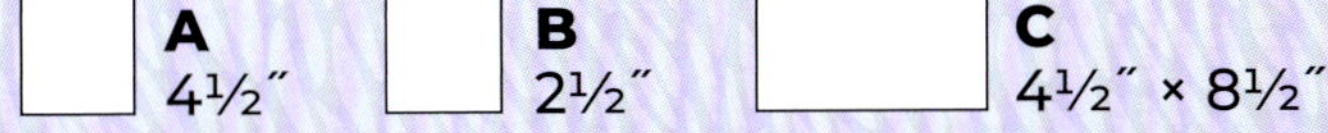

september 20

HOMEWARD BOUND

12″ × 12″

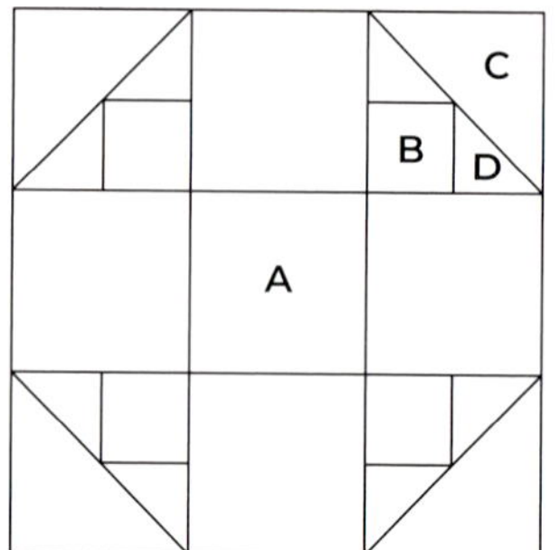

A 4½″

B 2½″

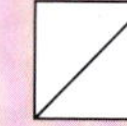

C 4⅞″

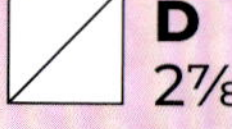

D 2⅞″

april 13

IRISH CHAIN VARIATION

16″ × 16″

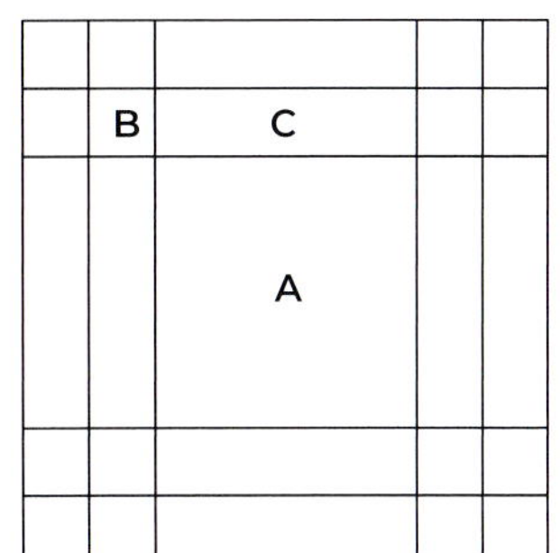

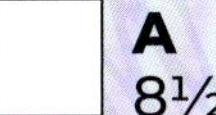

A
8½″

B
2½″

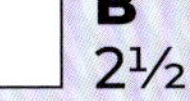

C
2½″ × 8½″

september 19

LOST GOSLIN

12″ × 12″

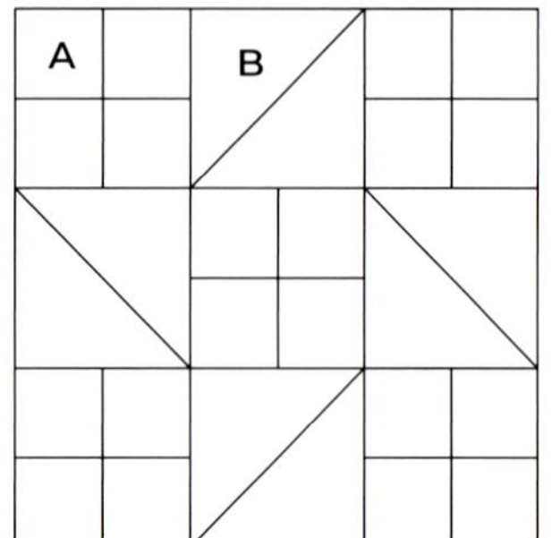

A
2½″

B
4⅞″

april 14

RISING SUN BLOCK

18″ × 18″

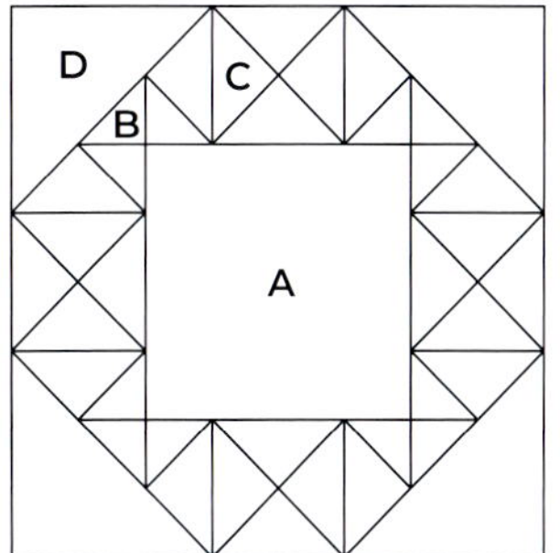

A 9½″

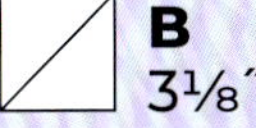

B 3⅛″

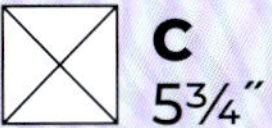

C 5¾″

D 7⅝″

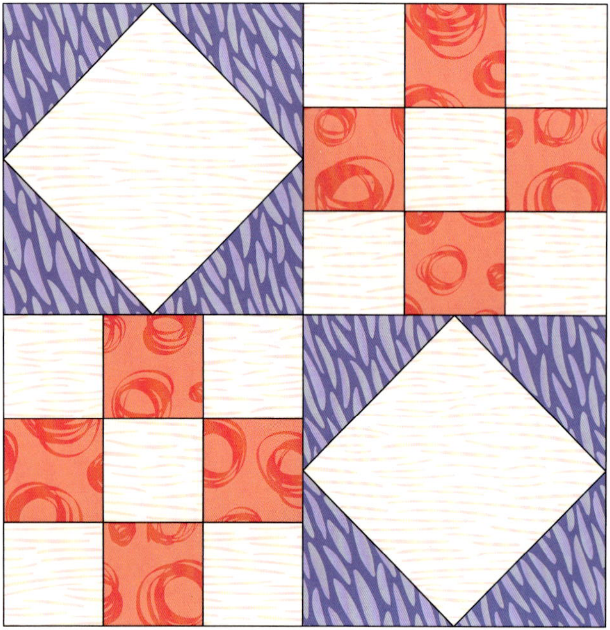

september 18

GOOSE CREEK

12″ × 12″

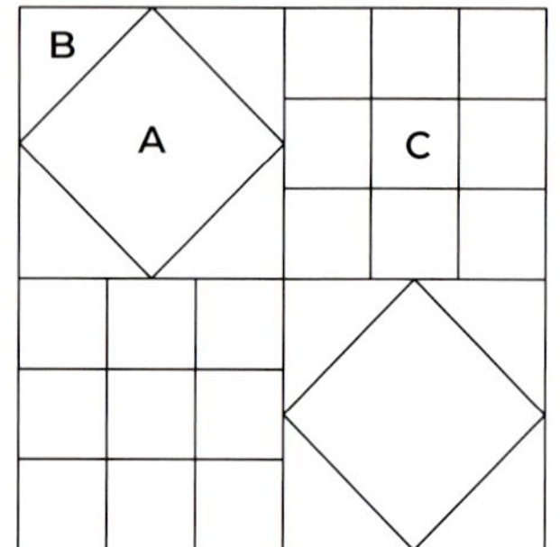

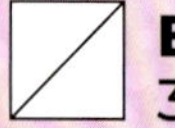
A
4¾″

B
3⅞″

C
2½″

april 15

RISING SUN VARIATION

18″ × 18″

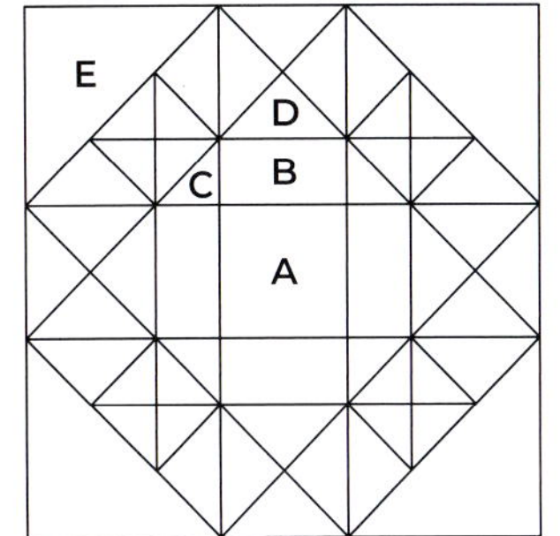

A
5″

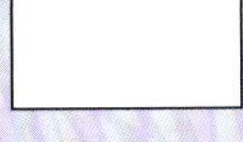

B
2¾″ × 5″

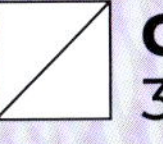

C
3⅛″

D
5¾″

E
7⅝″

september 17

LADIES AID

12″ × 12″

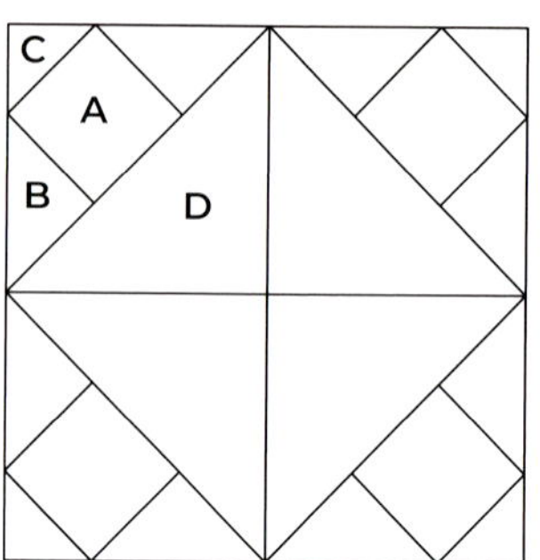

A
3 3/8″

B
5 1/4″

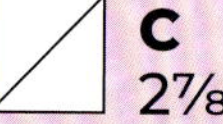

C
2 7/8″

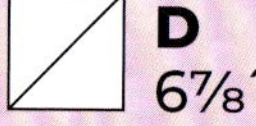

D
6 7/8″

april 16

KIMONO

12″ × 14″

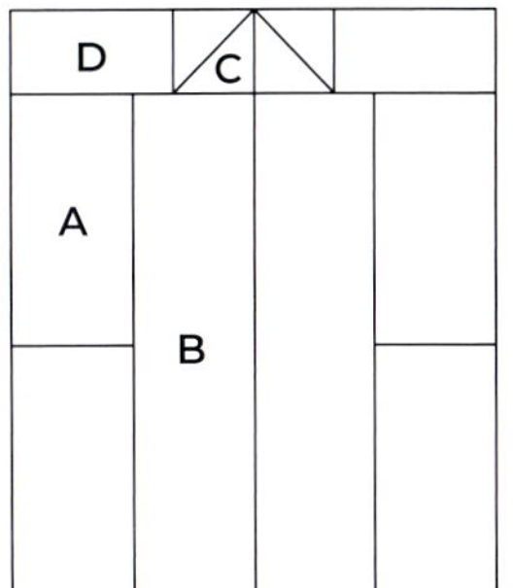

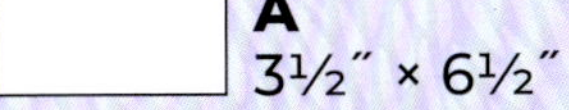

A
3½″ × 6½″

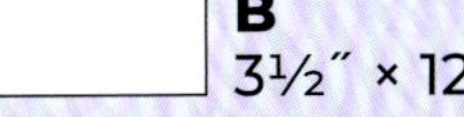

B
3½″ × 12½″

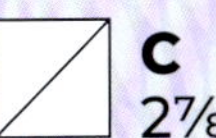

C
2⅞″

D
2½″ × 4½″

september 16

BEAR TRACKS

12″ × 12″

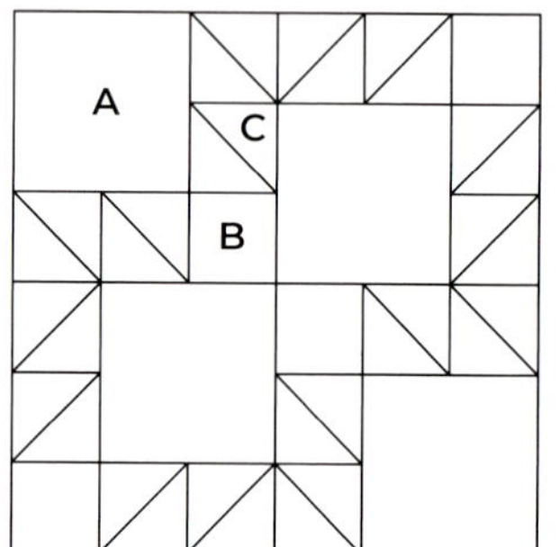

A
4½″

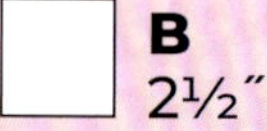

B
2½″

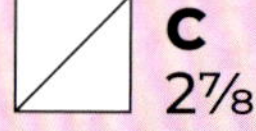

C
2⅞″

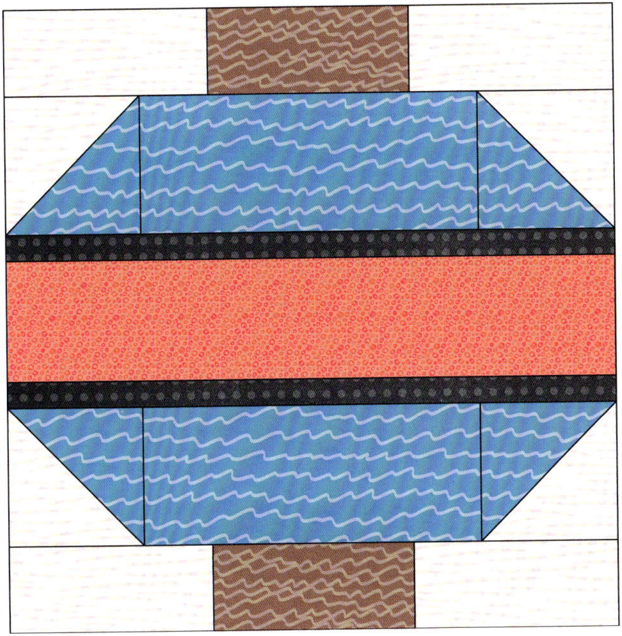

april 17

JAPANESE LANTERN

9″ × 9″

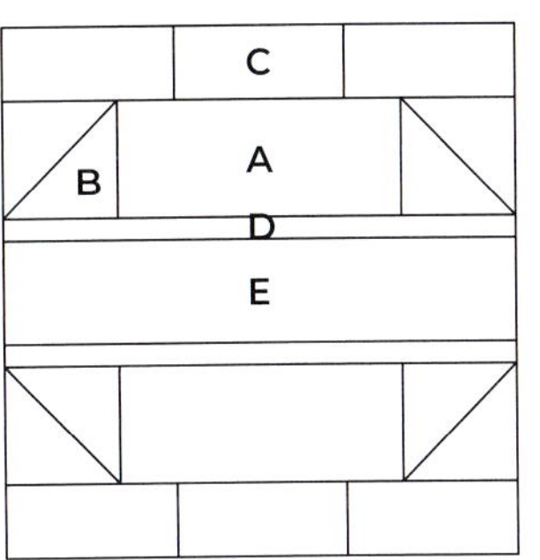

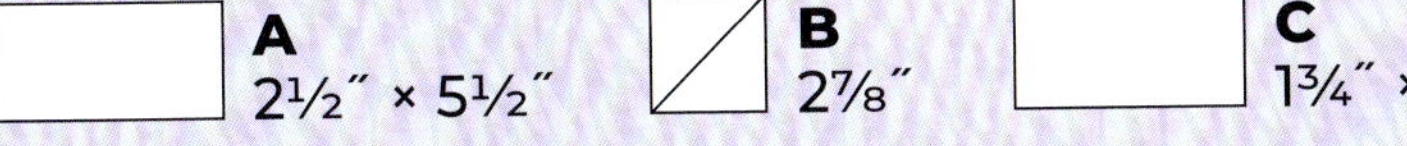

A 2½″ × 5½″

B 2⅞″

C 1¾″ × 3½″

D ⅞″ × 9½″

E 2¼″ × 9½″

september 15

MARKET SQUARE

12″ × 12″

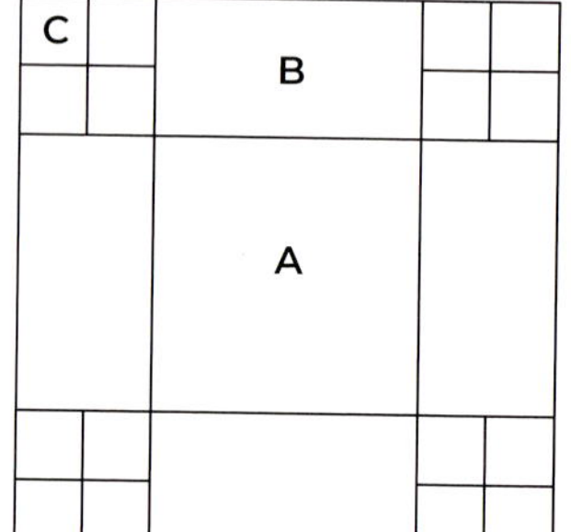

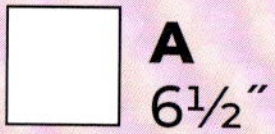

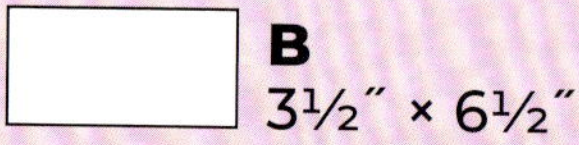

A
6½″

B
3½″ × 6½″

C
2″

april 18

DOUBLE SQUARES BLOCK

12″ × 12″

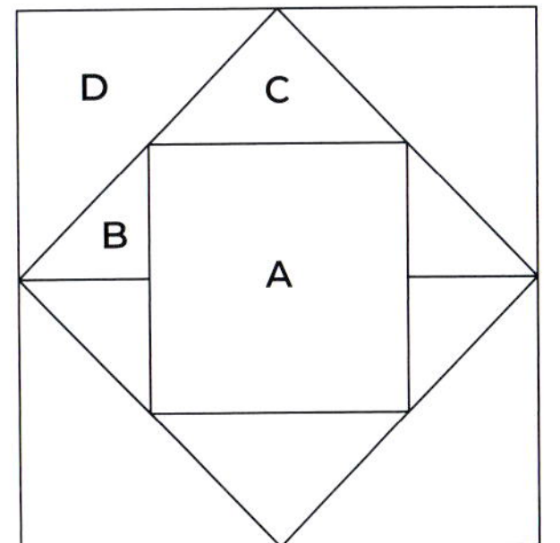

A	6½″
 **B**	3⅞″
 **C**	7¼″
 **D**	6⅞″

september 14

BLUE AND WHITE

12″ × 12″

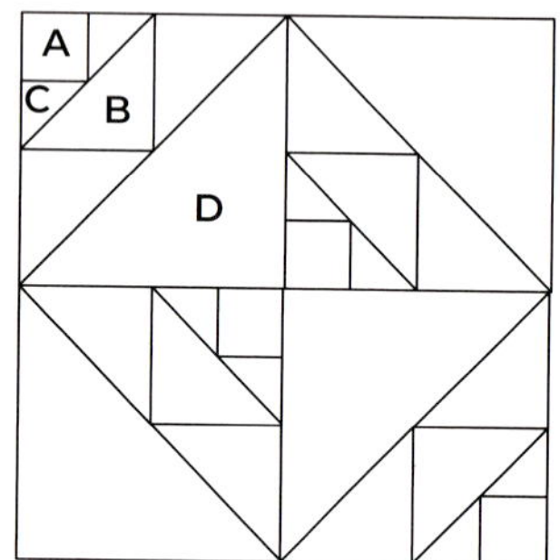

A
2″

B
3⅞″

C
2⅜″

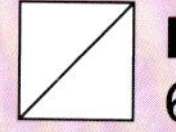

D
6⅞″

april 19

BIRD TRACKS

12″ × 12″

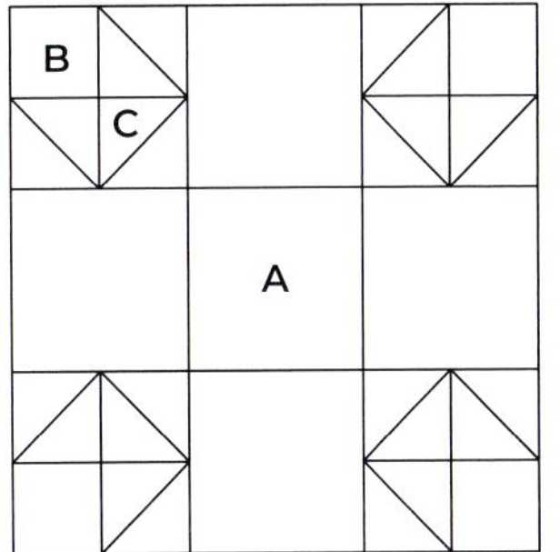

A
4½″

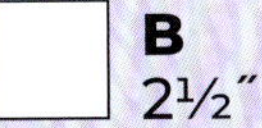

B
2½″

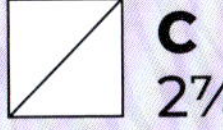

C
2⅞″

september 13

ANVIL BLOCK

12″ × 12″

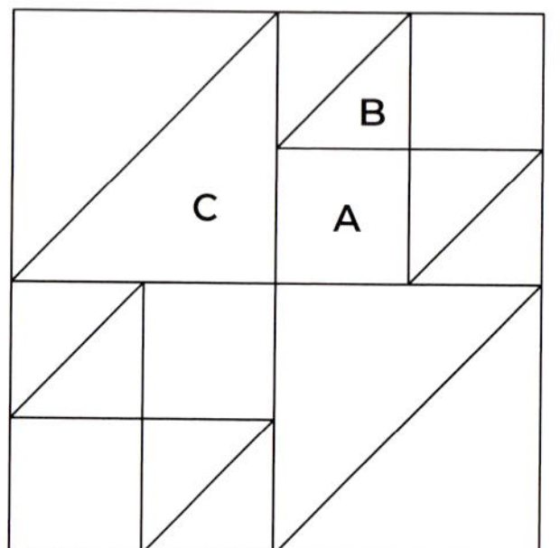

A
3½″

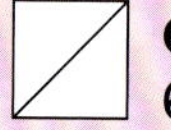

B
3⅞″

C
6⅞″

april 20

SISTER'S CHOICE

15″ × 15″

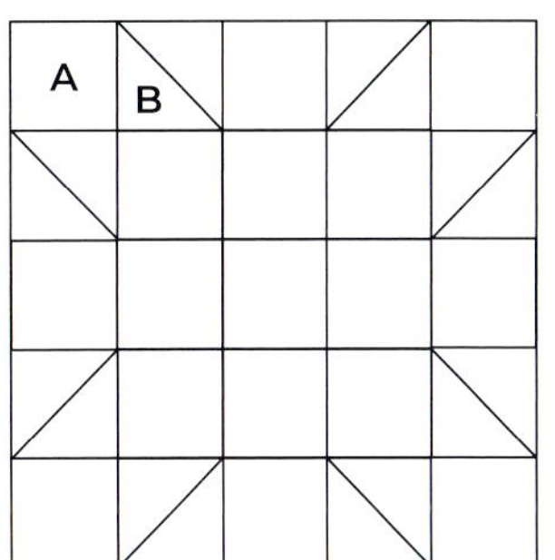

A
3½″

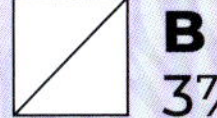

B
3⅞″

september 12

BIRDS IN THE AIR

6″ × 6″

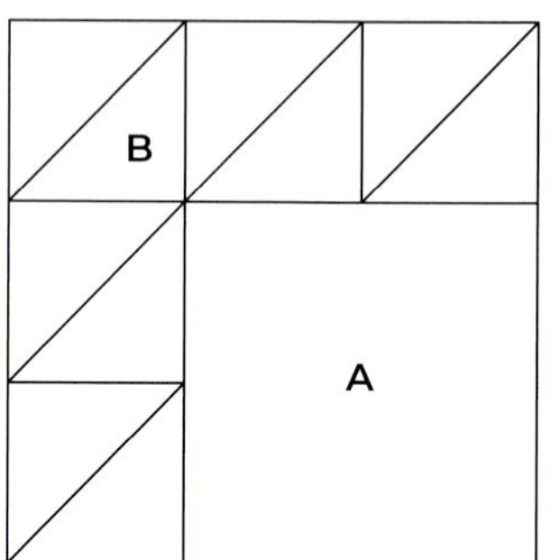

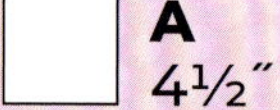

A
4½″

B
2⅞″

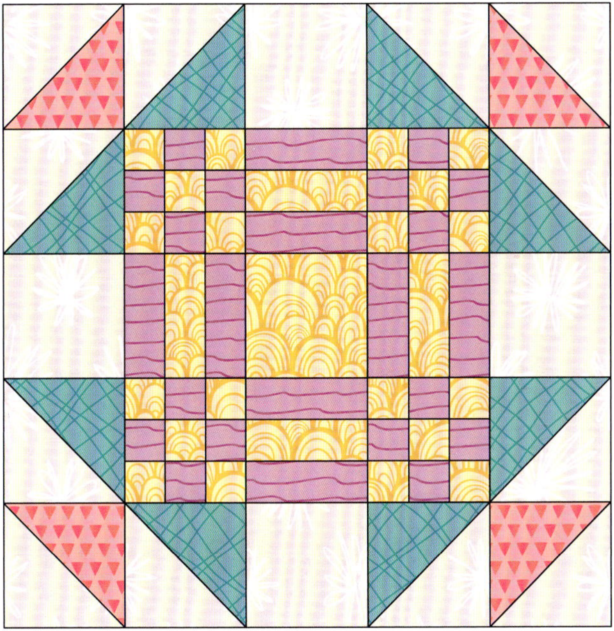

april 21

GOOSE IN THE POND

15″ × 15″

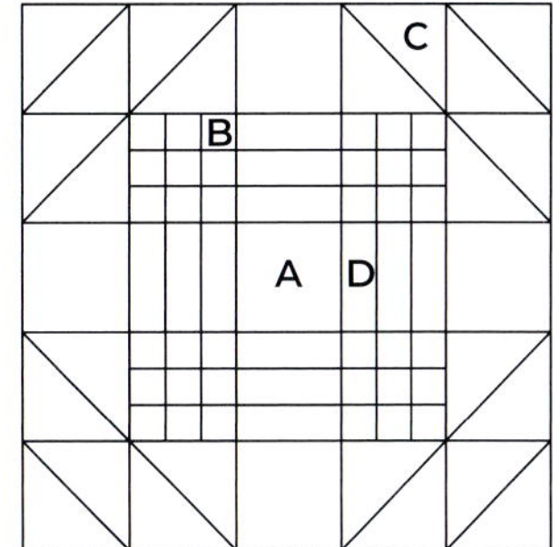

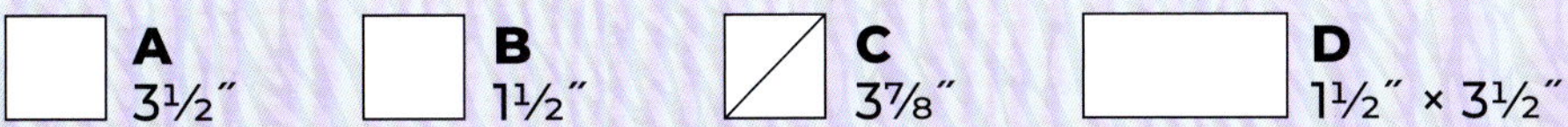

A
3½″

B
1½″

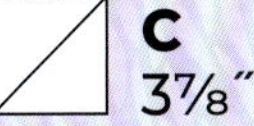

C
3⅞″

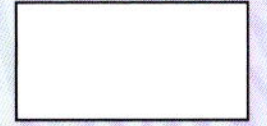

D
1½″ × 3½″

september 11

CRISS CROSS

14″ × 14″

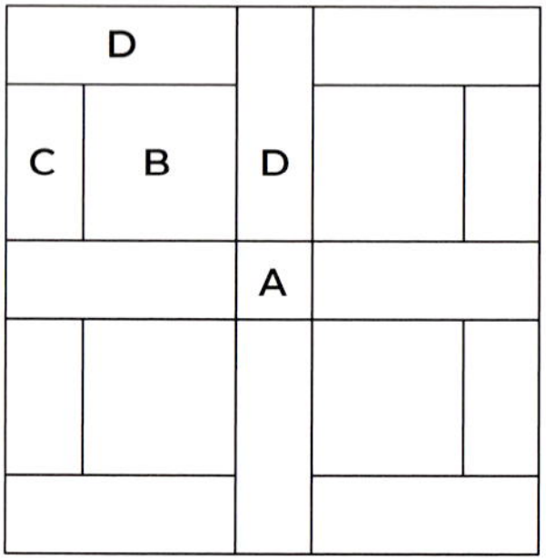

D

C B D

A

A
2½″

B
4½″

C
2½″ × 4½″

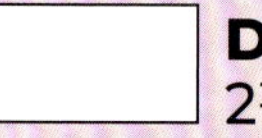

D
2½″ × 6½″

april 22

GEORGETOWN SQUARE

15″ × 15″

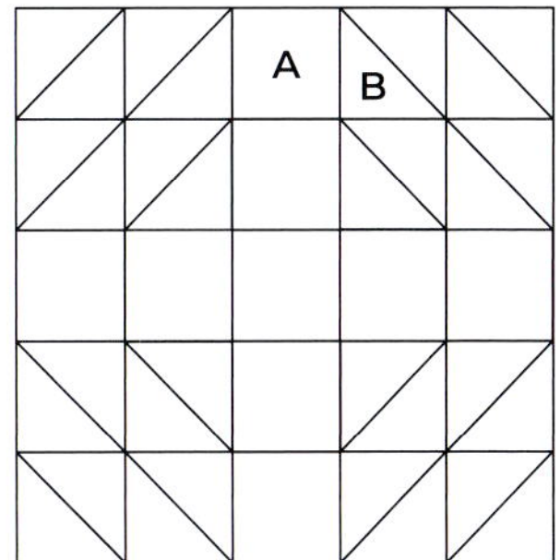

A
3½″

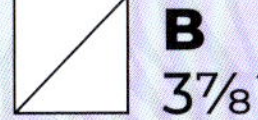

B
3⅞″

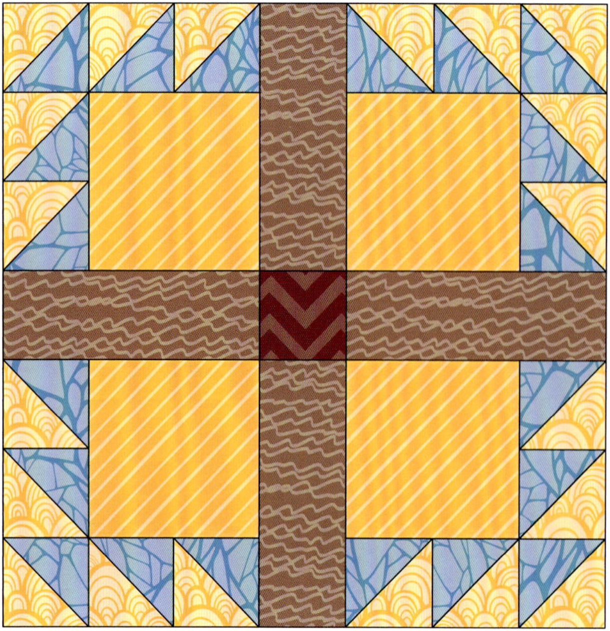

september 10

HEN AND CHICKS

14″ × 14″

C
B
D
A

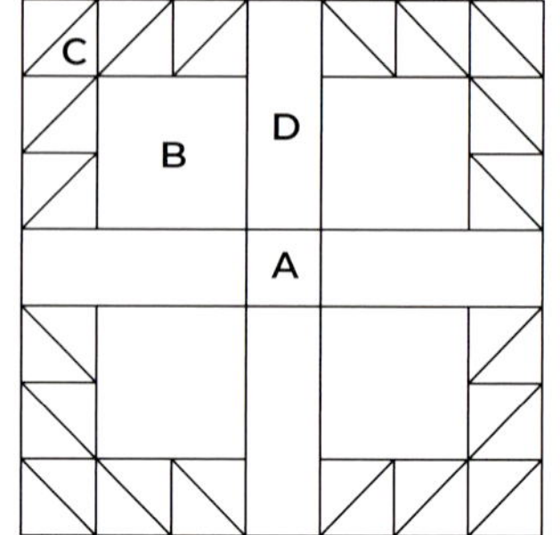

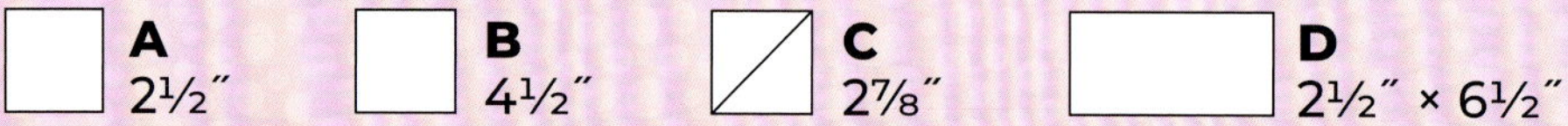

A
2½″
B
4½″
C
2⅞″
D
2½″ × 6½″

april 23

TEA FOR FOUR

15″ × 15″

C
D
B
A

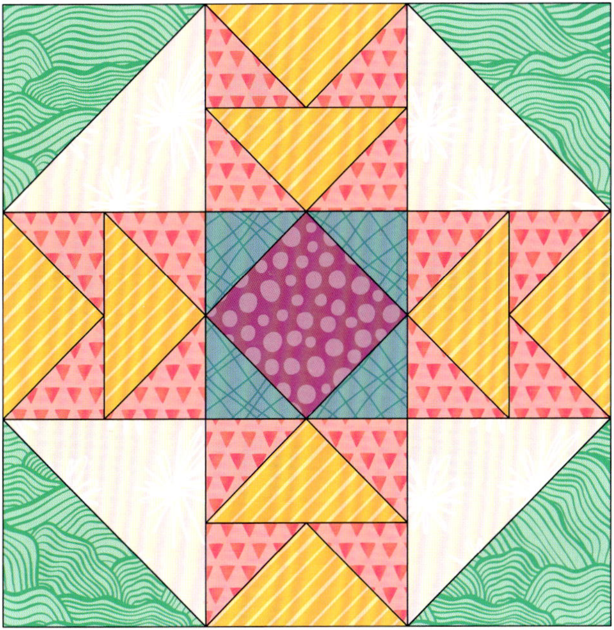

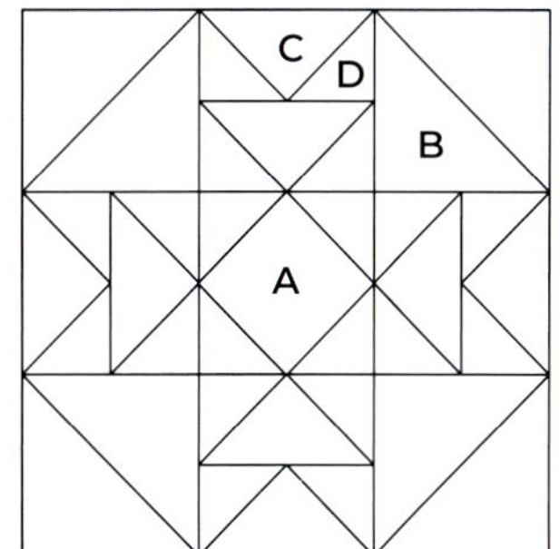

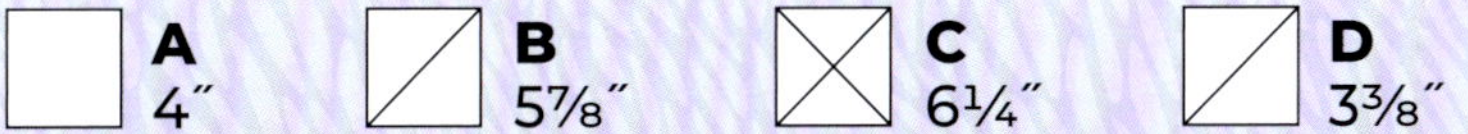

A
4″
B
5⅞″
C
6¼″
D
3⅜″

september 9

JUICY APPLE BLOCK

8″ × 8″

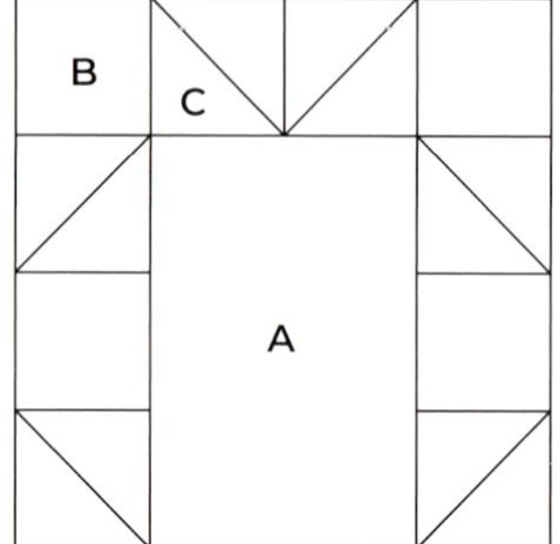

A
4½″ × 6½″

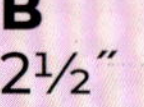

B
2½″

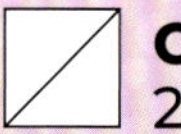

C
2⅞″

april 24

FIVE SPOT

15″ × 15″

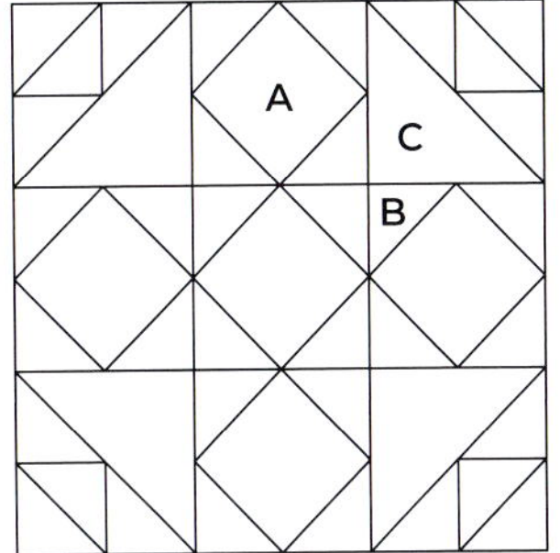

A
4″

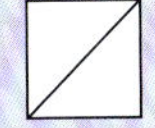

B
3⅜″

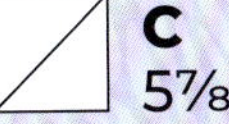

C
5⅞″

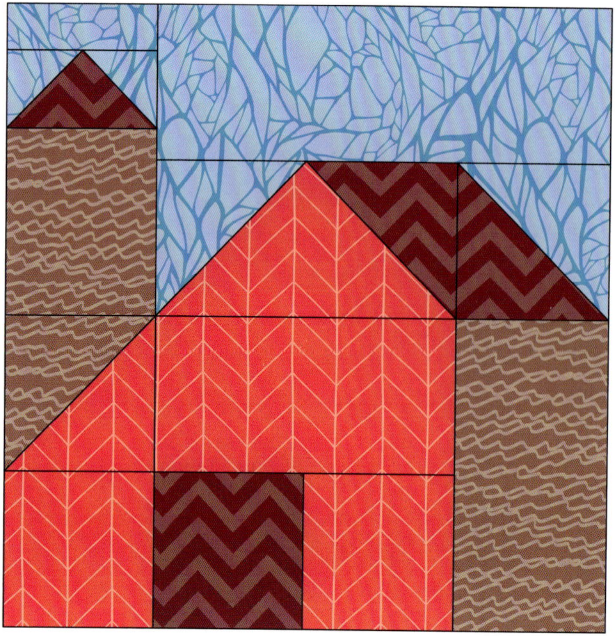

september 8

APPLE BARN BLOCK
10″ × 10″

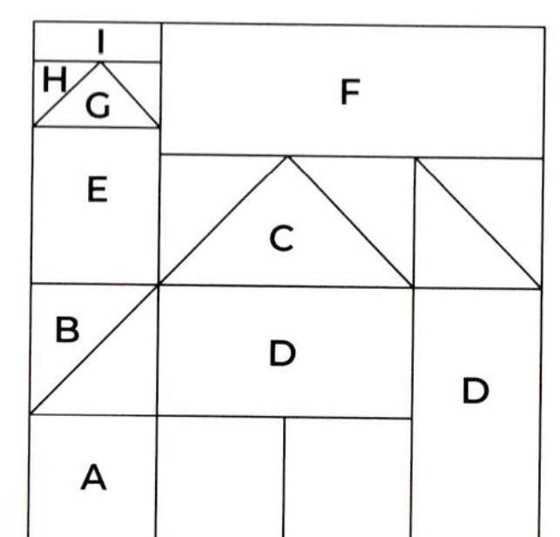

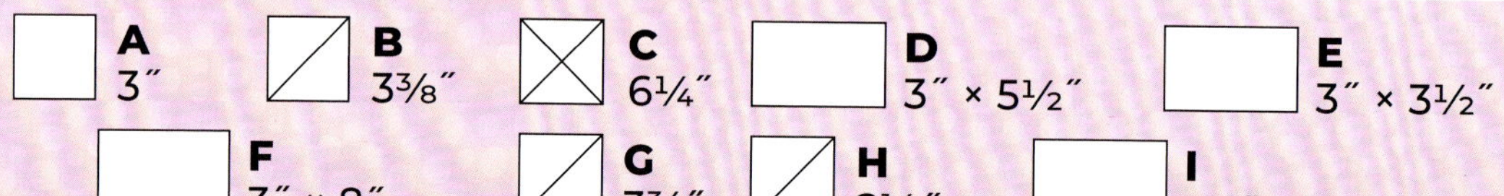

april 25

PRAIRIE QUEEN

15″ × 15″

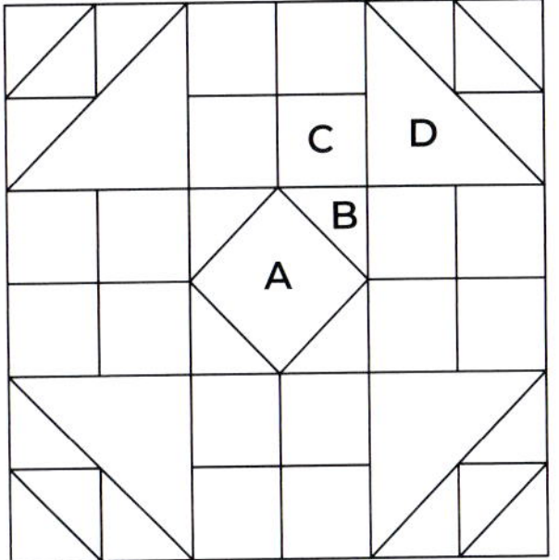

A
4″

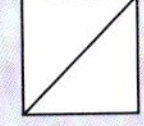

B
3⅜″

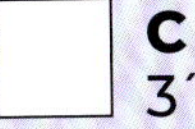

C
3″

D
5⅞″

september 7

SPLIT STAR

12″ × 12″

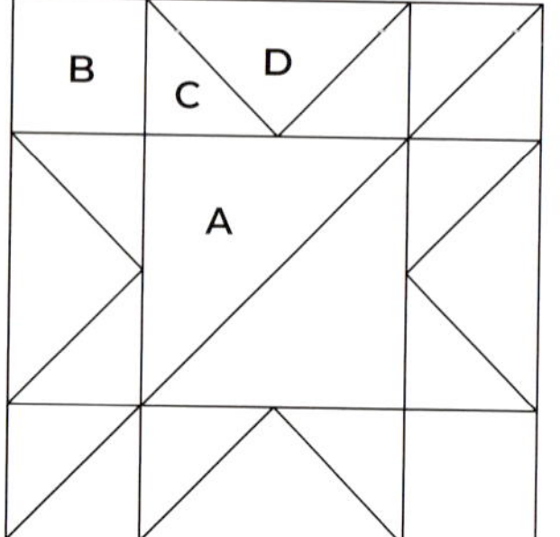

A 6⅞″

B 3½″

C 3⅞″

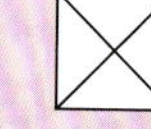

D 7¼″

april 26

BEGINNER'S DELIGHT

15″ × 15″

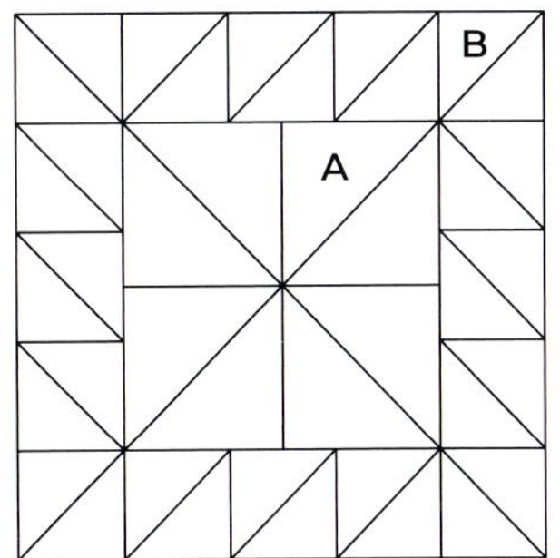

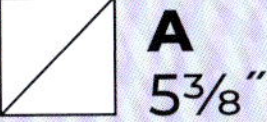

A
5⅜″

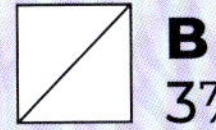

B
3⅞″

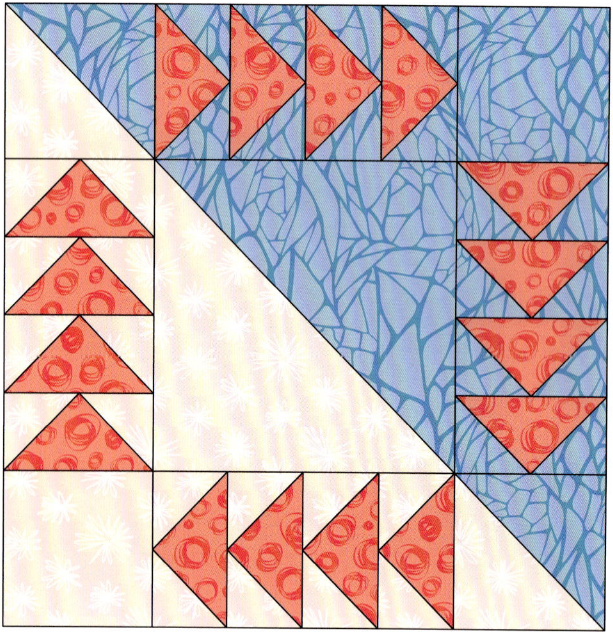

september 6

ROUNDABOUT GEESE

12″ × 12″

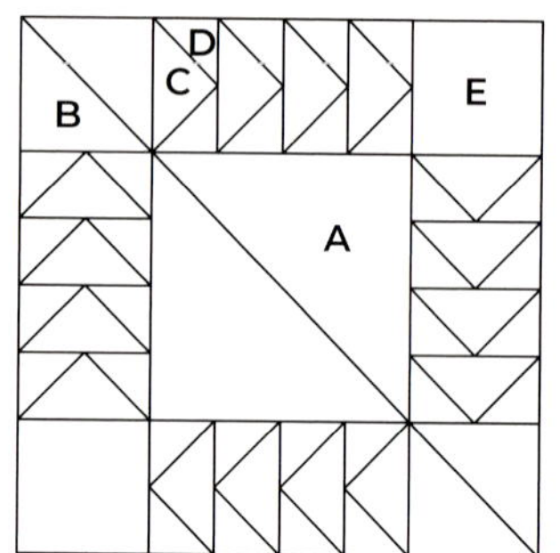

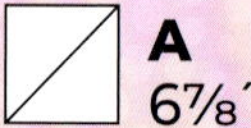

A
6⅞″

B
3⅞″

C
4¼″

D
2⅜″

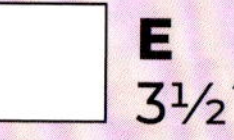

E
3½″

april 27

TURKEY IN THE STRAW

18″ × 18″

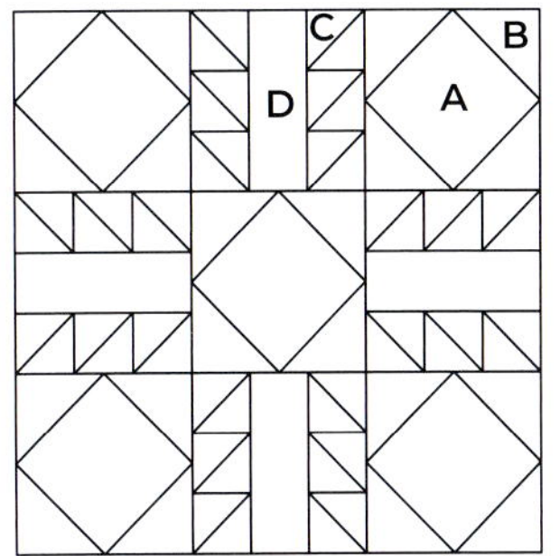

A 4¾″

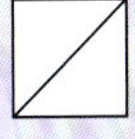

B 3⅞″

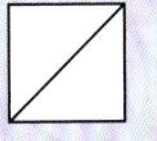

C 2⅞″

D 2½″ × 6½″

september 5

ECONOMY BLOCK
8″ × 8″

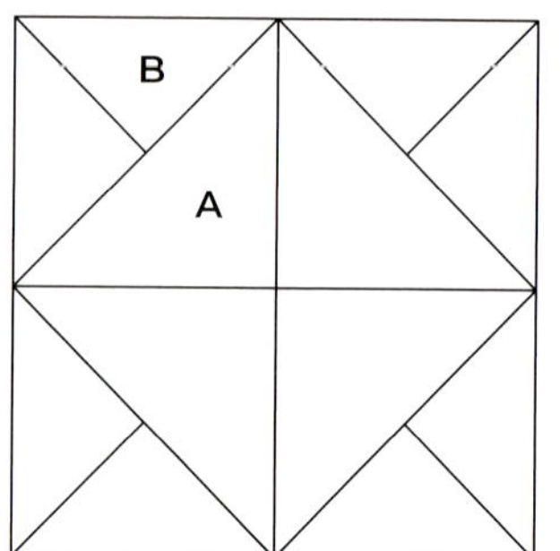

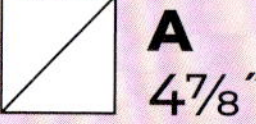

A
4⅞″

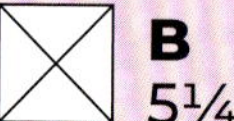

B
5¼″

april 28

FAR WEST

18″ × 18″

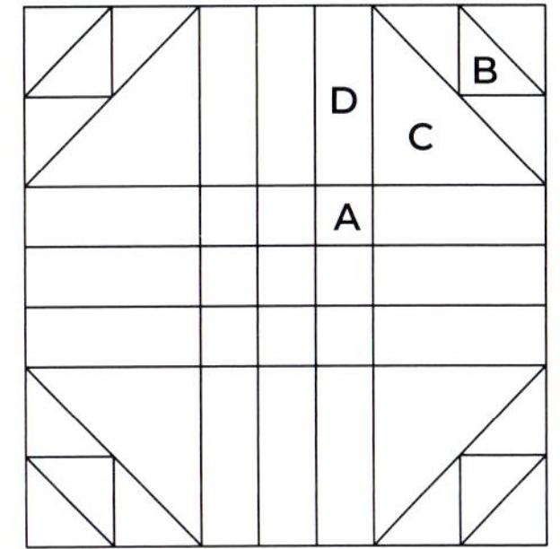

A
2½″

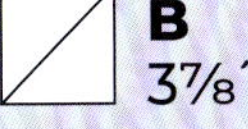

B
3⅞″

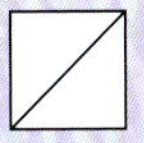

C
6⅞″

D
2½″ × 6½″

september 4

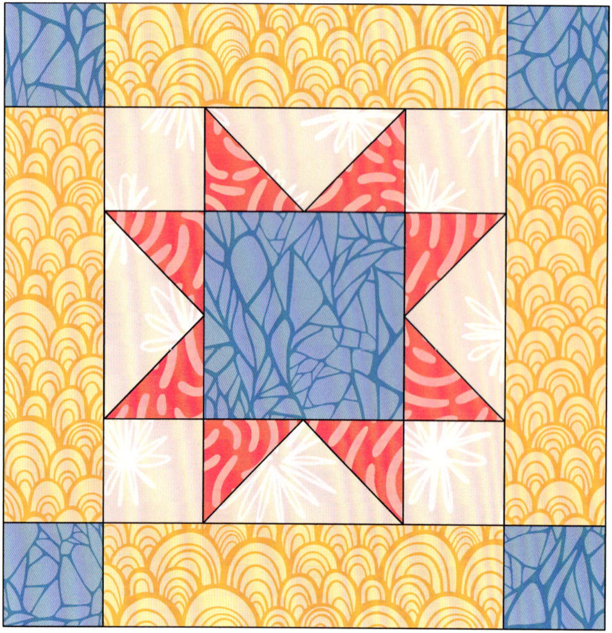

SAWTOOTH STARS

15″ × 15″

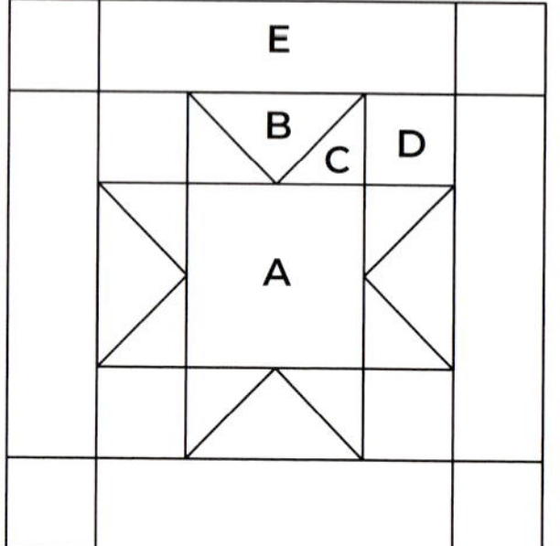

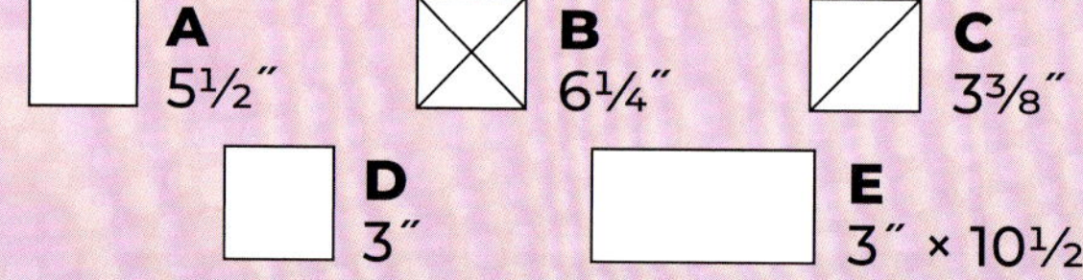

april 29

SOUVENIR BLOCK

15″ × 15″

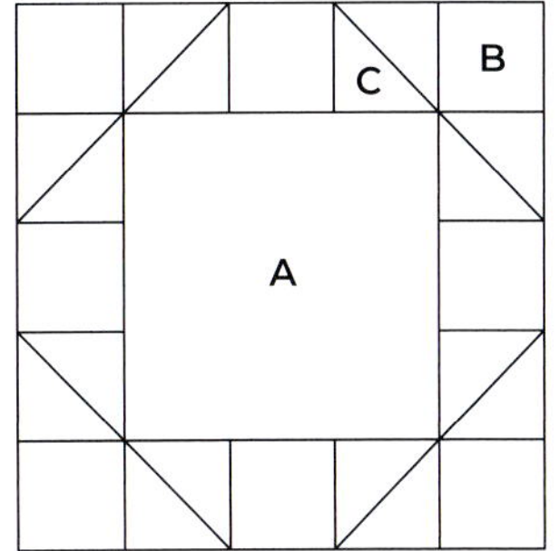

A
9½″

B
3½″

C
3⅞″

september 3

ROLLING STAR BLOCK

15″ × 15″

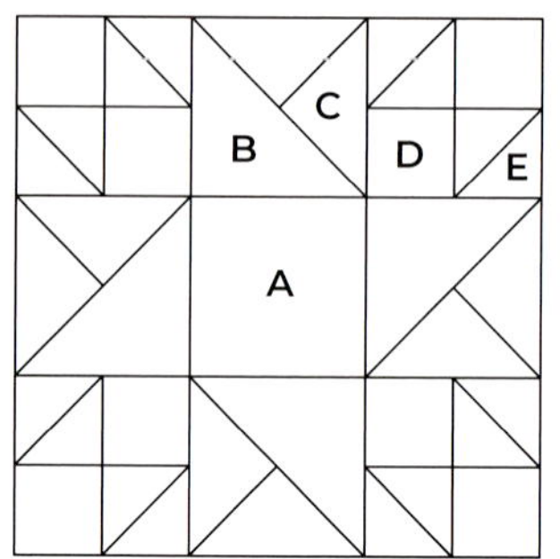

A 5½″

B 5⅞″

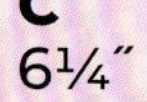

C 6¼″

D 3″

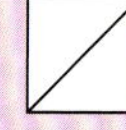

E 3⅜″

april 30

COUNTRY FENCES

15″ × 15″

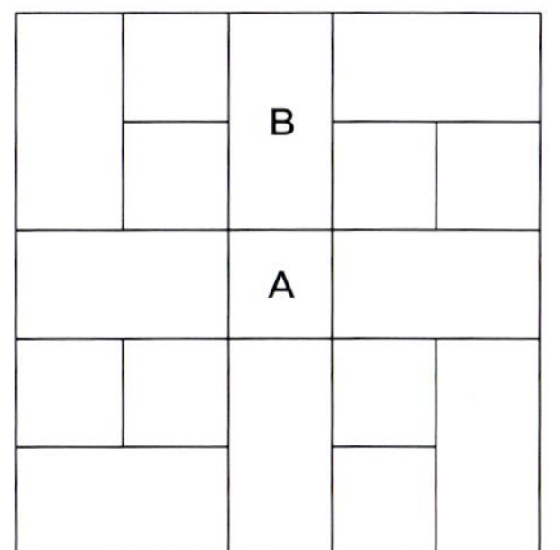

A
3½″

B
3½″ × 6½″

september 2

GOLDEN BLOOMS

10″ × 10″

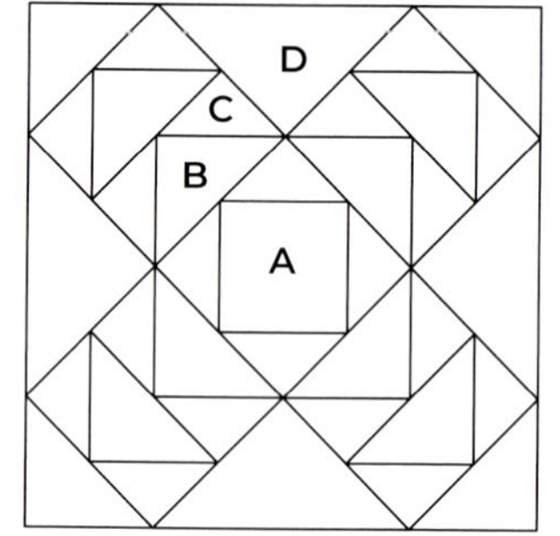

A 3″

B 3⅜″

C 3¾″

D 6¼″

may 1

BABY BUNTING

18″ × 18″

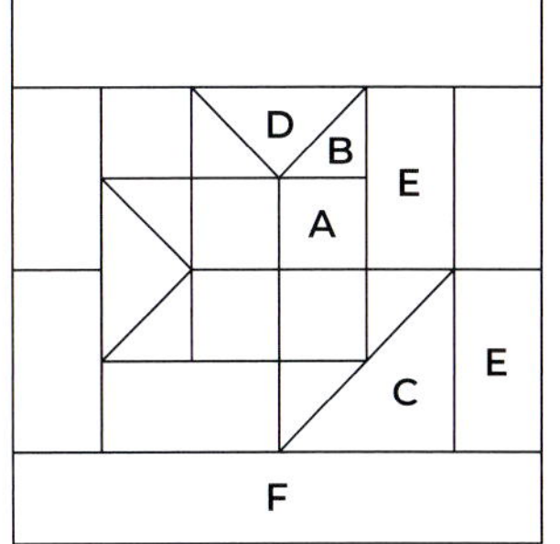

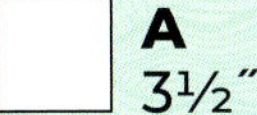

A
3½″

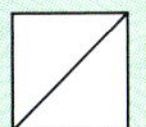

B
3⅞″

C
6⅞″

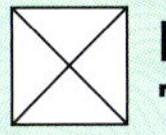

D
7¼″

E
3½″ × 6½″

F
3½″ × 18½″

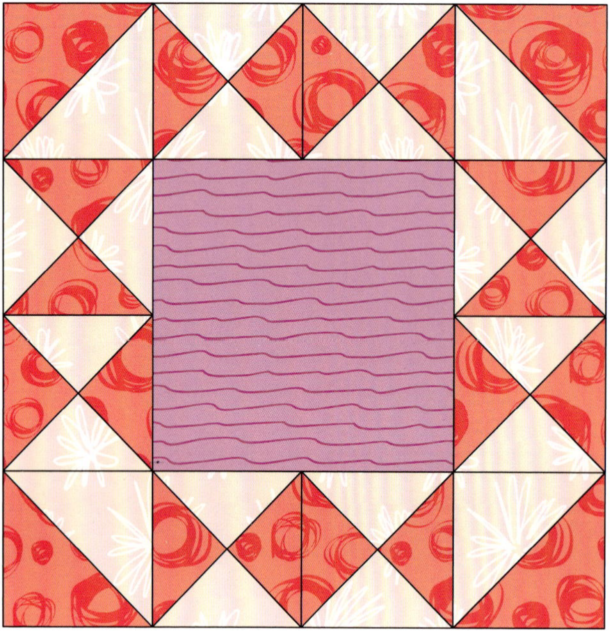

september 1

SQUARE AND STAR
12″ × 12″

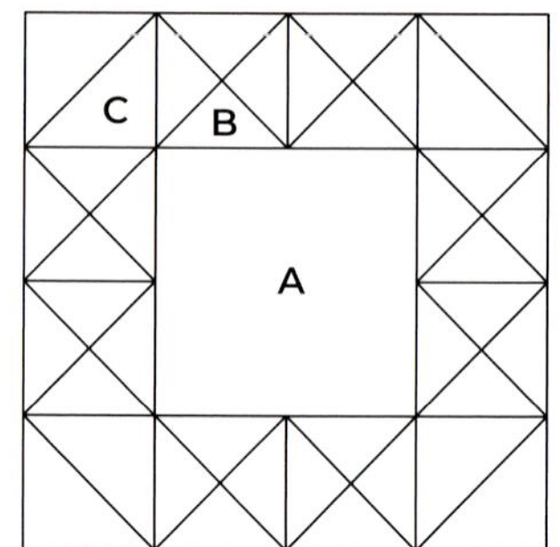

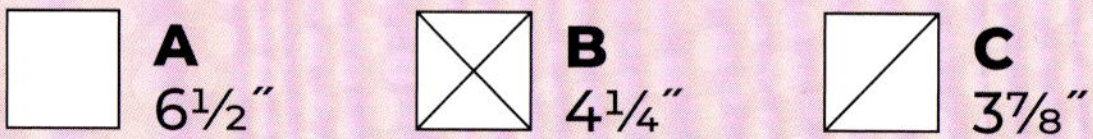

A
6½″

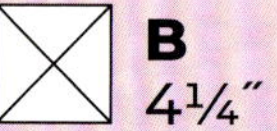

B
4¼″

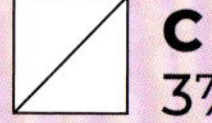

C
3⅞″

may 2

BRAVE WORLD

18″ × 18″

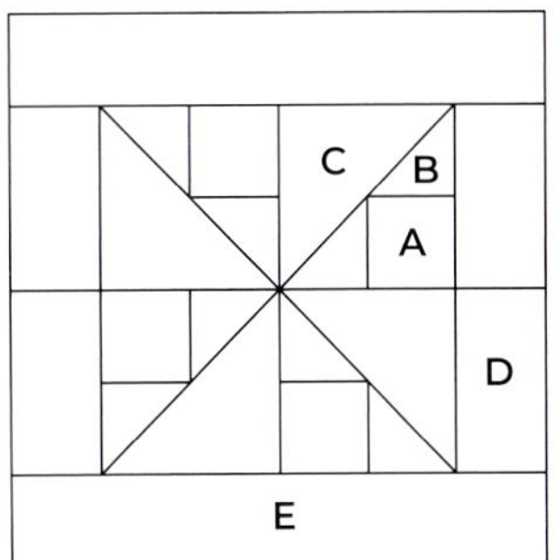

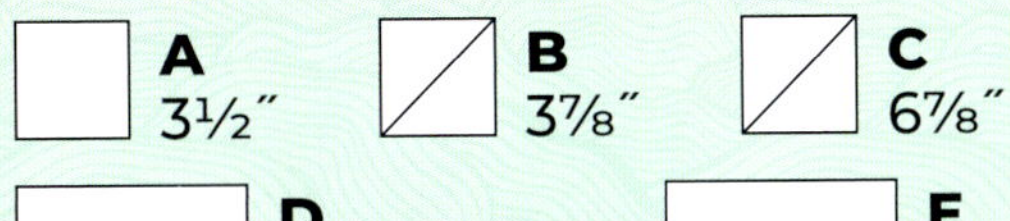

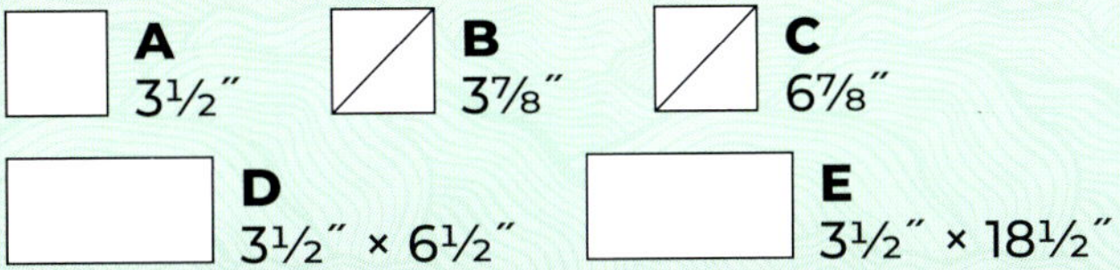

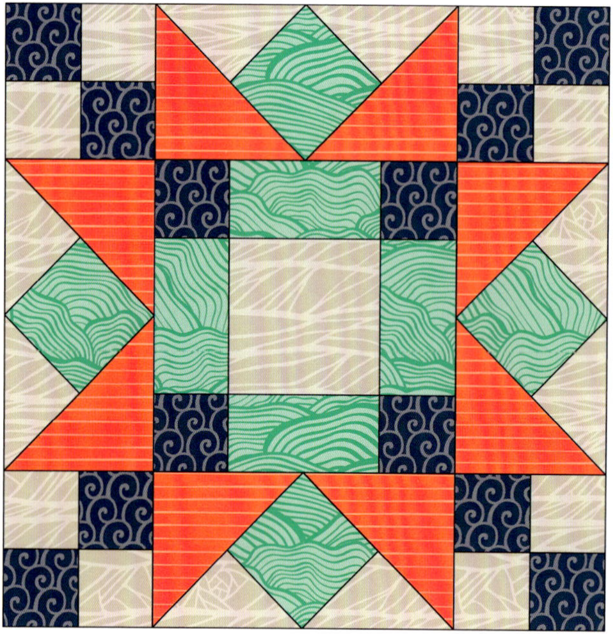

august 31

KITTY CORNER STAR

12″ × 12″

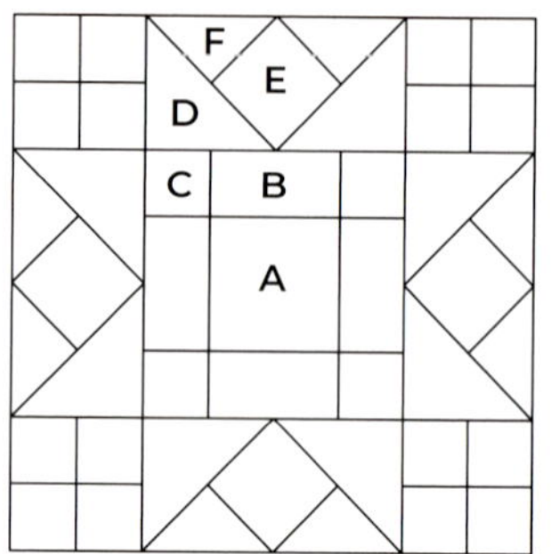

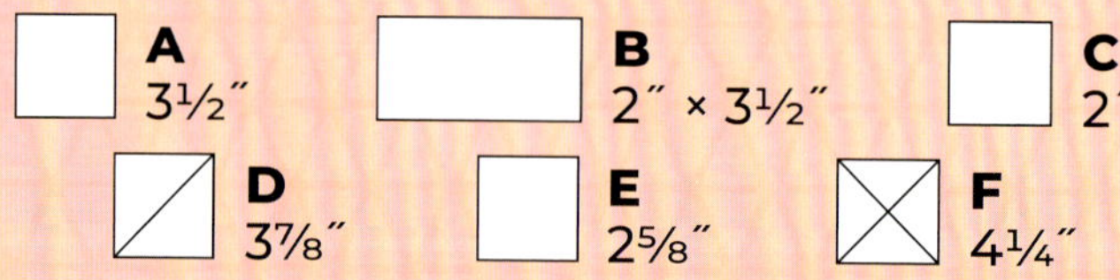

may 3

BROKEN DISHES

18″ × 18″

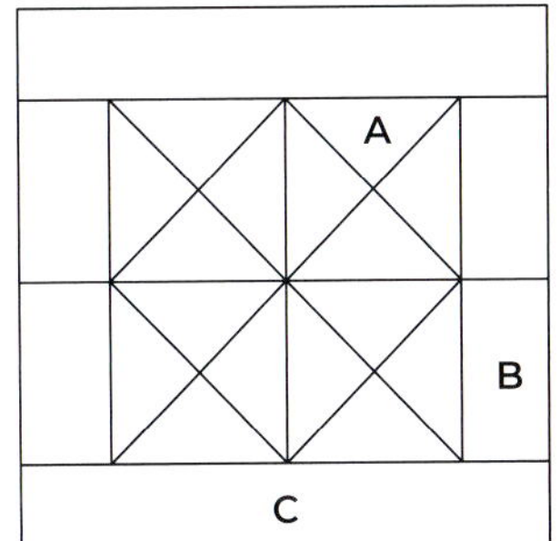

A 7¼″

B 3½″ × 6½″

C 3½″ × 18½″

august 30

SAWTOOTH STAR VARIATION

12″ × 12″

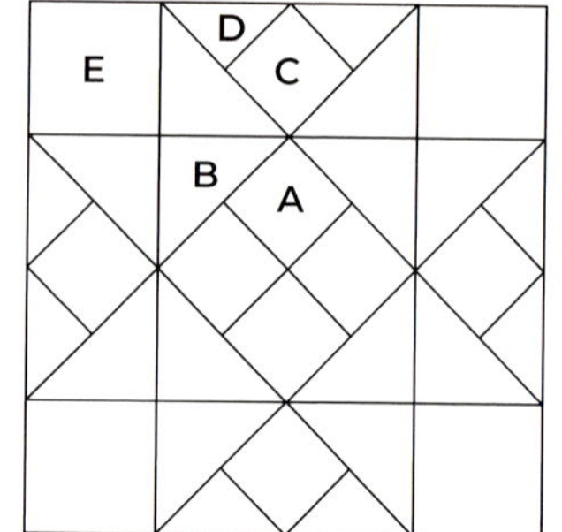

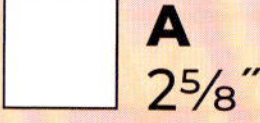

A
2⅝″

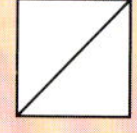

B
3⅞″

C
2⅝″

D
4¼″

E
3½″

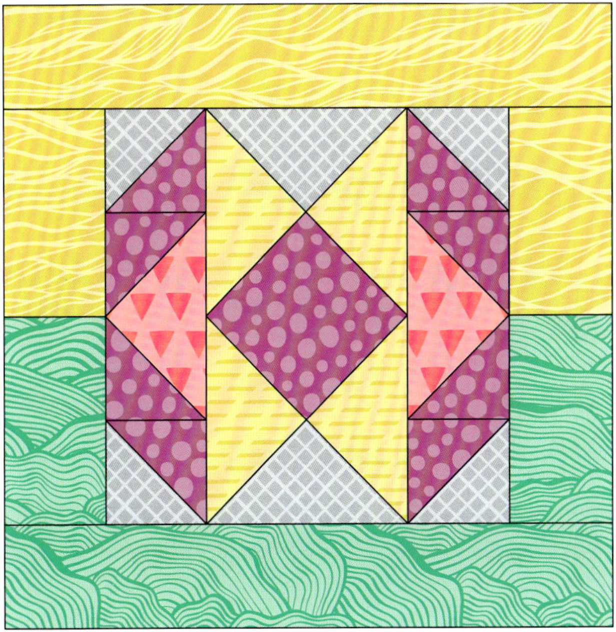

may 4

BUTTERFLY BLOCK
18″ × 18″

C
B
A
D
E

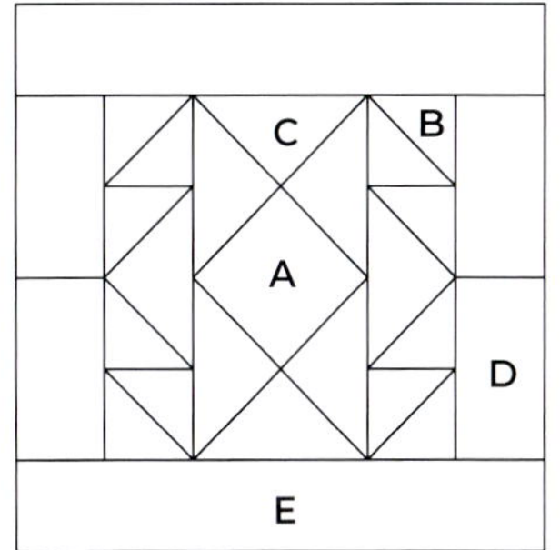

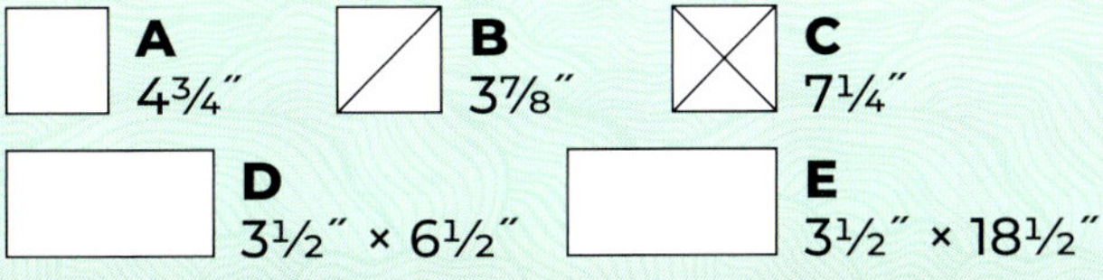

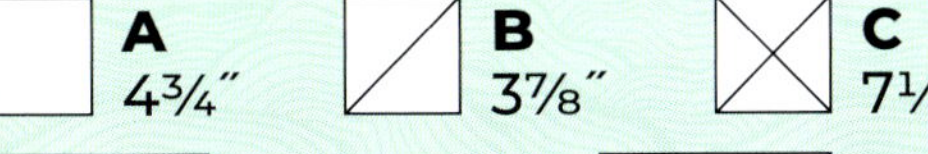

A
4¾″
B
3⅞″
C
7¼″
D
3½″ × 6½″
E
3½″ × 18½″

august 29

SAWTOOTH STAR

12″ × 12″

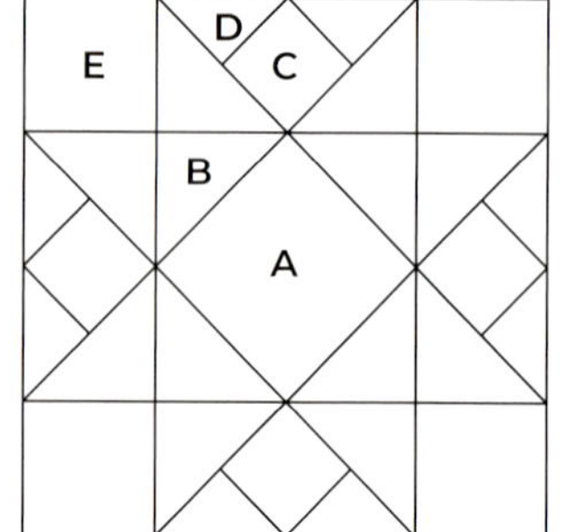

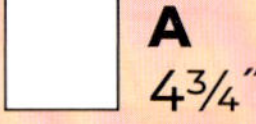

A
4 3/4″

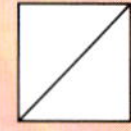

B
3 7/8″

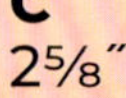

C
2 5/8″

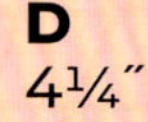

D
4 1/4″

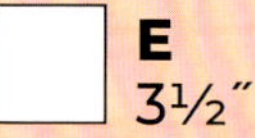

E
3 1/2″

may 5

CHEYENNE

18″ × 18″

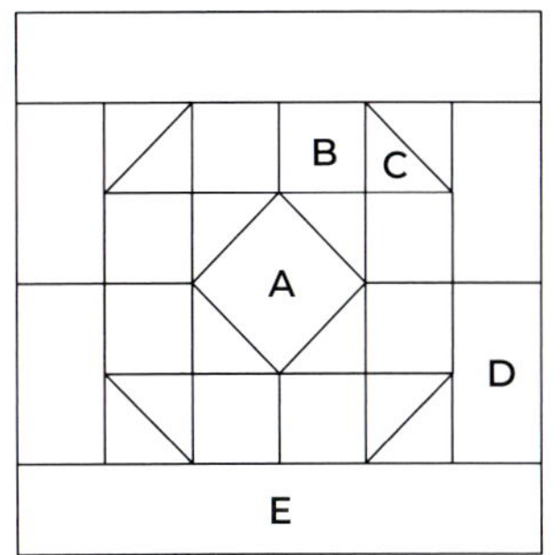

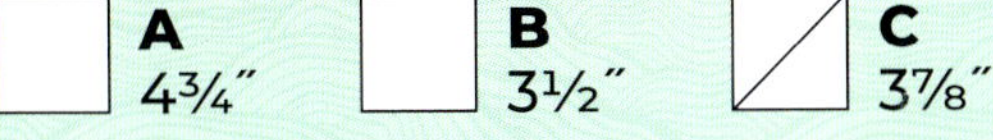

august 28

HIT OR MISS STAR

12″ × 12″

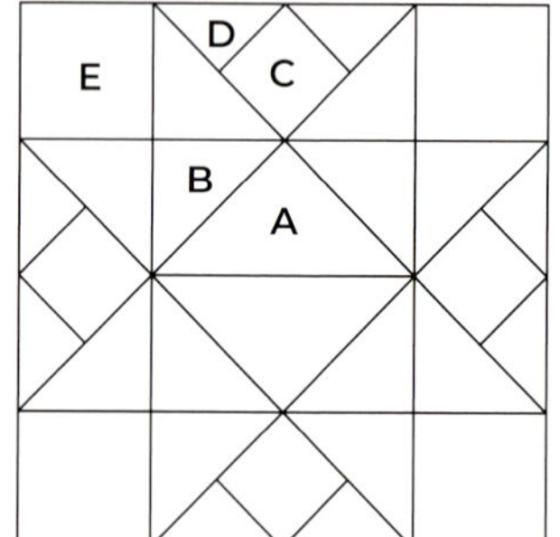

A 7¼″

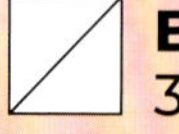

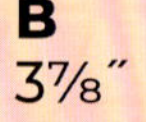

B 3⅞″

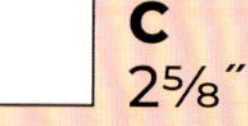

C 2⅝″

D 4¼″

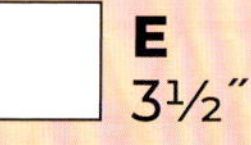

E 3½″

may 6

CROSS PATCH

18″ × 18″

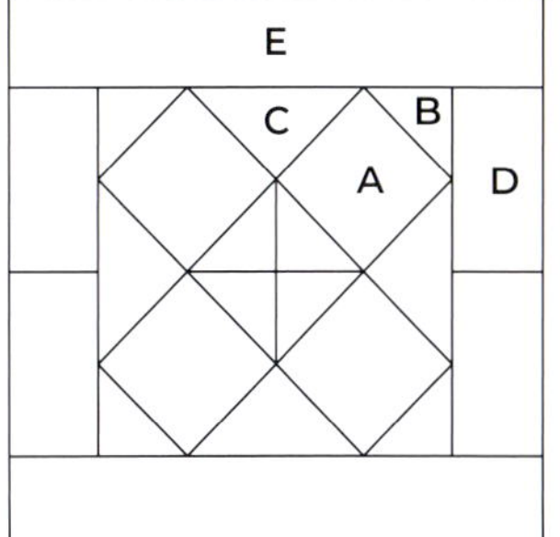

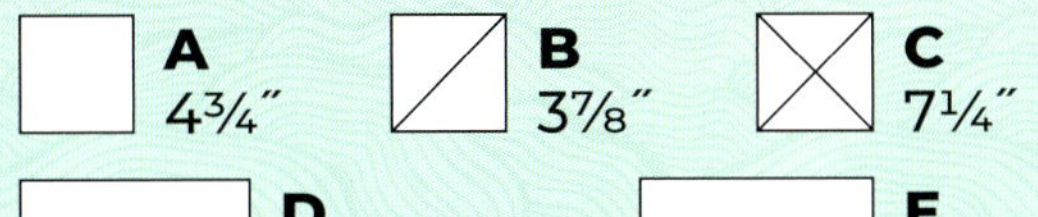

august 27

HOME CIRCLE

15″ × 15″

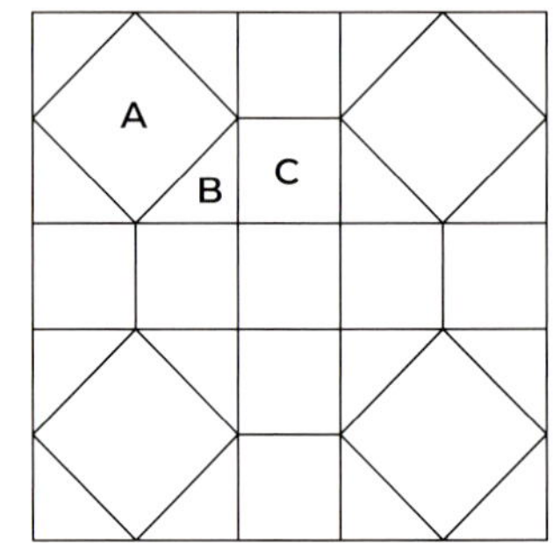

A 4¾″

B 3⅞″

C 3½″

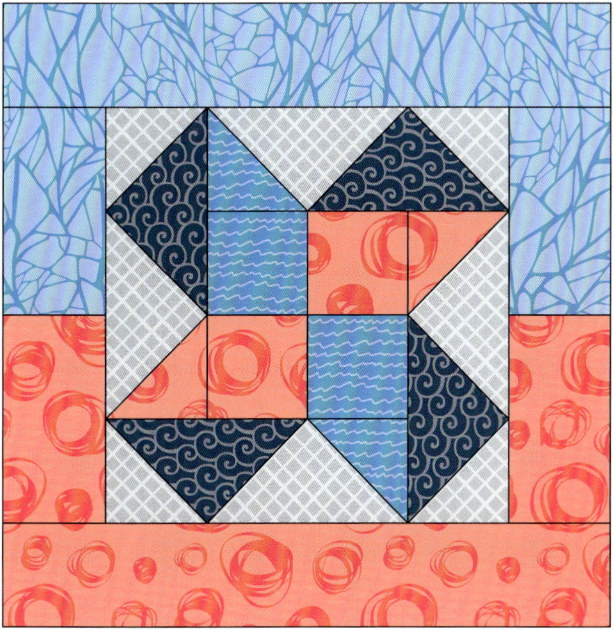

may 7

FOURTH OF JULY

18″ × 18″

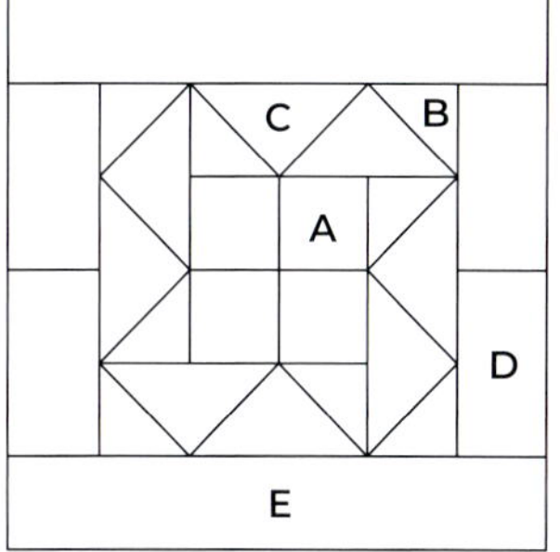

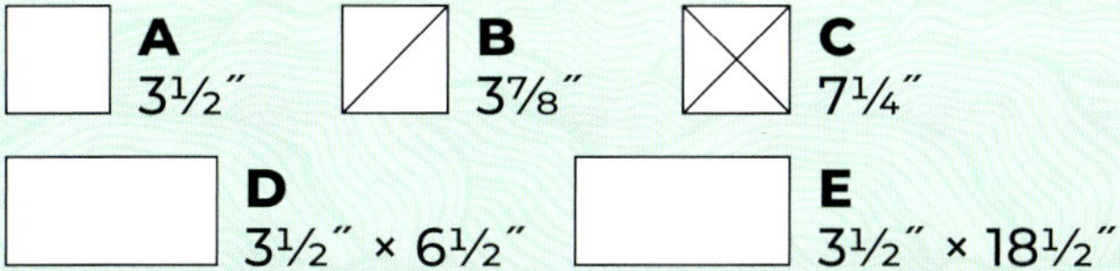

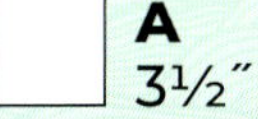

A
3½″

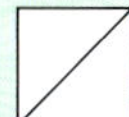

B
3⅞″

C
7¼″

D
3½″ × 6½″

E
3½″ × 18½″

august 26

MONKEY WRENCH

15″ × 15″

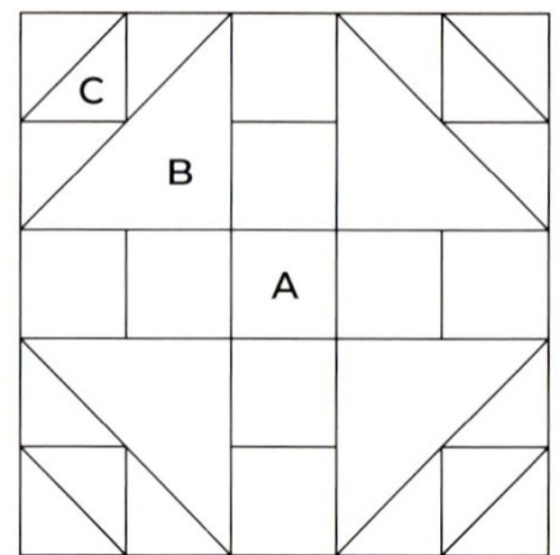

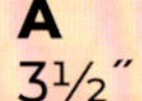

A
3½″

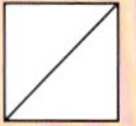

B
6⅞″

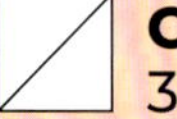

C
3⅞″

may 8

LOUISIANA

18″ × 18″

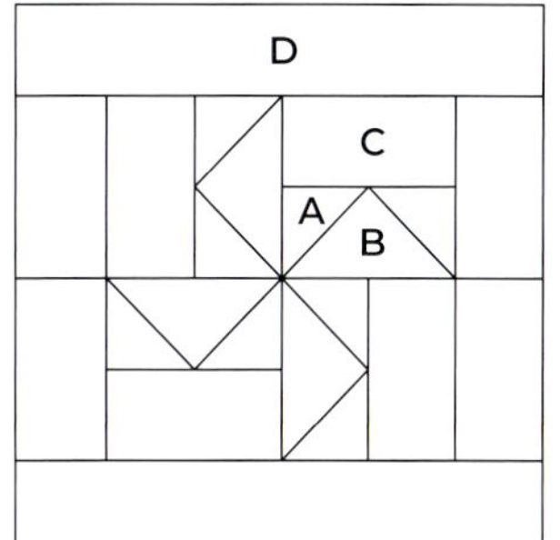

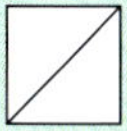

A
3⅞″

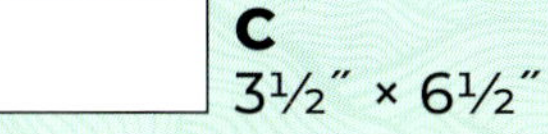

B
7¼″

C
3½″ × 6½″

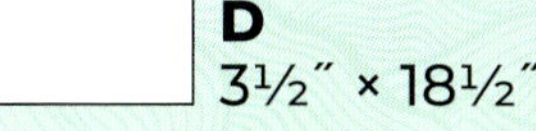

D
3½″ × 18½″

august 25

YOUNG MAN'S FANCY

15″ × 15″

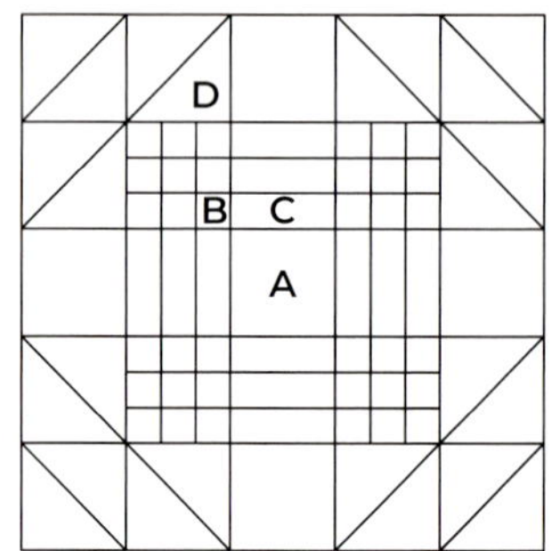

A 3½″

B 1½″

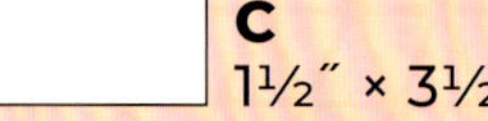

C 1½″ × 3½″

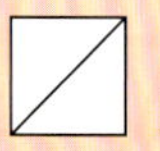

D 3⅞″

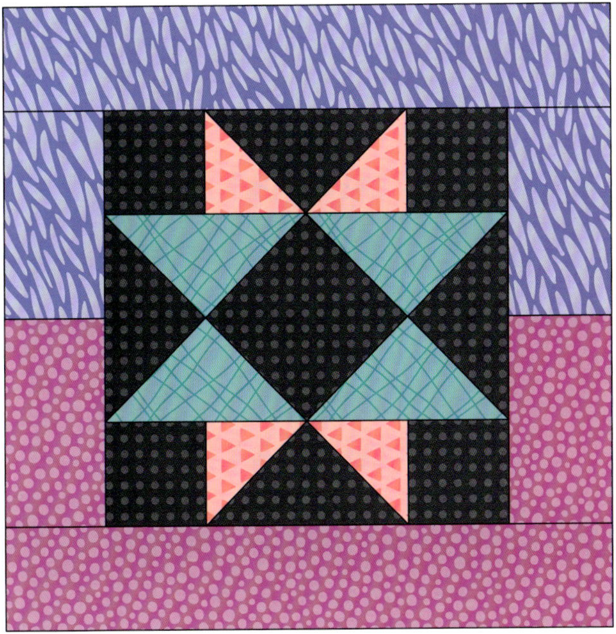

may 9

MOSAIC BLOCK

18″ × 18″

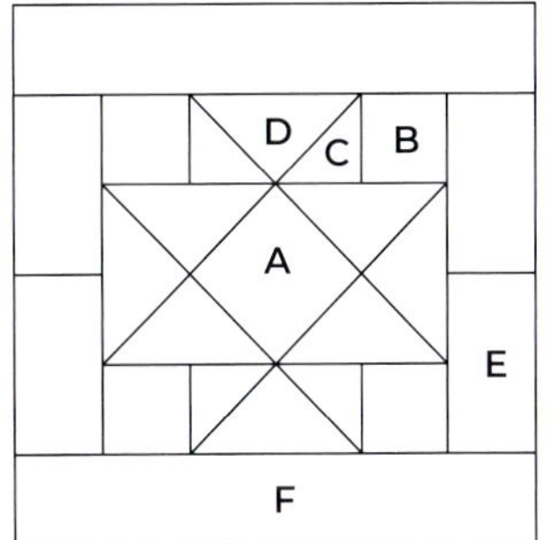

A
$4^3/_4$″

B
$3^1/_2$″

C
$3^7/_8$″

D
$7^1/_4$″

E
$3^1/_2$″ × $6^1/_2$″

F
$3^1/_2$″ × $18^1/_2$″

august 24

NEXT DOOR NEIGHBOR

16″ × 16″

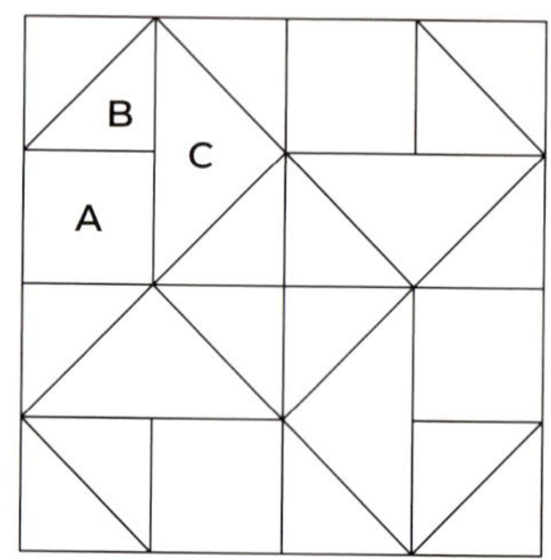

A 4½″

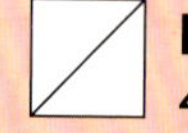

B 4⅞″

C 9¼″

may 10

PEACE AND PLENTY

18″ × 18″

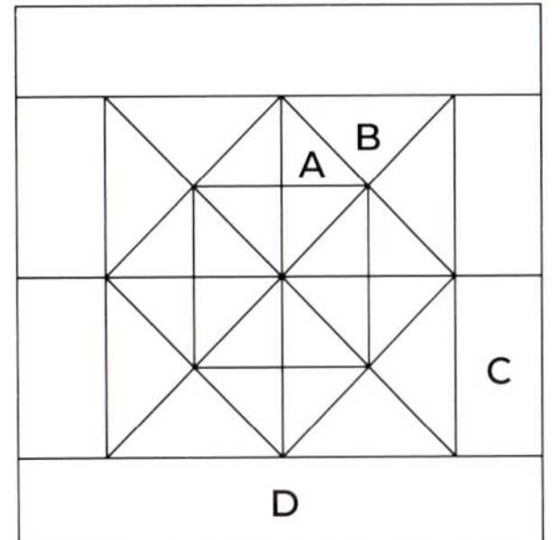

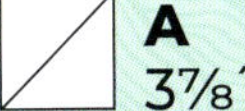

A
3⅞″

B
7¼″

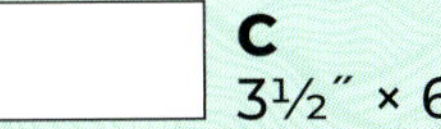

C
3½″ × 6½″

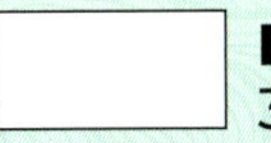

D
3½″ × 18½″

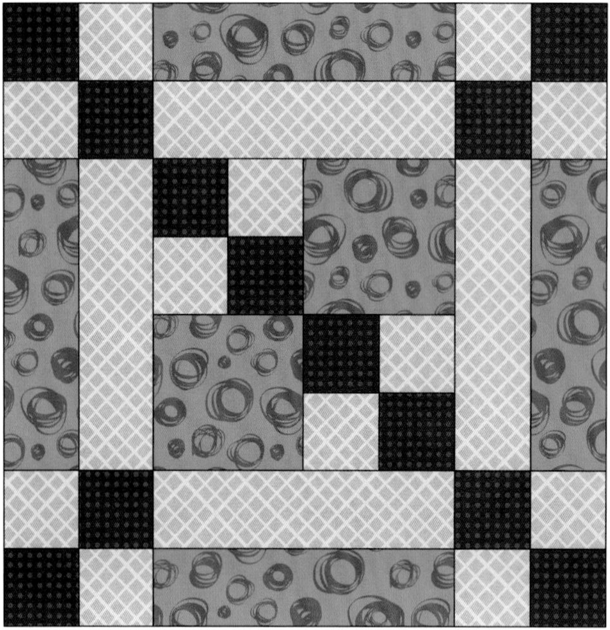

august 23

DOUBLE FOUR PATCH

12″ × 12″

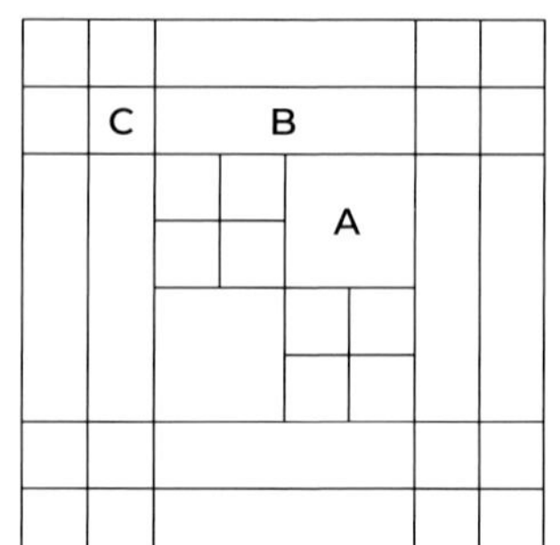

A
3½″

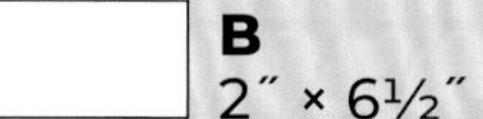

B
2″ × 6½″

C
2″

may 11

SCHOOL GIRL PUZZLE

18″ × 18″

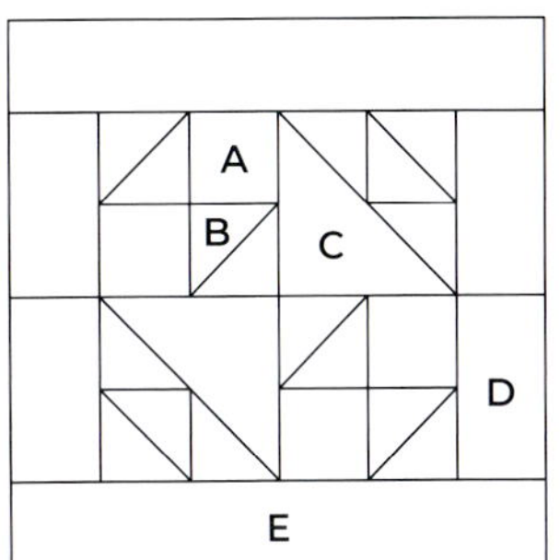

A
3½″

B
3⅞″

C
6⅞″

D
3½″ × 6½″

E
3½″ × 18½″

august 22

COVERLET BLOCK

12″ × 12″

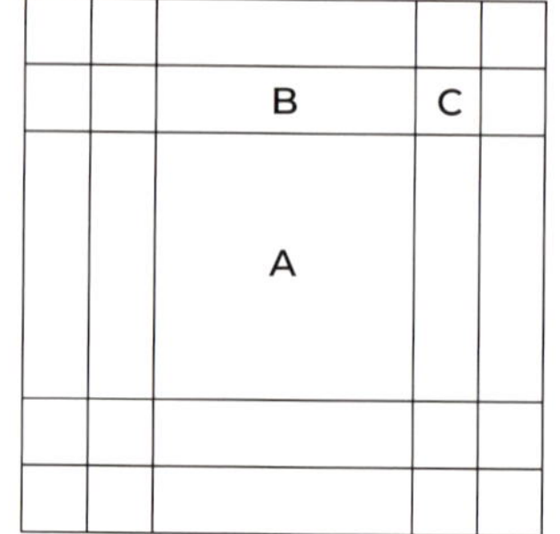

A
6½″

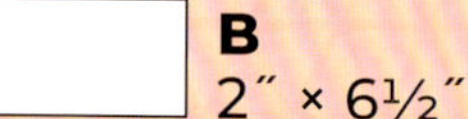

B
2″ × 6½″

C
2″

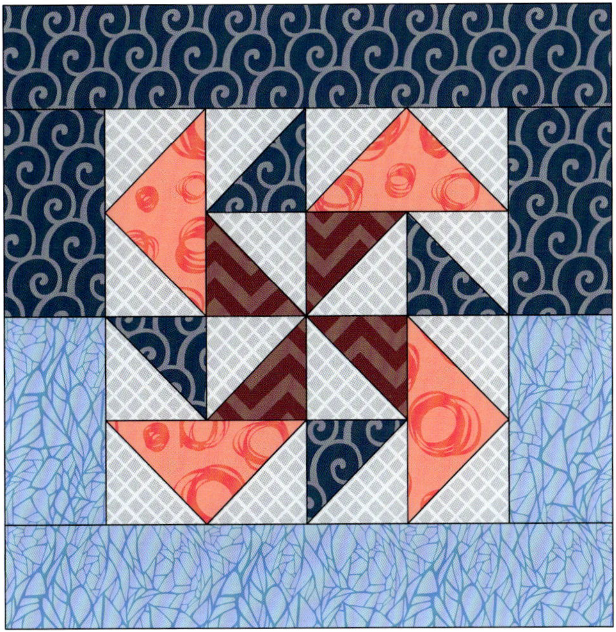

may 12

YANKEE PUZZLE

18″ × 18″

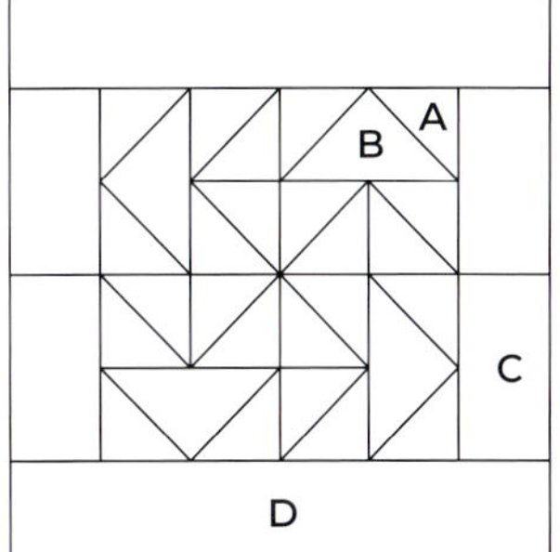

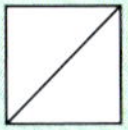

A
3⅞″

B
7¼″

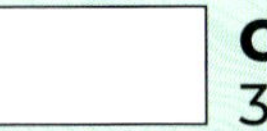

C
3½″ × 6½″

D
3½″ × 18½″

august 21

DOUBLE T
18″ × 18″

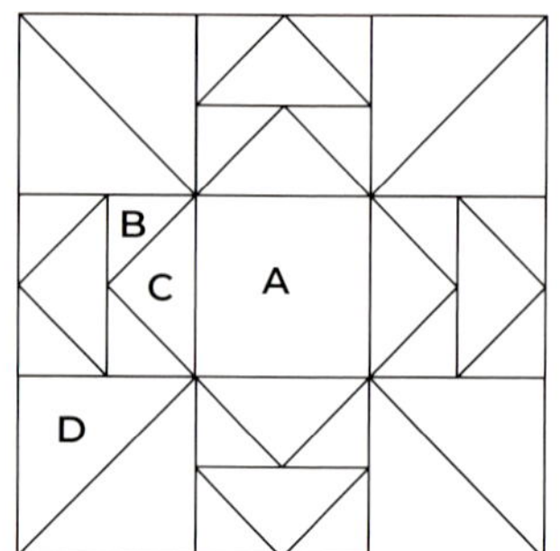

A
6½″

B
3⅞″

C
7¼″

D
6⅞″

may 13

COLORBURST SQUARES #1

10″ × 10″

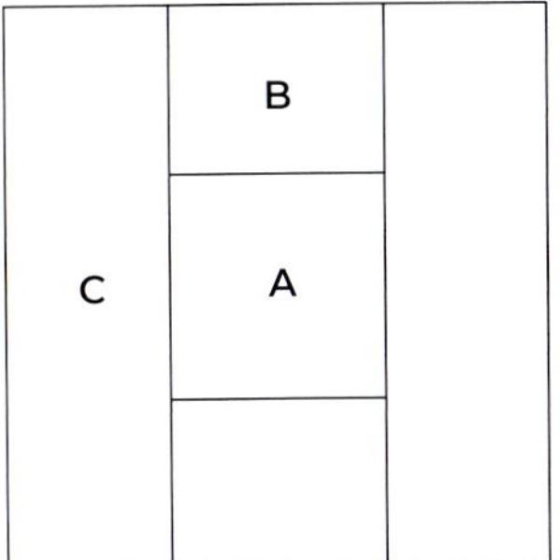

A
4½″

B
3½″ × 4½″

C
3½″ × 10½″

august 20

DOUBLE STARS

18″ × 18″

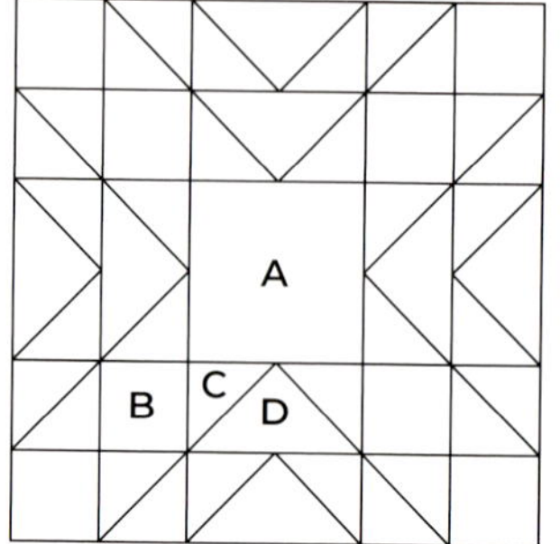

A
6½″

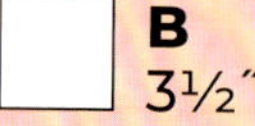

B
3½″

C
3⅞″

D
7¼″

may 14

COLORBURST SQUARES #2

10″ × 10″

A
4½″

B
2½″ × 4½″

C
2½″ × 10½″

D
4½″ × 10½″

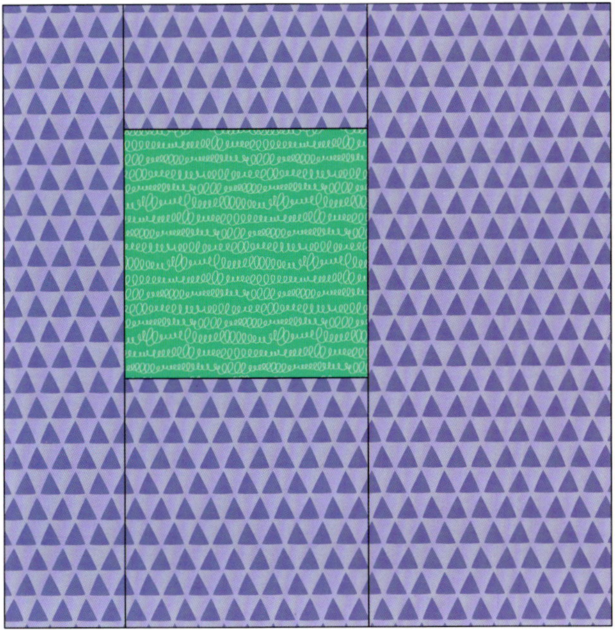

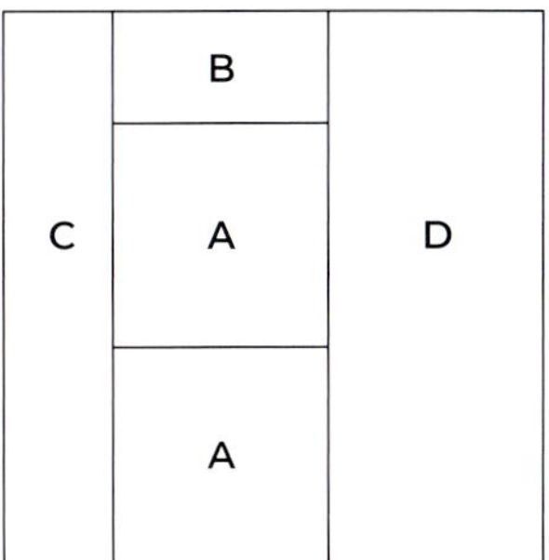

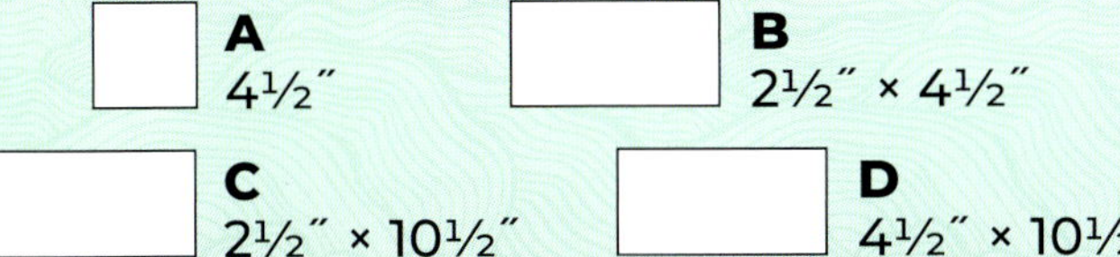

august 19

GARDEN PATH

12″ × 12″

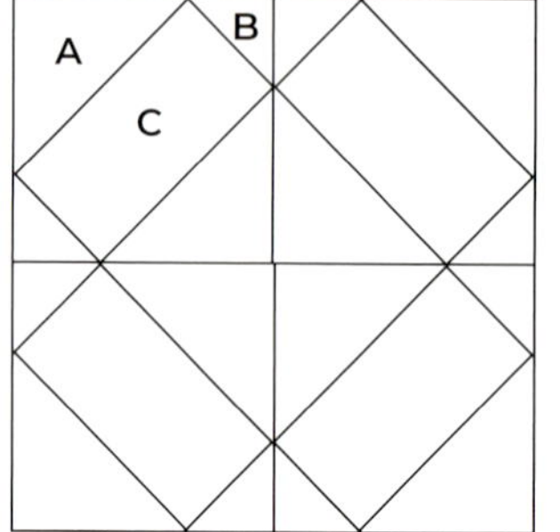

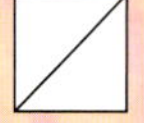

A
4⅞″

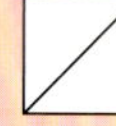

B
2⅞″

C
3⅜″ × 6¼″

may 15

COLORBURST SQUARES #3

10″ × 10″

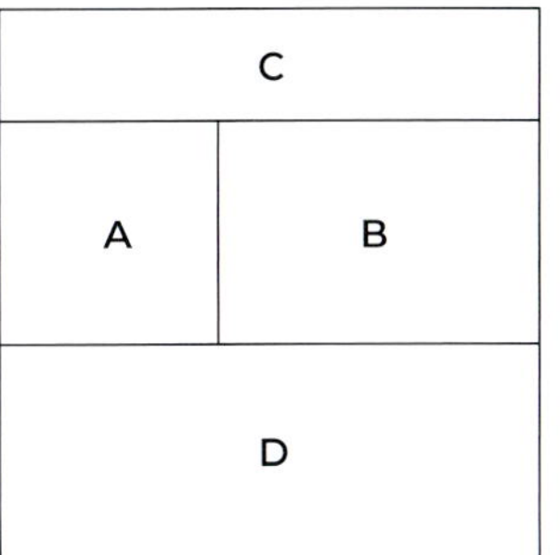

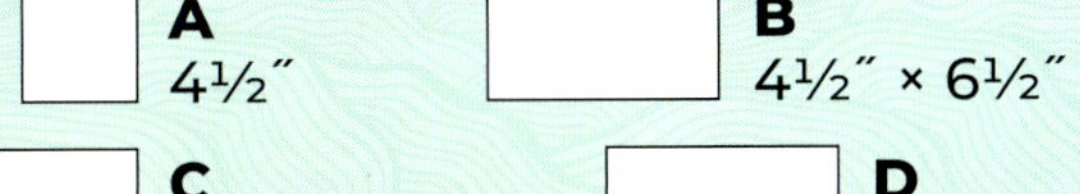

A
4½″

B
4½″ × 6½″

C
2½″ × 10½″

D
4½″ × 10½″

august 18

FOUR SEASONS

12″ × 12″

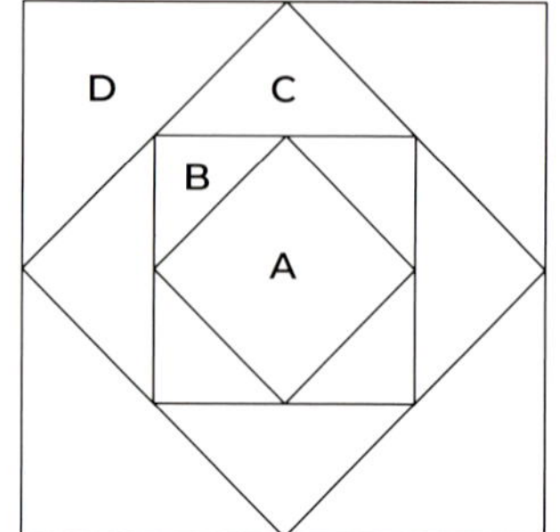

A
4¾″

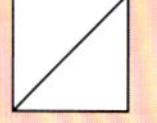

B
3⅞″

C
7¼″

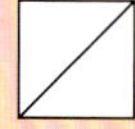

D
6⅞″

may 16

FLOWER BASKET VARIATION

10″ × 10″

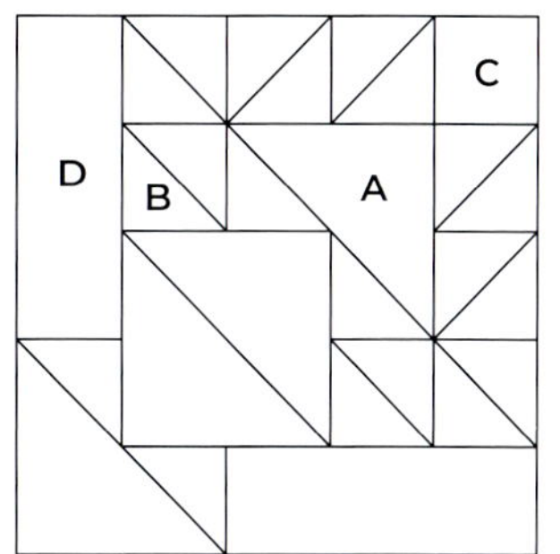

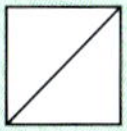

A 4⅞″

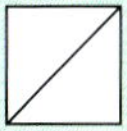

B 2⅞″

C 2½″

D 2½″ × 6½″

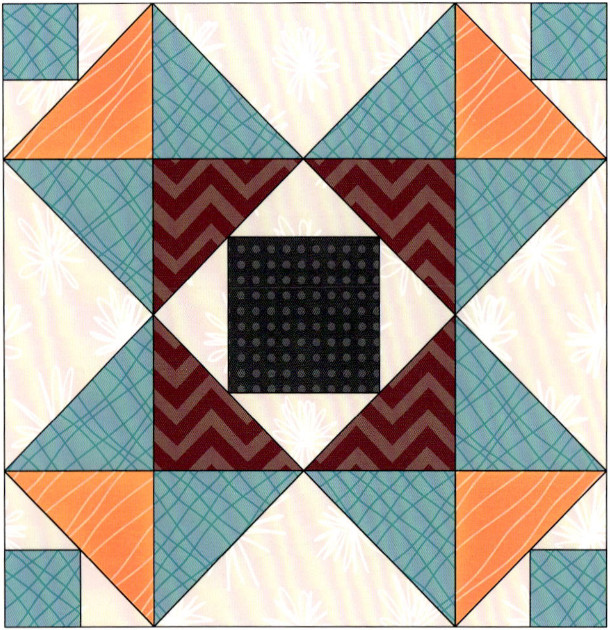

august 17

CASTLE MOSAIC

16″ × 16″

B
F
C
E
D
A

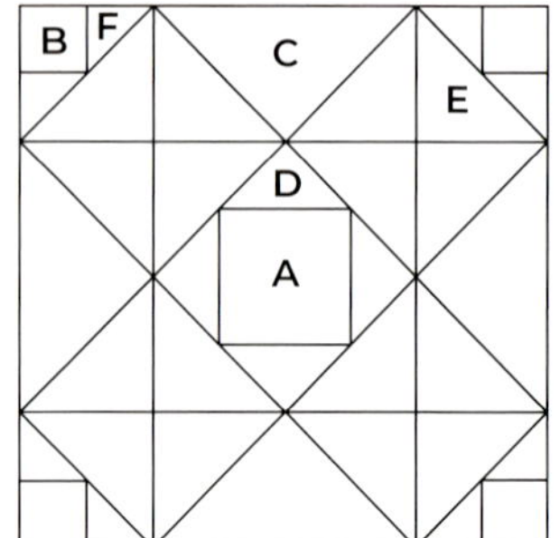

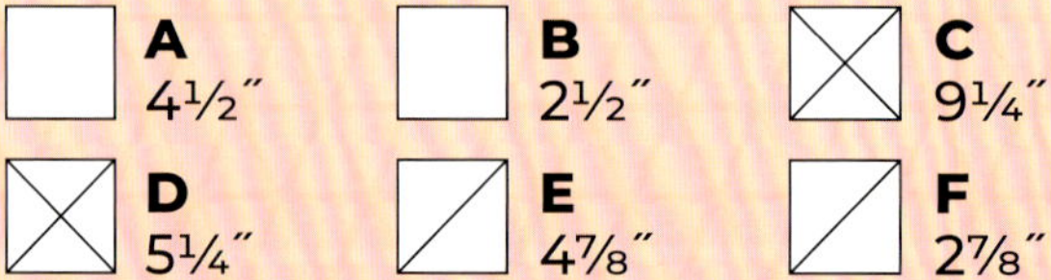

A
4½″
B
2½″
C
9¼″
D
5¼″
E
4⅞″
F
2⅞″

may **17**

FRUIT BASKET

10″ × 10″

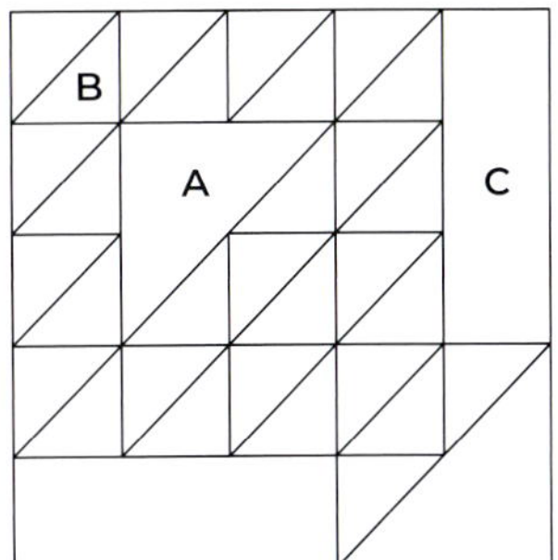

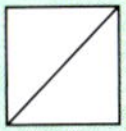

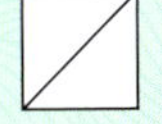

A
4⅞″

B
2⅞″

C
2½″ × 6½″

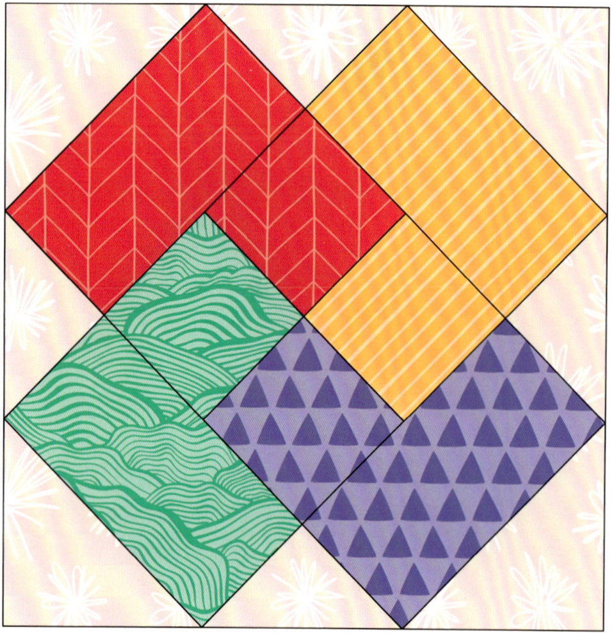

august 16

CARD TRICK
9″ × 9″

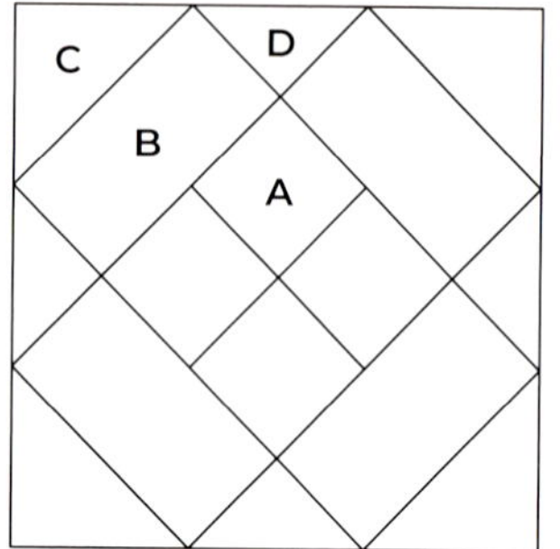

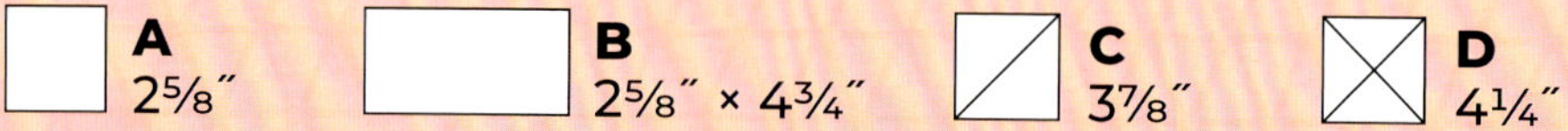

A
2⅝″

B
2⅝″ × 4¾″

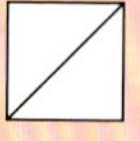

C
3⅞″

D
4¼″

may 18

GRANDMOTHER'S BASKET

10″ × 10″

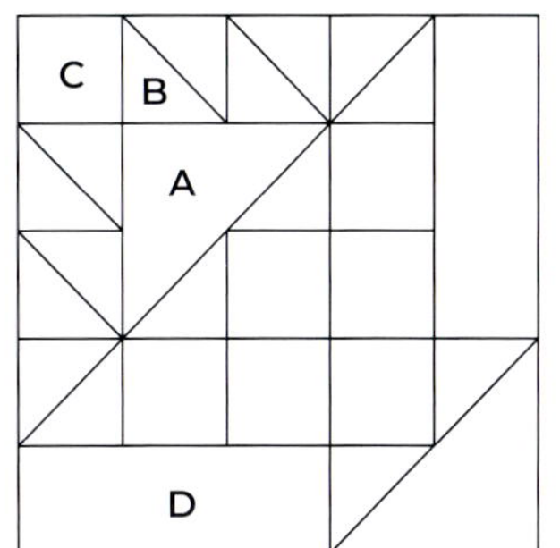

A 4⅞″

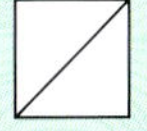

B 2⅞″

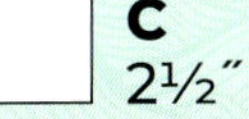

C 2½″

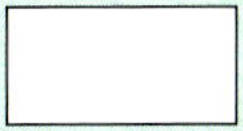

D 2½″ × 6½″

august 15

GARDEN PARTY

12″ × 12″

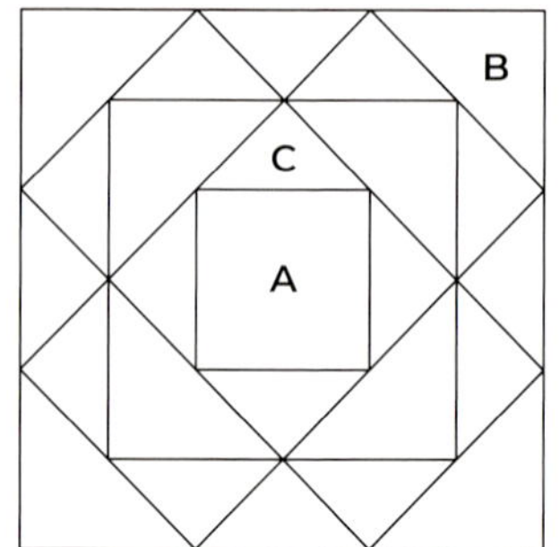

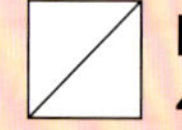

A
4½″

B
4⅞″

C
5¼″

may 19

HANGING BASKET
10″ × 10″

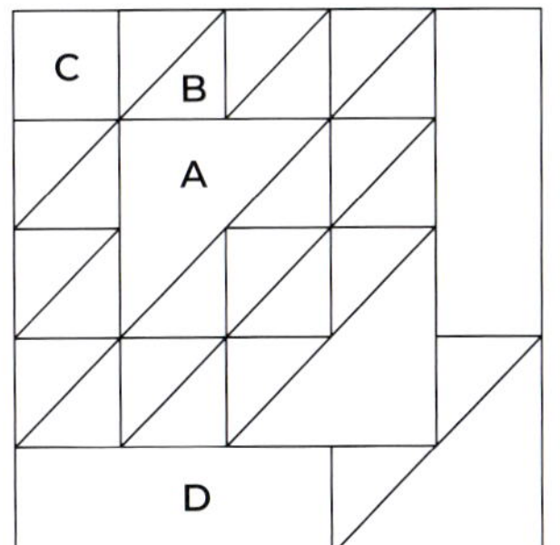

A 4⅞″

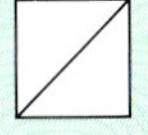

B 2⅞″

C 2½″

D 2½″ × 6½″

august 14

CAT'S CRADLE

10″ × 10″

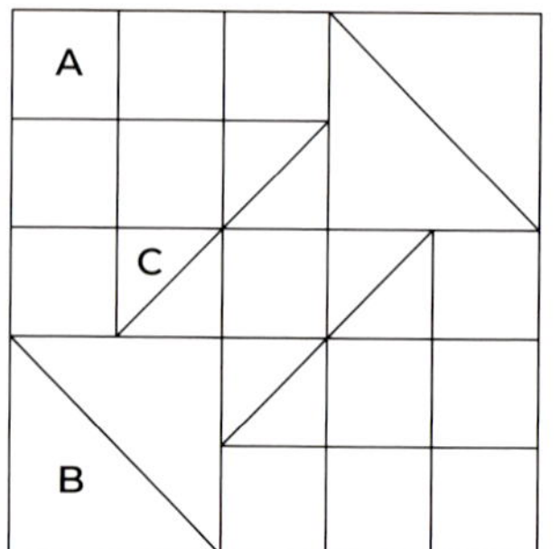

A
2½″

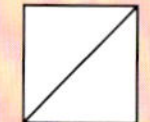

B
4⅞″

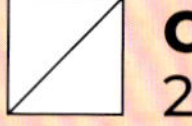

C
2⅞″

may 20

CONTRARY WIFE

12″ × 12″

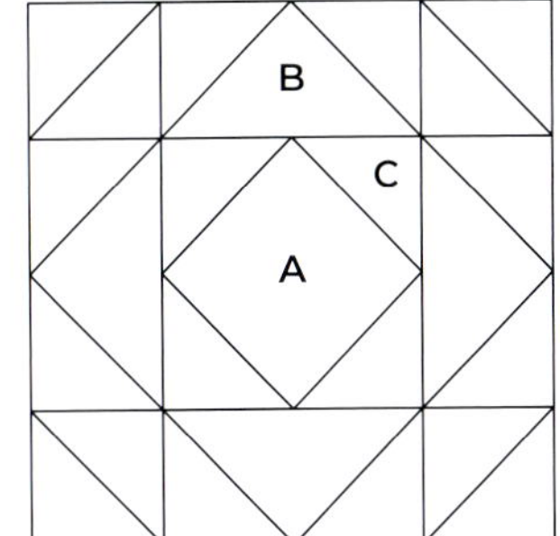

A 4¾″

B 7¼″

C 3⅞″

august 13

FOUR KNAVES

12″ × 12″

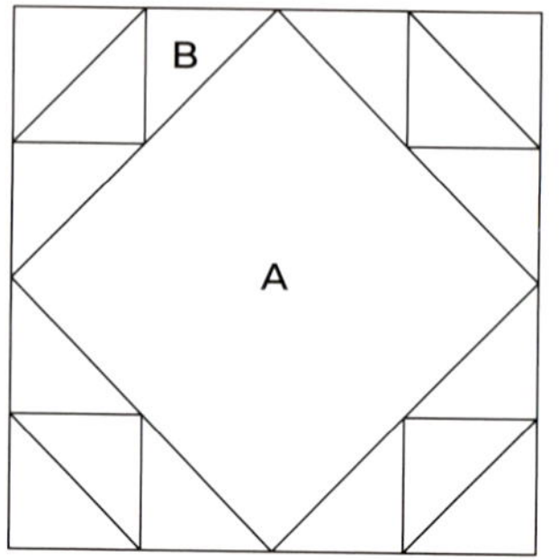

A
9″

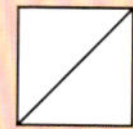

B
3⅞″

may 21

COUNTRY LANES VARIATION

12″ × 12″

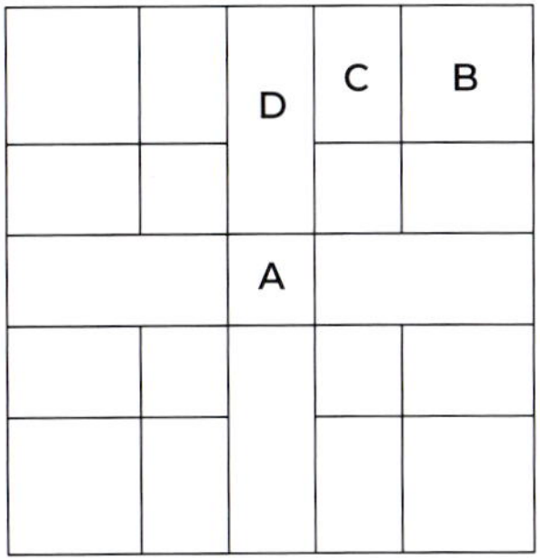

D C B

A

A
2½″

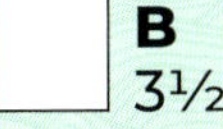

B
3½″

C
2½″ × 3½″

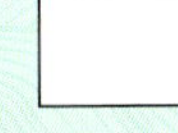

D
2½″ × 5½″

august 12

BASKET OF SQUARES
18″ × 18″

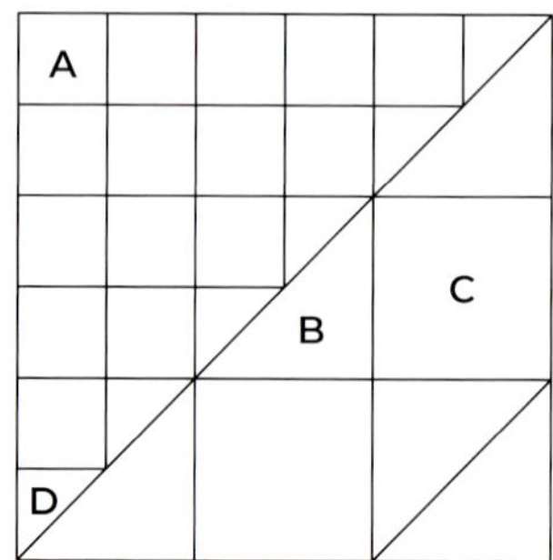

A
3½″

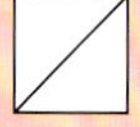

B
6⅞″

C
6½″

D
3⅞″

may 22

ANTIQUE ALBUM

16″ × 16″

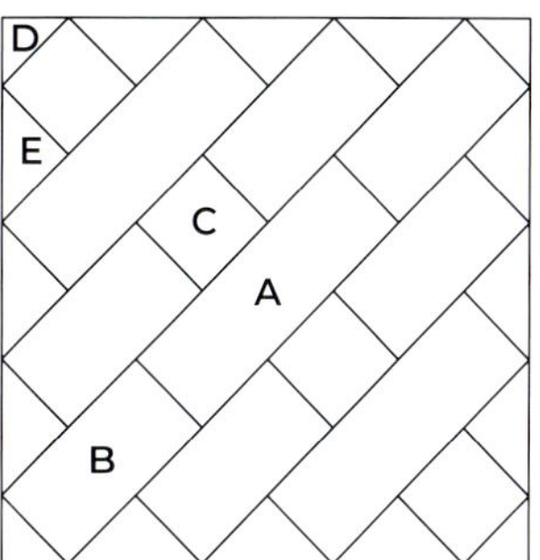

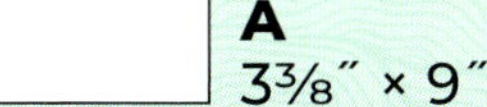

A
3⅜″ × 9″

B
3⅜″ × 6⅛″

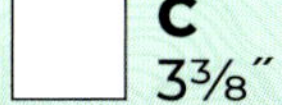

C
3⅜″

D
2⅞″

E
5¼″

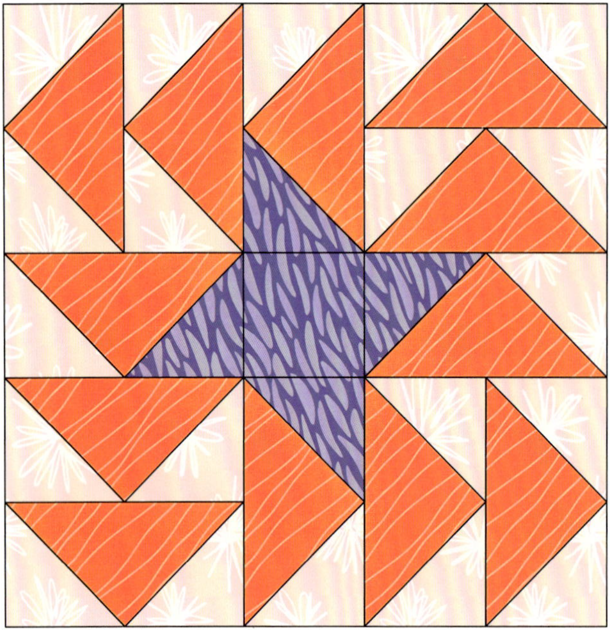

august 11

STAR STRUCK GEESE

10″ × 10″

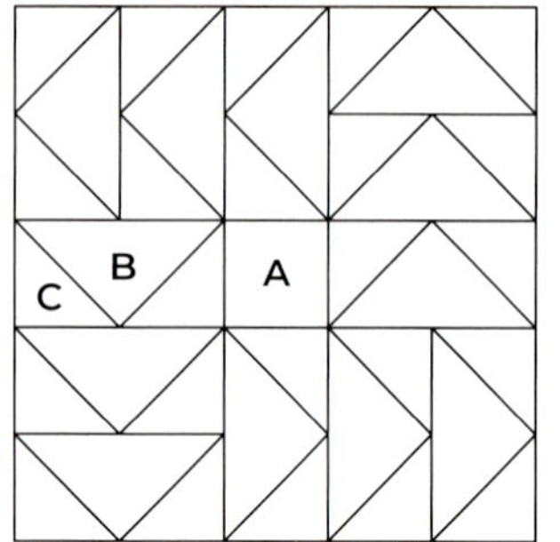

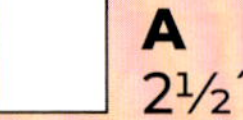

A
2½″

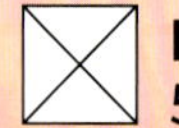

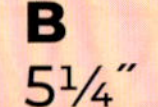

B
5¼″

C
2⅞″

may 23

EASY LOGS BLOCK #1

8″ × 8″

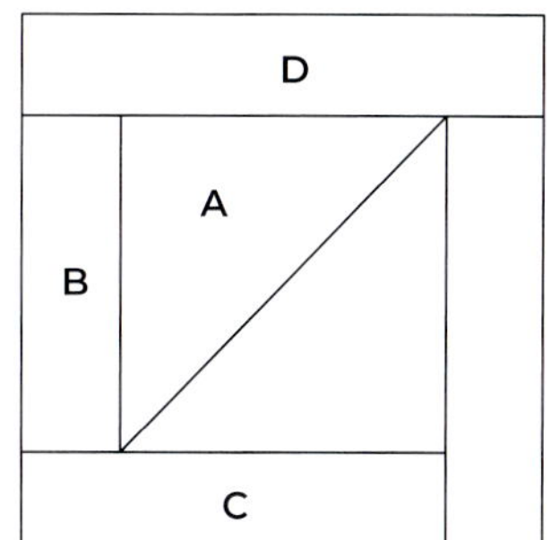

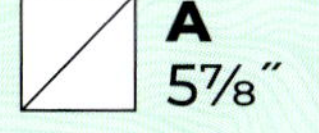

A
5⅞″

B
2″ ×5½″

C
2″ × 7″

D
2″ × 8½″

august 10

MAY BASKET

10″ × 10″

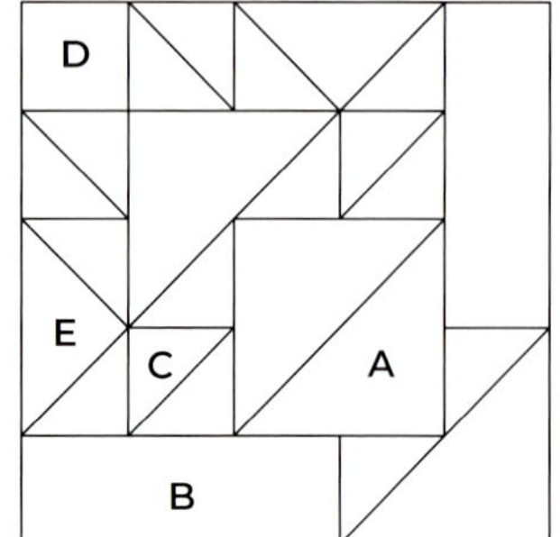

A
4⅞″

B
2½″ × 6½″

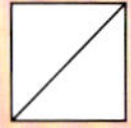

C
2⅞″

D
2½″

E
5¼″

may 24

EASY LOGS BLOCK #2

8″ × 8″

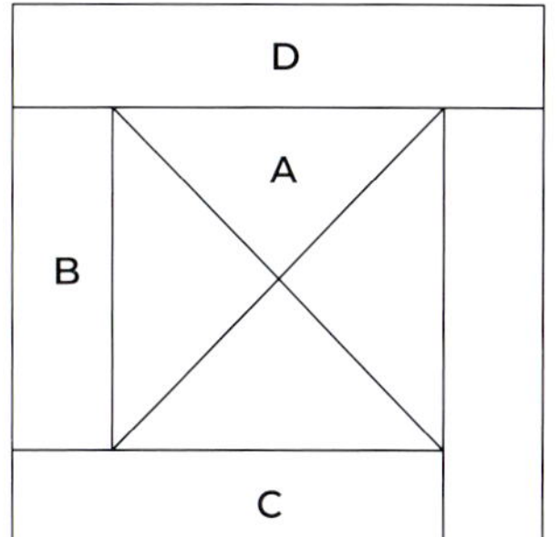

A
6¼″

B
2″ × 5½″

C
2″ × 7″

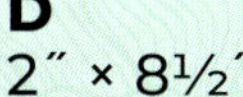

D
2″ × 8½″

august 9

HONEY'S CHOICE
10″ × 10″

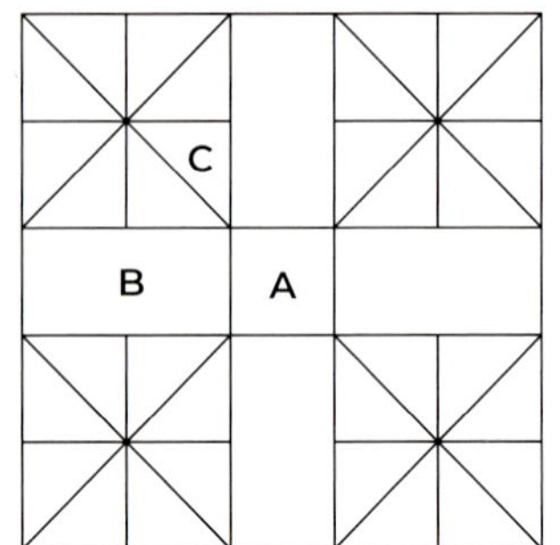

A
$2\frac{1}{2}$″

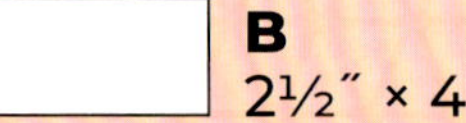
B
$2\frac{1}{2}$″ × $4\frac{1}{2}$″

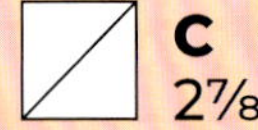
C
$2\frac{7}{8}$″

may 25

EASY LOGS BLOCK #3

8″ × 8″

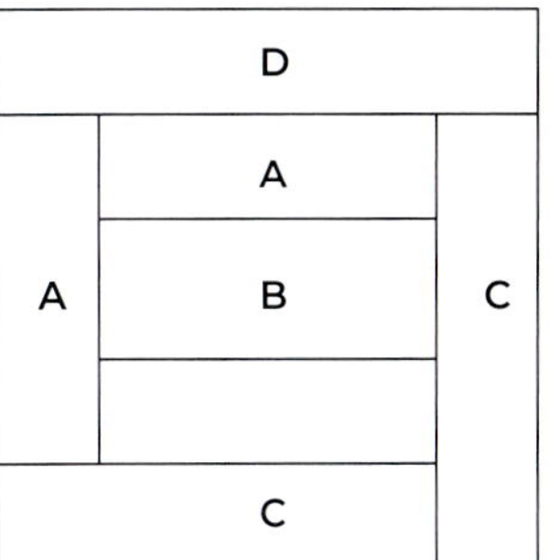

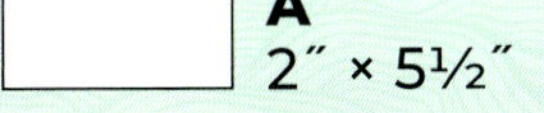

A
2″ × 5½″

B
2½″ × 5½″

C
2″ × 7″

D
2″ × 8½″

august 8

HEAVENLY PROBLEMS

10″ × 10″

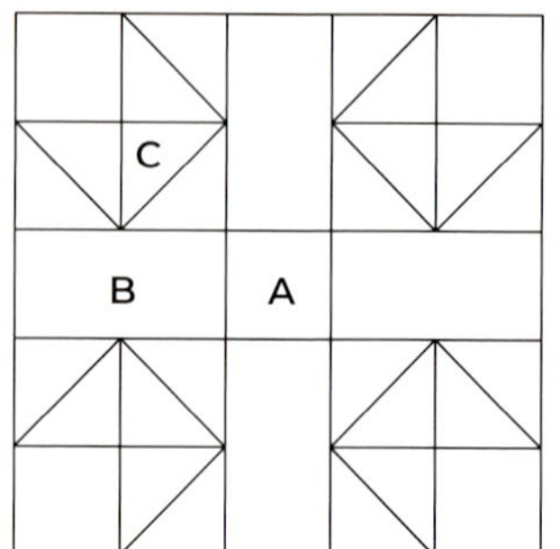

A
2½″

B
2½″ × 4½″

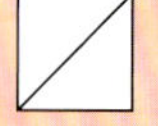

C
2⅞″

may 26

EASY LOGS BLOCK #4

8″ × 8″

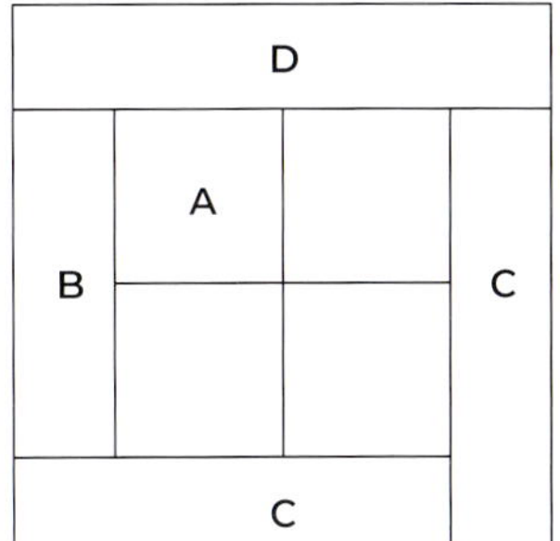

A
3″

B
2″ × 5½″

C
2″ × 7″

D
2″ × 8½″

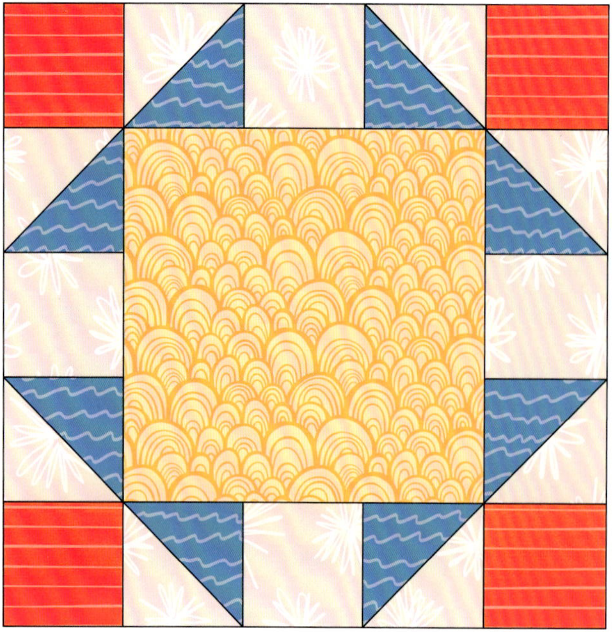

august 7

FIVE PATCH FRAME

10″ × 10″

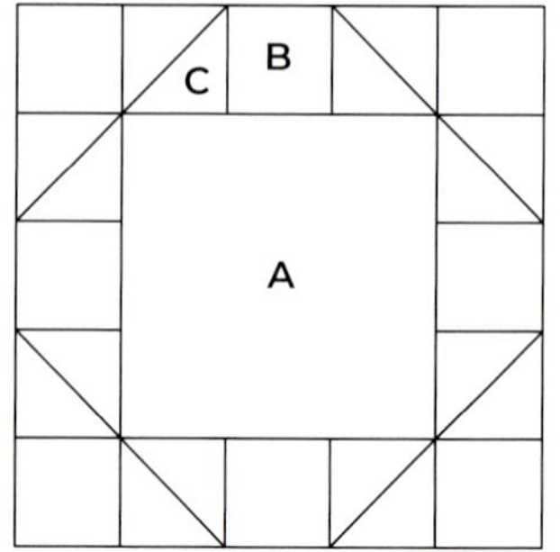

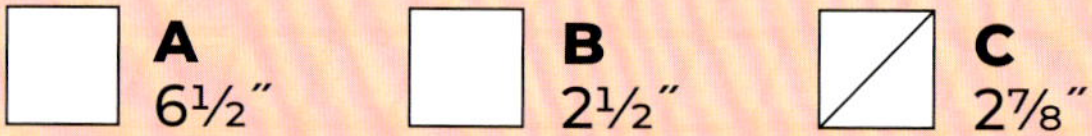

A
6½″

B
2½″

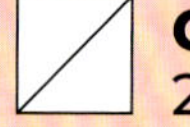

C
2⅞″

may 27

EASY LOGS BLOCK #5

8″ × 8″

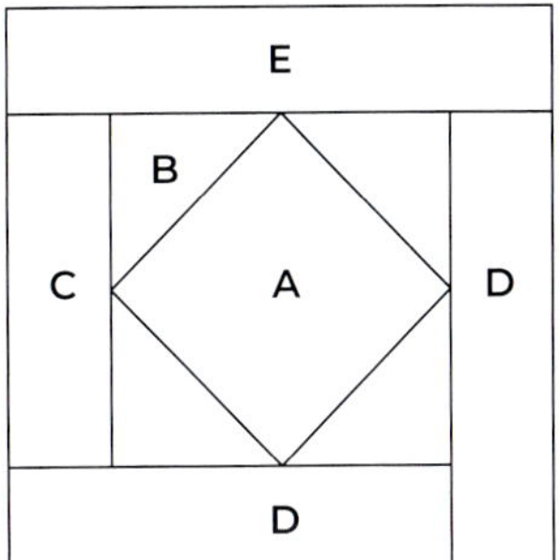

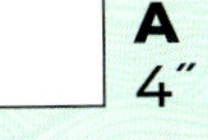

A
4″

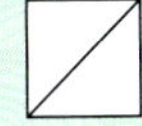

B
3⅜″

C
2″ × 5½″

D
2″ × 7″

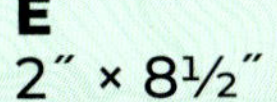

E
2″ × 8½″

august 6

FARMER'S DAUGHTER

10″ × 10″

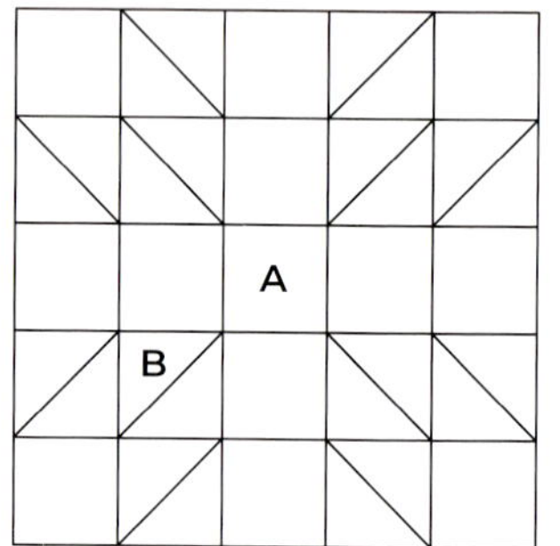

A
2½″

B
2⅞″

may 28

ALBUM SQUARES BLOCK

14″ × 14″

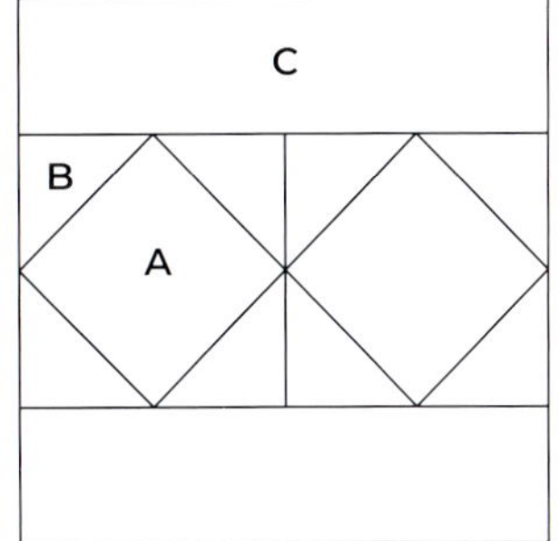

A
5½″

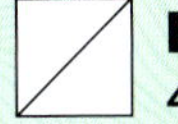

B
4⅜″

C
4″ × 14½″

august 5

DOUBLE V

10″ × 10″

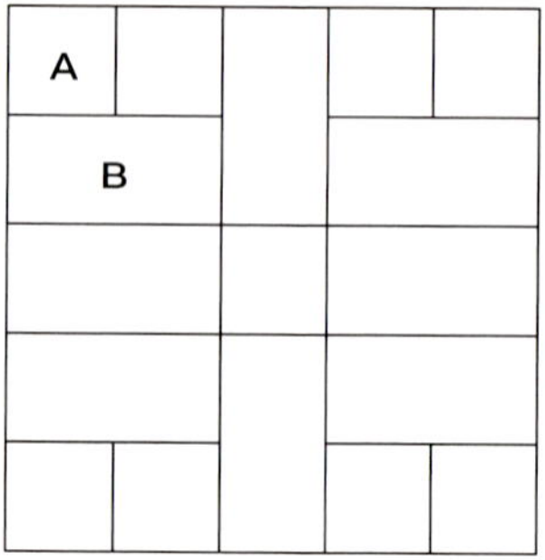

A

B

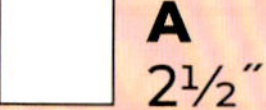

A
$2\frac{1}{2}$″

B
$2\frac{1}{2}$″ × $4\frac{1}{2}$″

may 29

SQUARES ON POINT
14″ × 14″

C
D
A
B

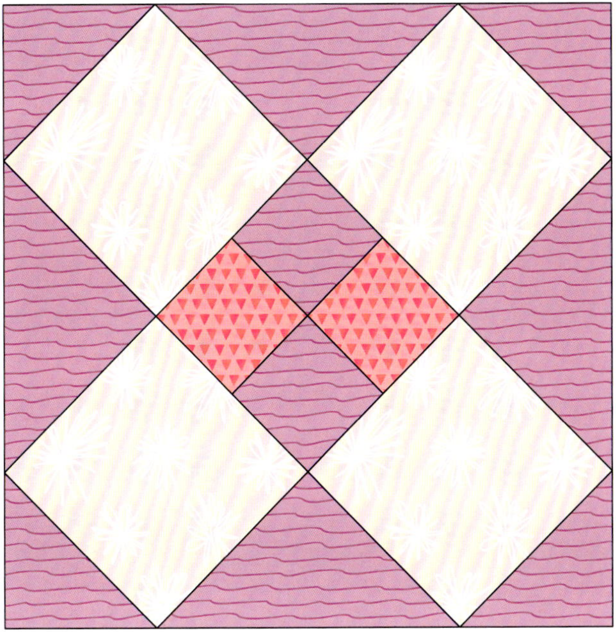

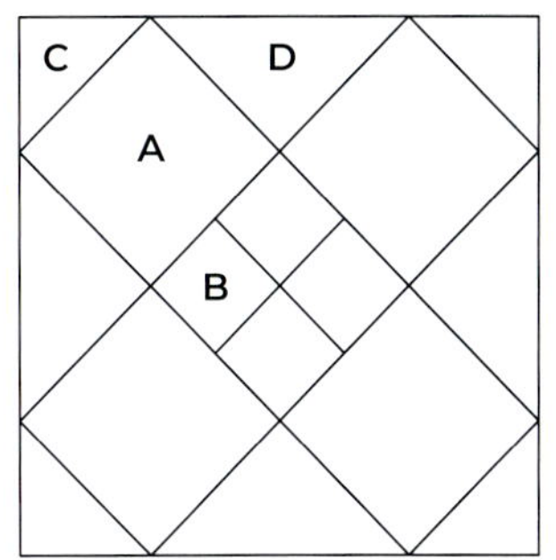

A
5½″
B
3″
C
4⅜″
D
8¼″

august 4

FLYING SQUARES

10″ × 10″

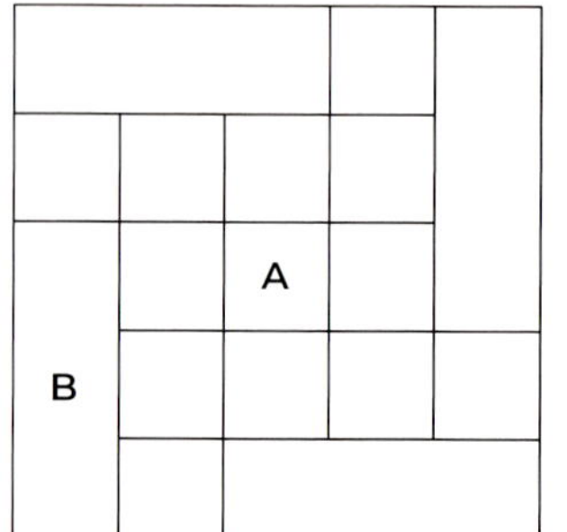

A
2½″

B
2½″ × 6½″

may 30

CROSSROADS

12″ × 12″

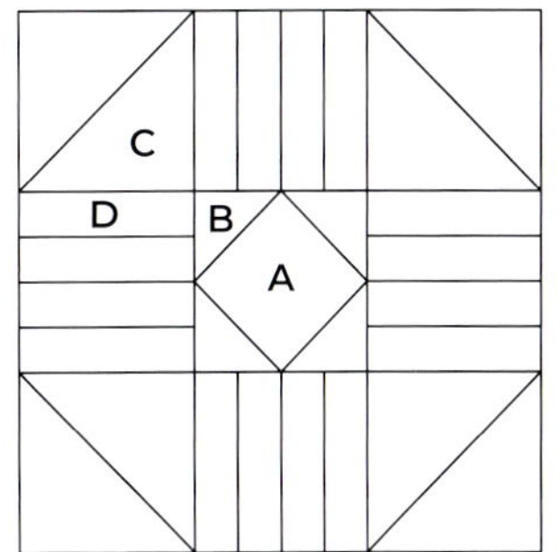

A
3⅜″

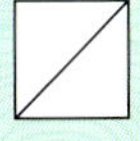

B
2⅞″

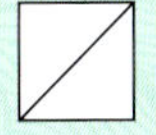

C
4⅞″

D
1½″ × 4½″

august 3

BEACON LIGHT

10″ × 10″

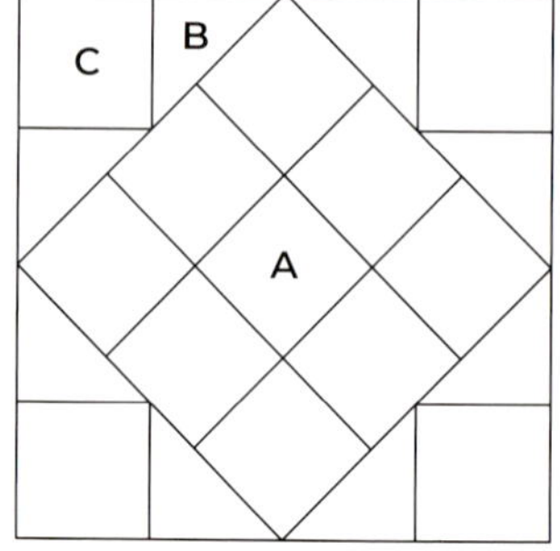

A	2⅞″
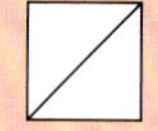 **B**	3⅜″
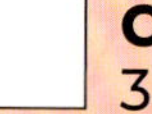 **C**	3″

may 31

MEMORY WREATH

12″ × 12″

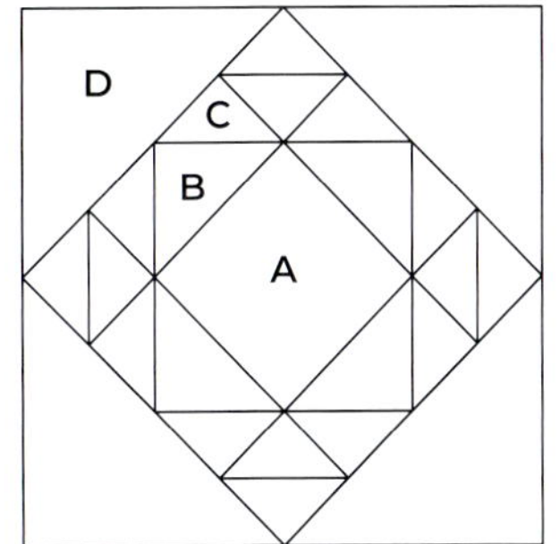

A 4¾″

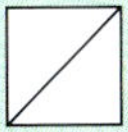

B 3⅞″

C 4¼″

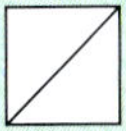

D 6⅞″

august 2

BASKET PUZZLE

10″ × 10″

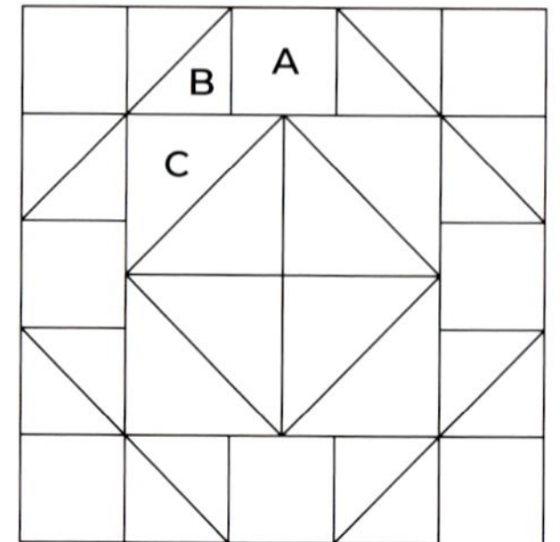

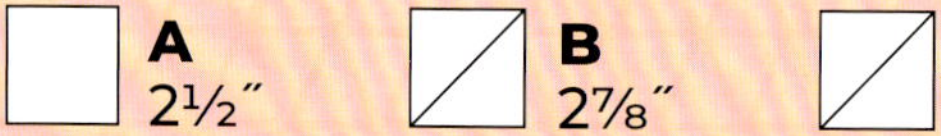

A
2½″

B
2⅞″

C
3⅞″

june 1

STEPS TO THE ALTAR

12″ × 12″

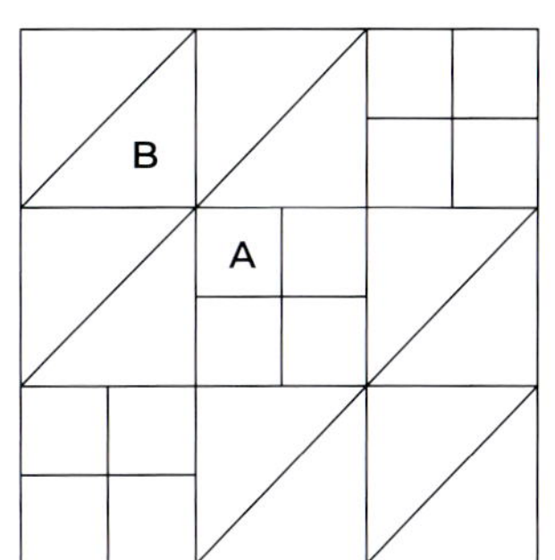

A
2½″

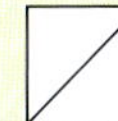

B
4⅞″

august 1

ALPINE CROSS

10″ × 10″

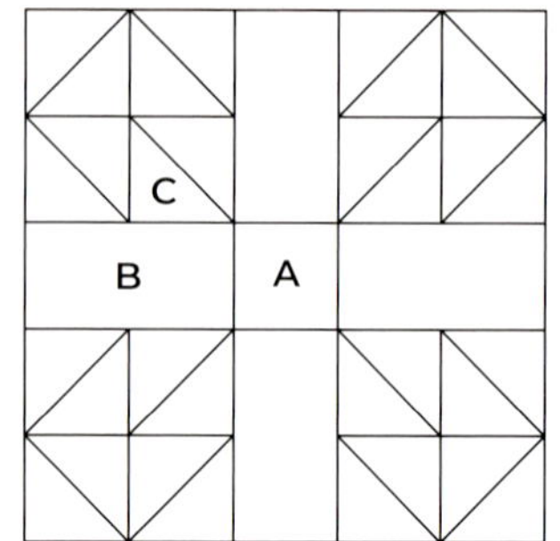

A
2½″

B
2½″ × 4½″

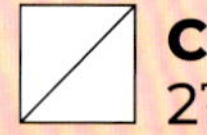

C
2⅞″

june 2

STAIRSTEPS BLOCK

12″ × 12″

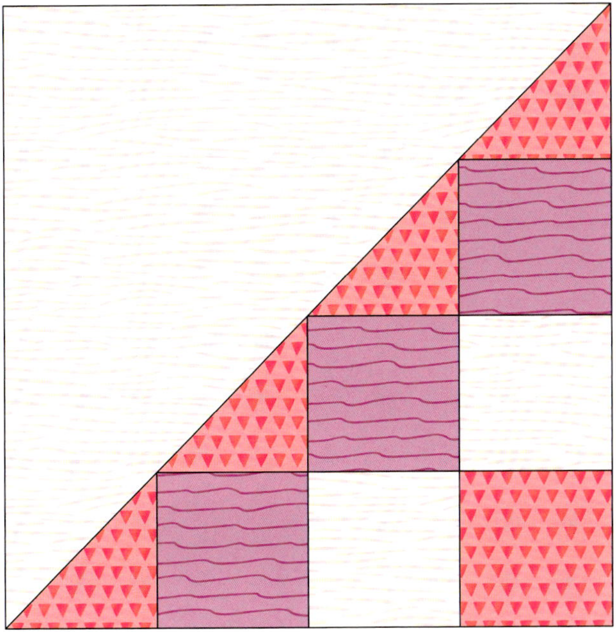

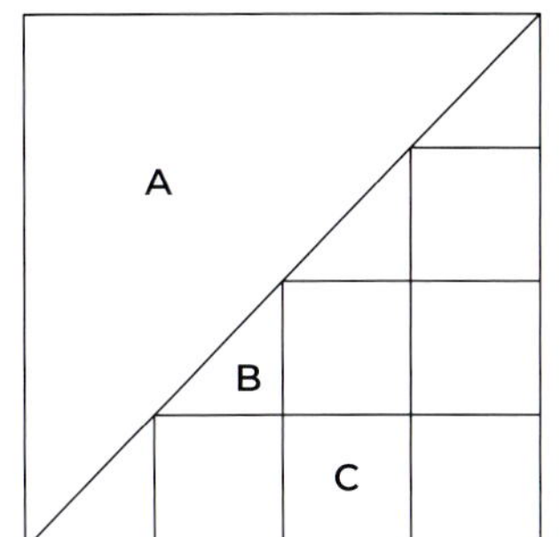

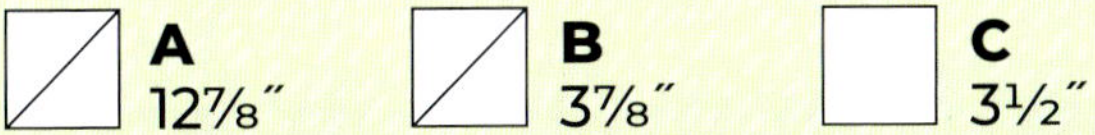

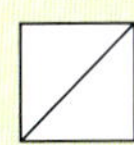

A
12⅞″

B
3⅞″

C
3½″

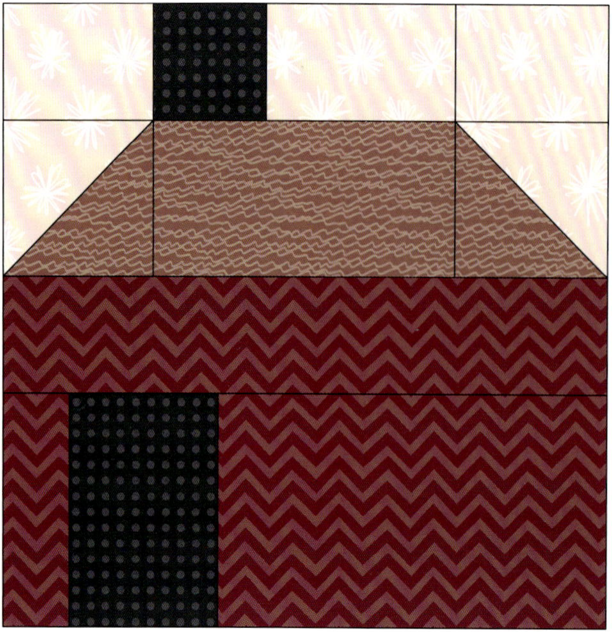

july 31

HOUSE BLOCK
8″ × 8″

A 1½″ × 3½″

B 2½″ × 3½″

C 5½″ × 3½″

D 2″ × 8½″

E 2½″ × 4½″

F 2⅞″

G 2½″ × 2″

H 3″ × 2″

I 2″

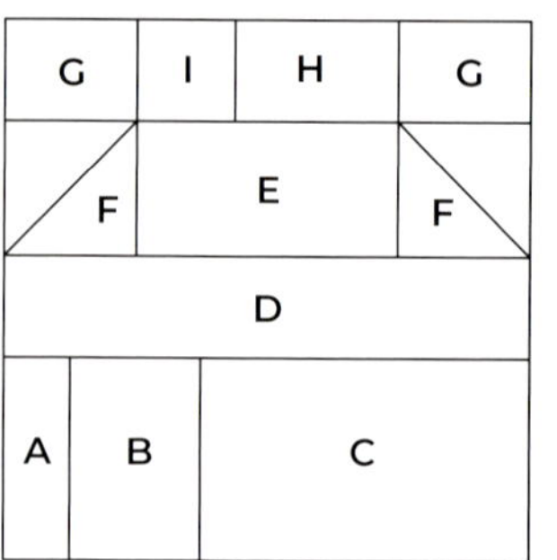

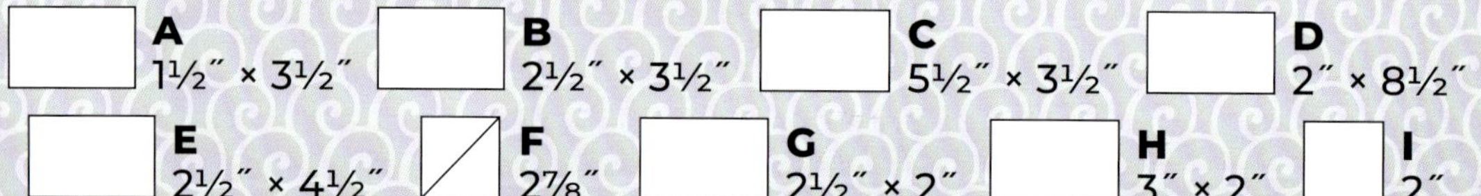

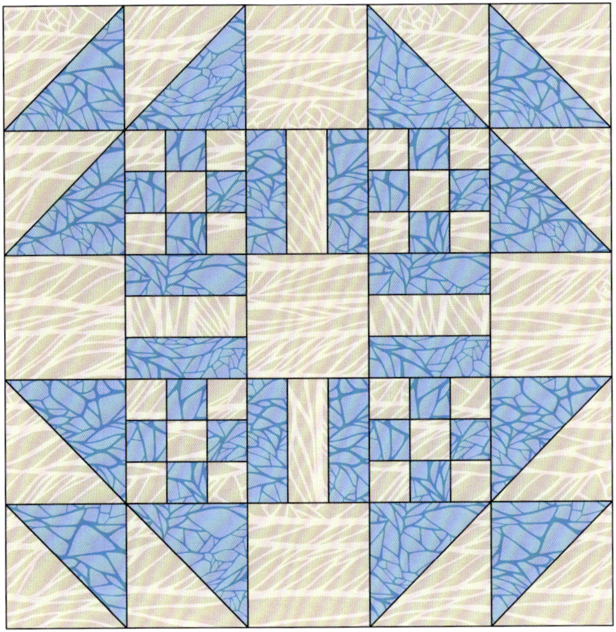

june 3

GOOSE IN THE POND VARIATION

15″ × 15″

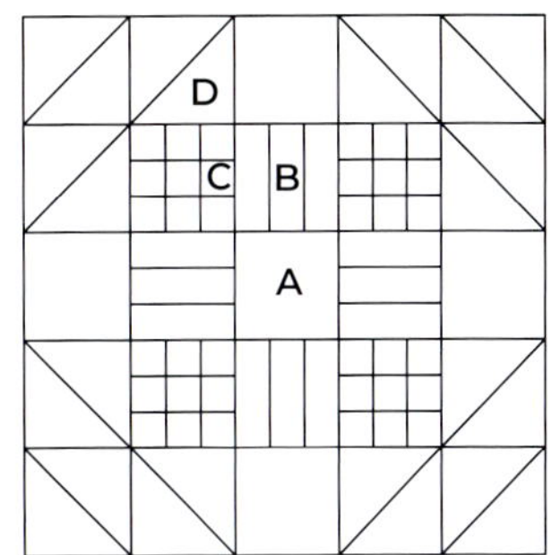

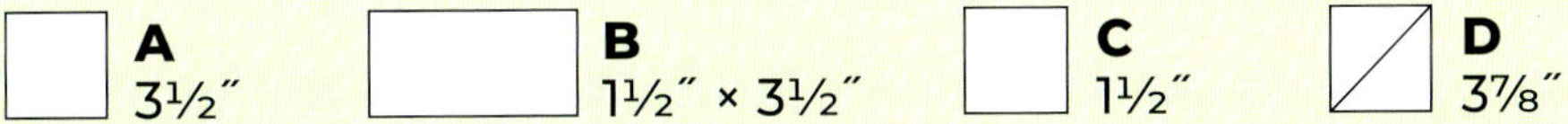

A
3½″

B
1½″ × 3½″

C
1½″

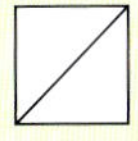

D
3⅞″

july 30

SAILBOAT BLOCK #3

8″ × 8″

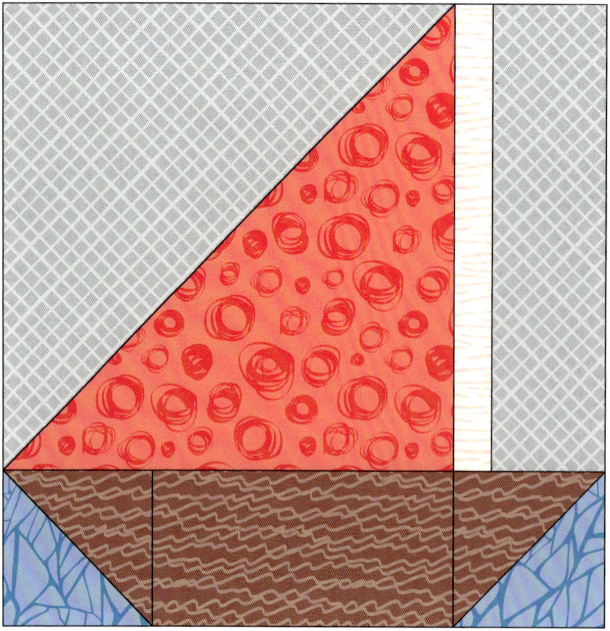

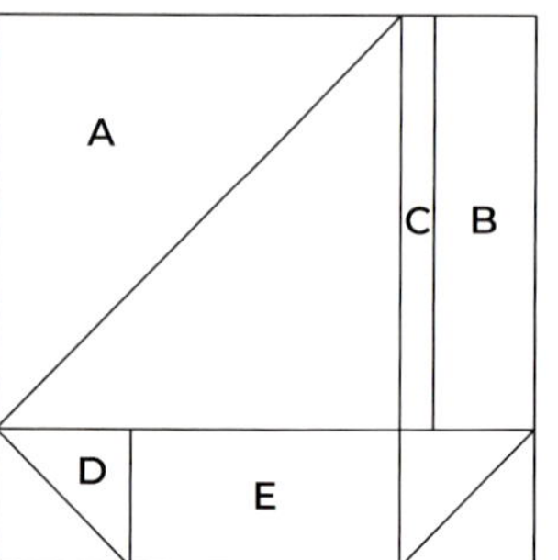

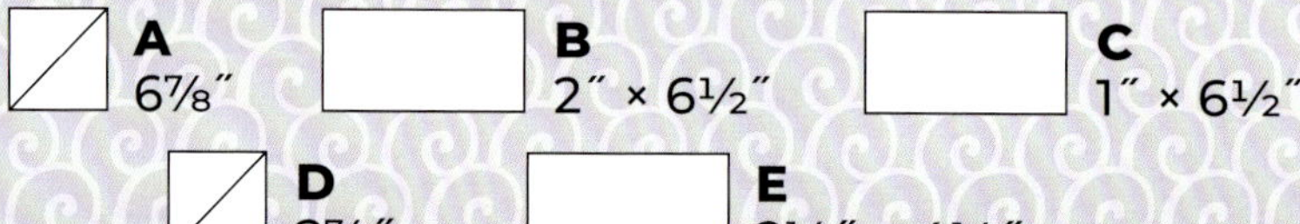

june 4

BIRD'S NEST

15″ × 15″

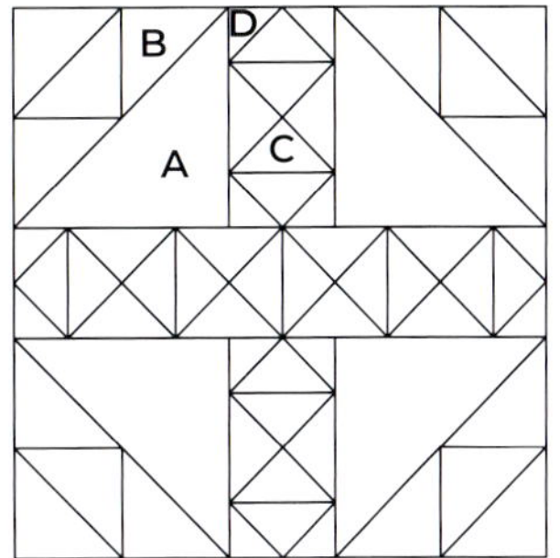

A 6⅞″

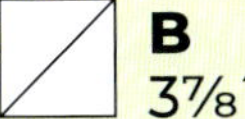

B 3⅞″

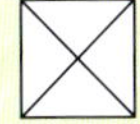

C 4¼″

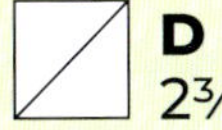

D 2⅜″

july 29

SAILBOAT BLOCK #2

8″ × 8″

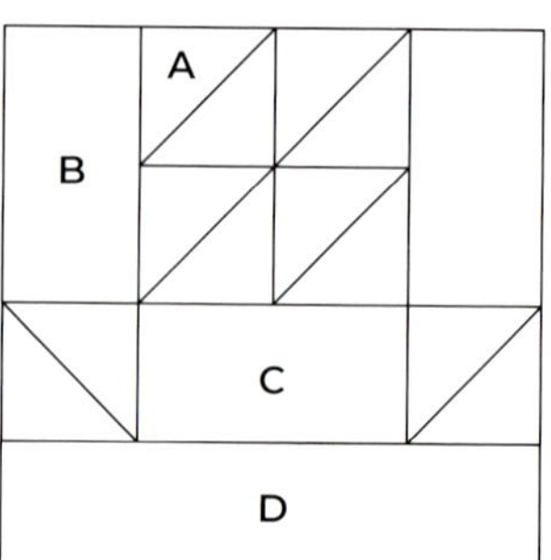

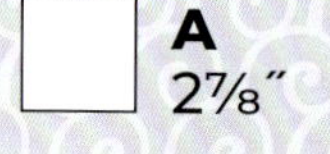

A
2⅞″

B
2½″ × 4½″

C
2½″ × 4½″

D
2½″ × 8½″

june 5

DUCK AND DUCKLINGS

15″ × 15″

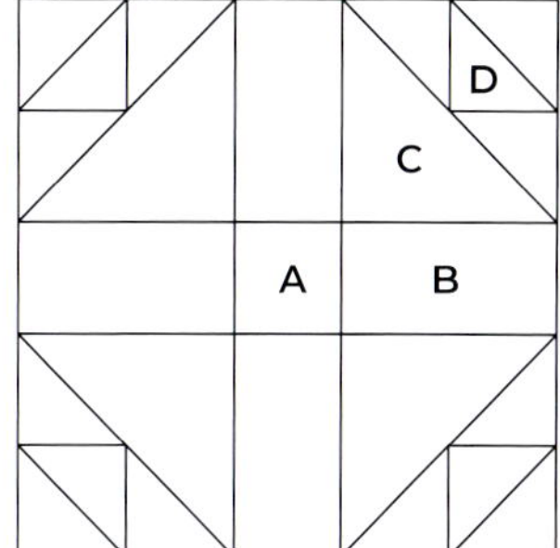

A
3½″

B
3½″ × 6½″

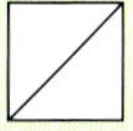

C
6⅞″

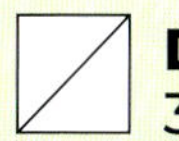

D
3⅞″

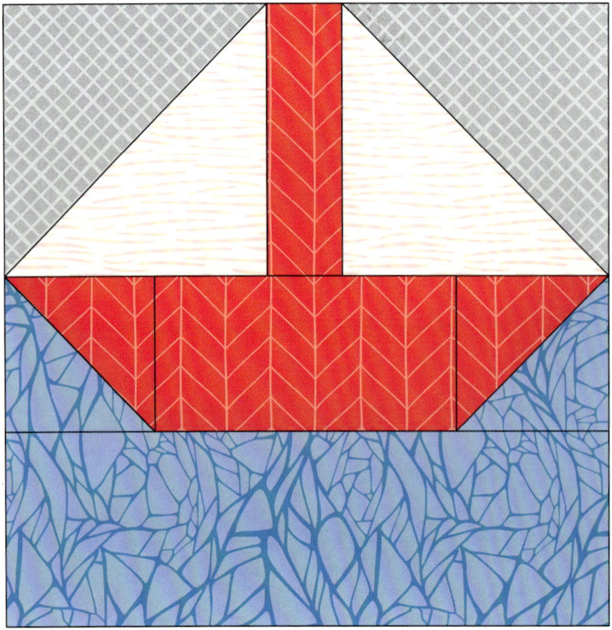

july 28

SAILBOAT BLOCK #1

8″ × 8″

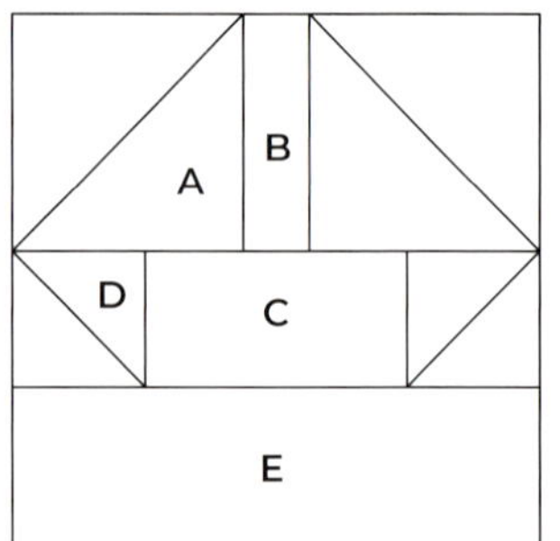

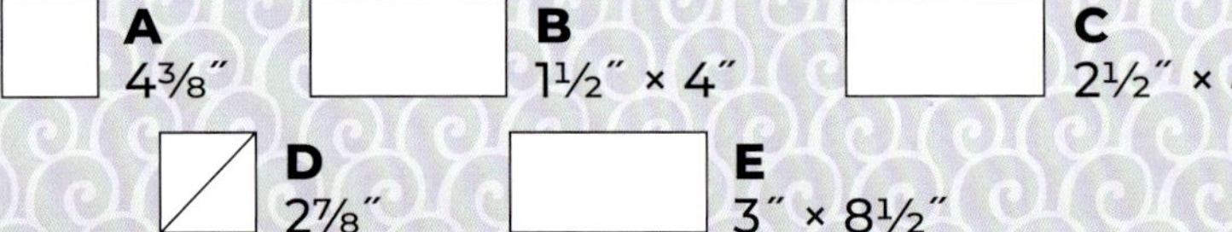

june 6

IRISH PUZZLE

10″ × 10″

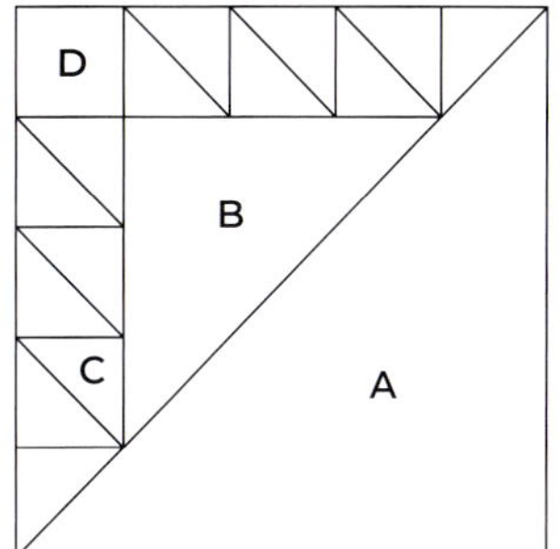

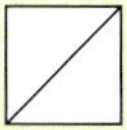

A
10⅞″

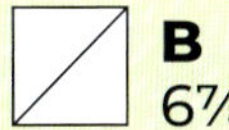

B
6⅞″

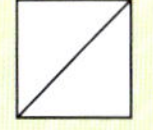

C
2⅞″

D
2½″

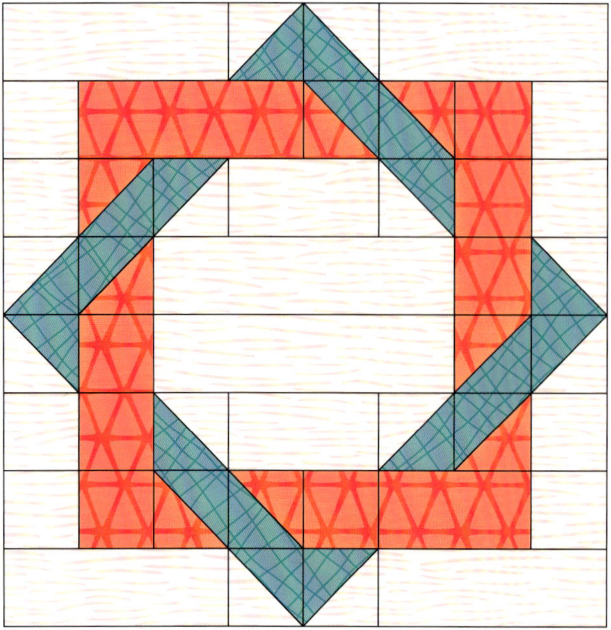

july 27

INTERLOCKED RINGS

16″ × 16″

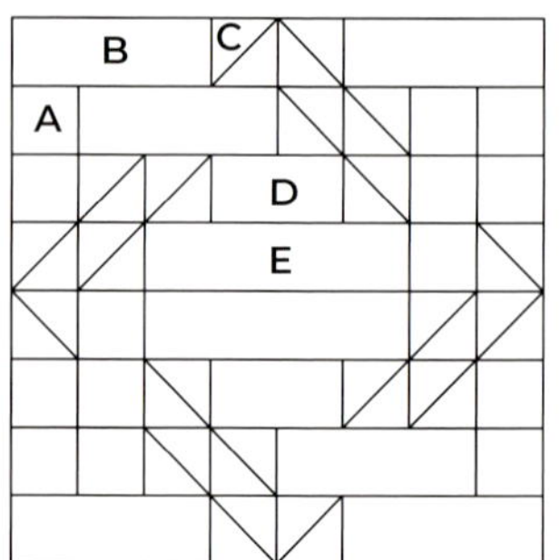

june 7

WINDBLOWN SQUARE

12″ × 12″

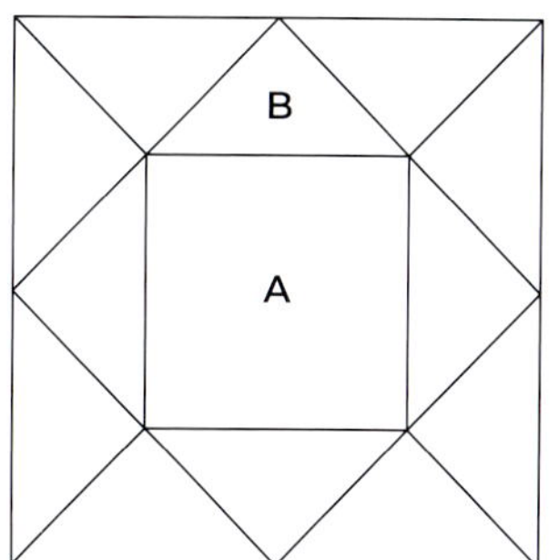

A
6½″

B
7¼″

july 26

FLYING GEESE VARIATION

12″ × 12″

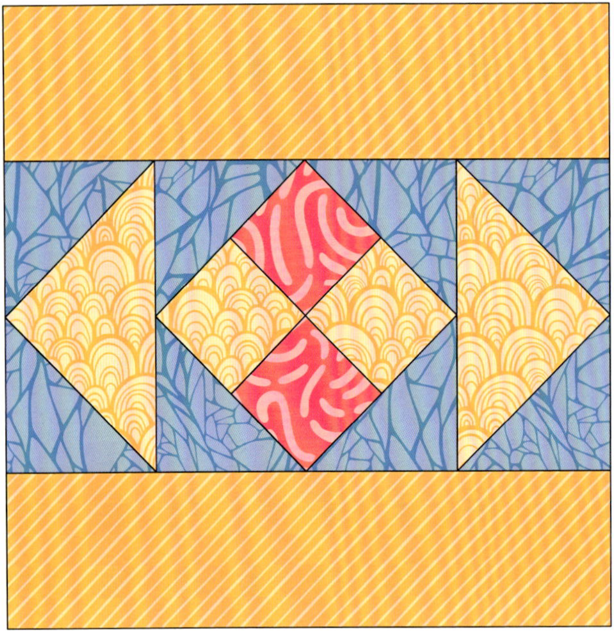

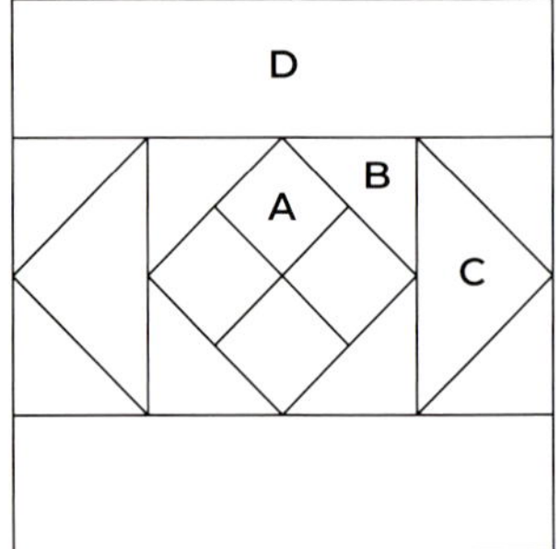

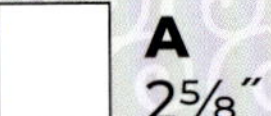

A
$2\frac{5}{8}$″

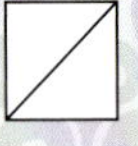

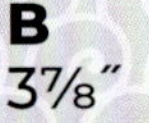

B
$3\frac{7}{8}$″

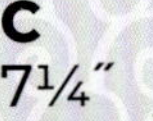

C
$7\frac{1}{4}$″

D
$3\frac{1}{2}$″ × $12\frac{1}{2}$″

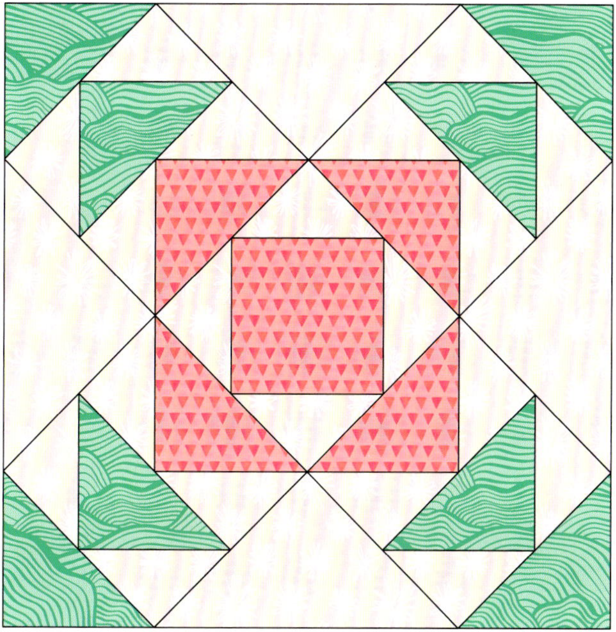

june 8

GEESE IN THE AIR

10″ × 10″

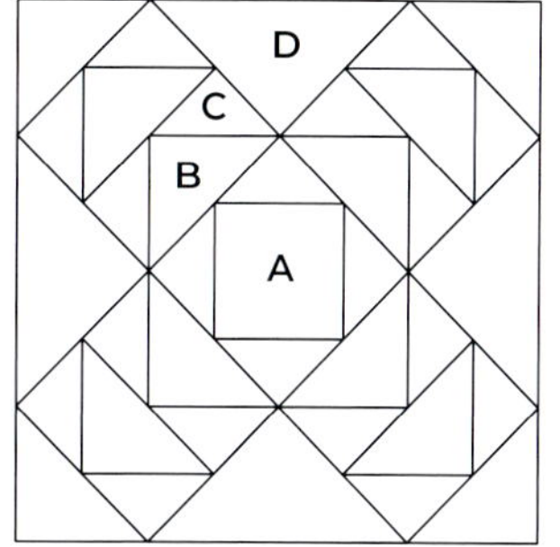

A 3″

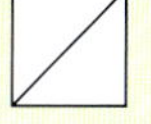

B 3⅜″

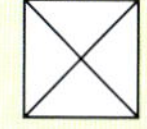

C 3¾″

D 6¼″

july 25

STAR CROSS

15″ × 15″

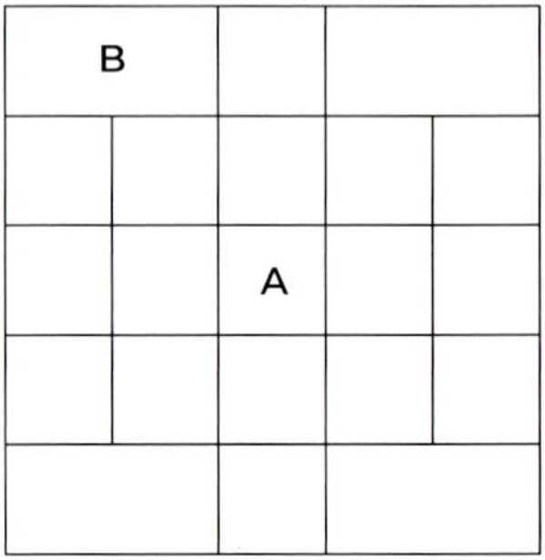

B

A

june 9

BORDERED PUSS IN THE CORNER

12″ × 12″

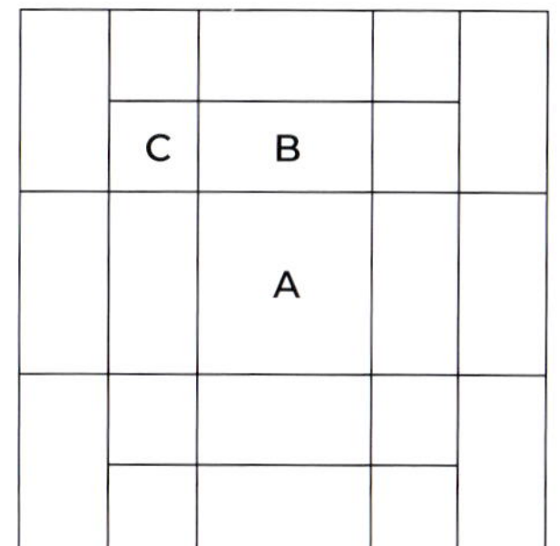

A
4½″

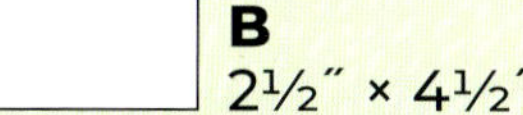

B
2½″ × 4½″

C
2½″

july 24

GARDEN STAR

15″ × 15″

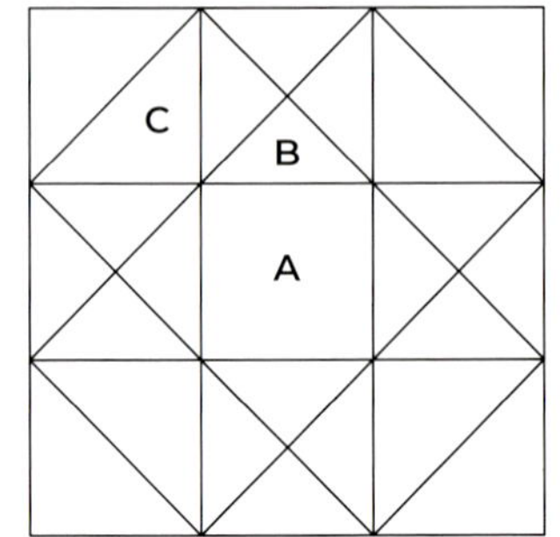

A
5½″

B
6¼″

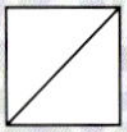

C
5⅞″

june 10

GRANDMOTHER'S CROSS

12″ × 12″

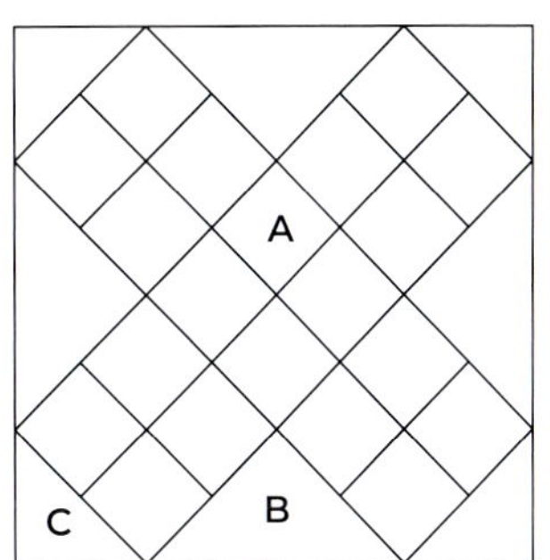

A 2⅝″

B 7¼″

C 3⅞″

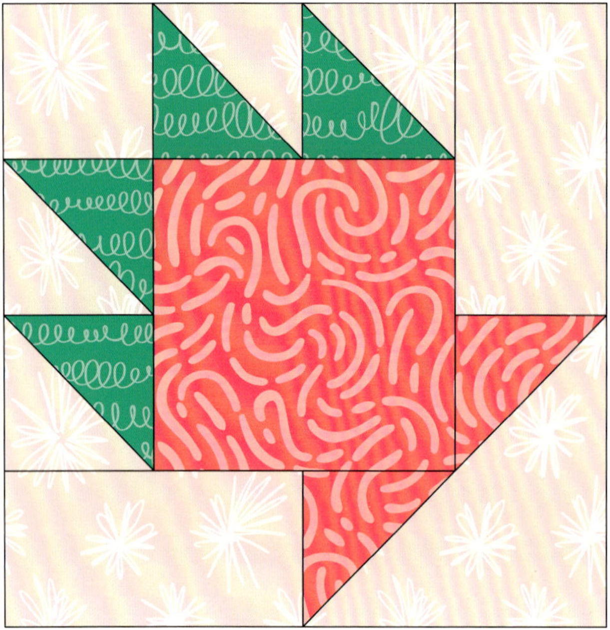

july 23

CACTUS POT

8″ × 8″

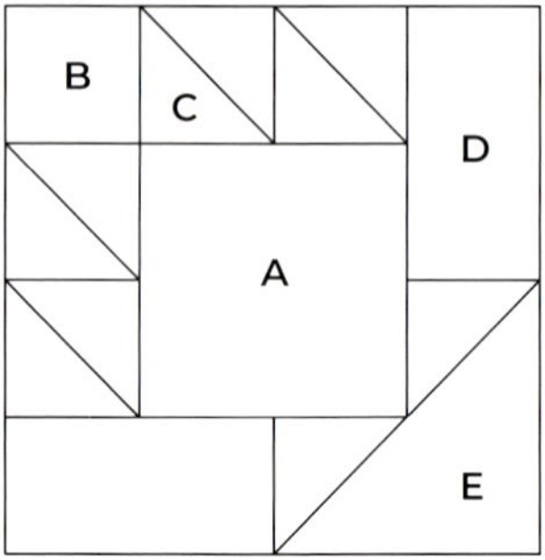

B
C
D
A
E

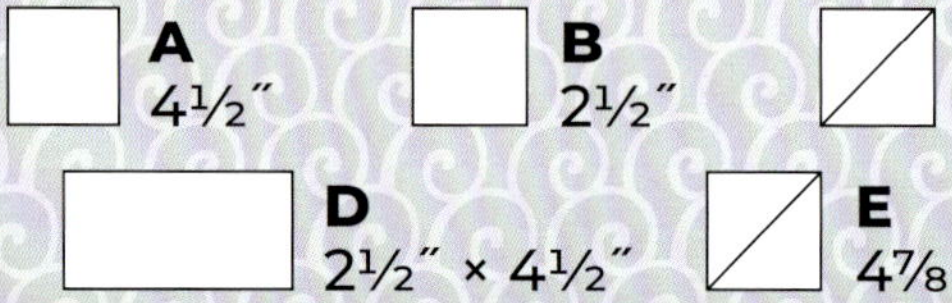

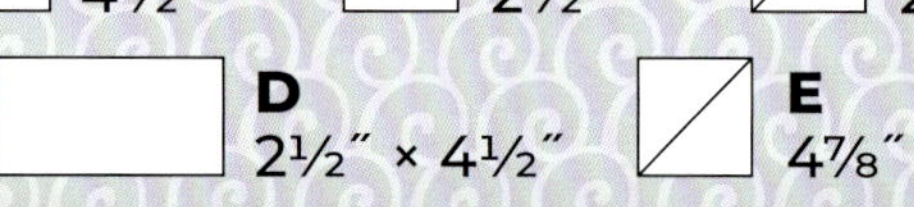

june 11

STAIRWAYS BLOCK

16″ × 16″

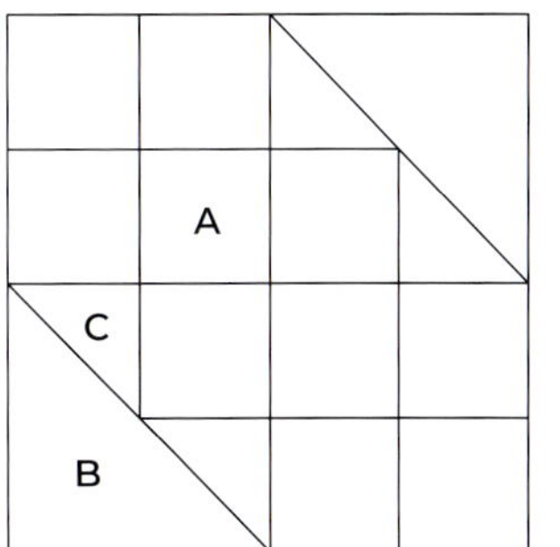

A
4½″

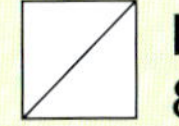

B
8⅞″

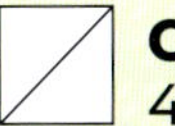

C
4⅞″

july 22

RIBBON STAR
12″ × 12″

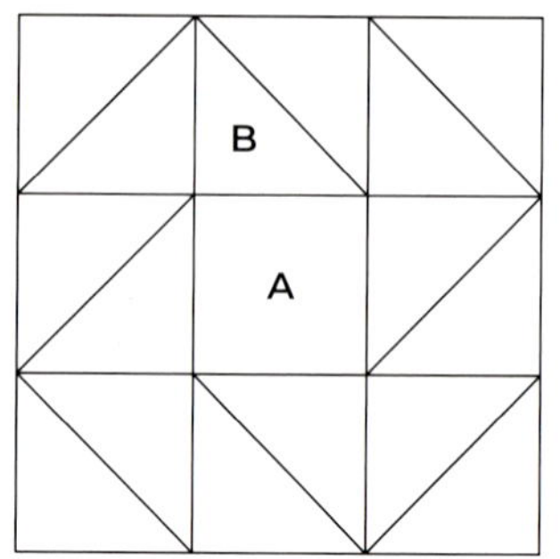

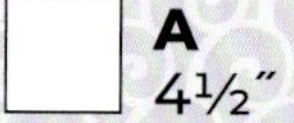
A
4½″

B
4⅞″

june 12

SPINNER BLOCK

8″ × 8″

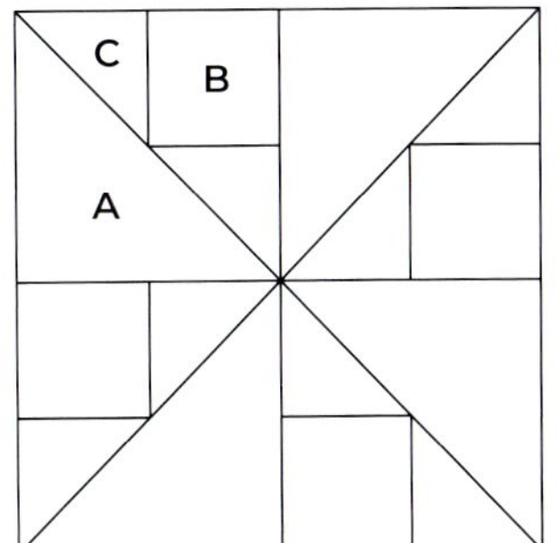

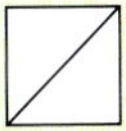

A
$4\frac{7}{8}$″

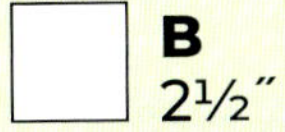

B
$2\frac{1}{2}$″

C
$2\frac{7}{8}$″

july 21

TREE EVERLASTING

12″ × 12″

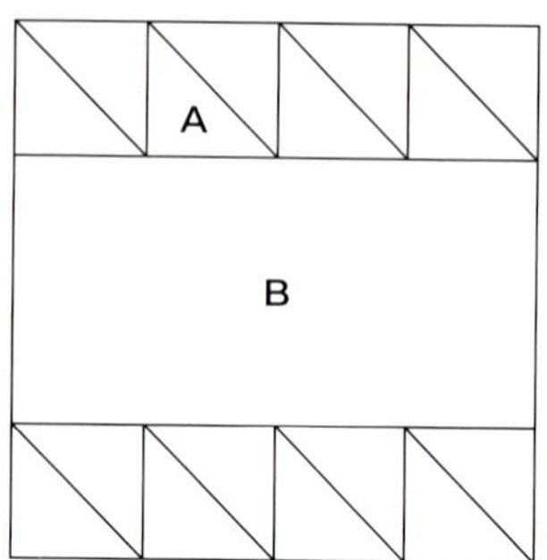

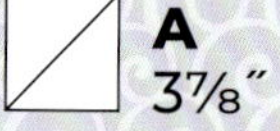

A
3⅞″

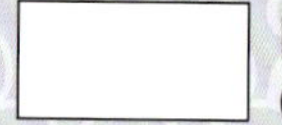

B
6½″ × 12½″

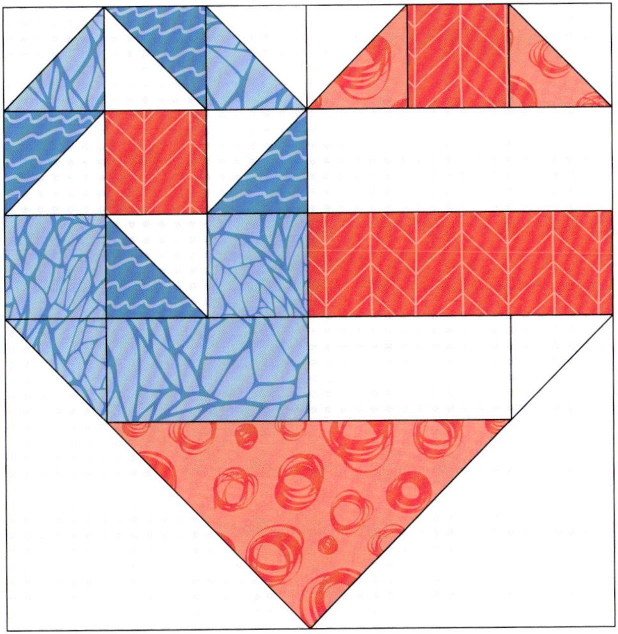

june 13

OLD GLORY STAR

18″ × 18″

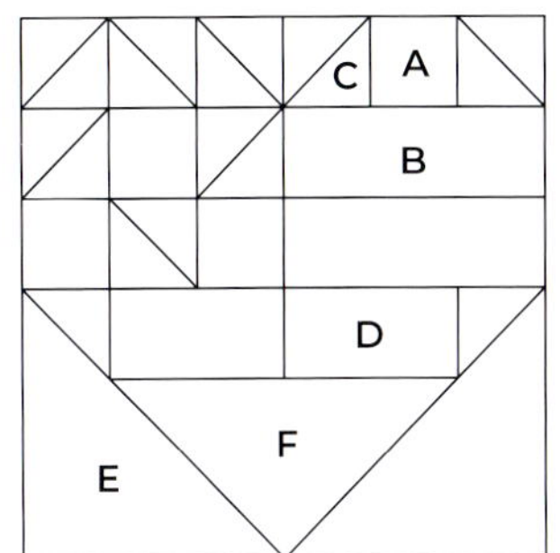

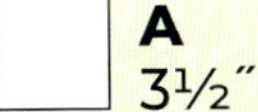

A
3½″

B
3½″ × 9½″

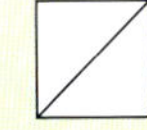

C
3⅞″

D
3½″ × 6½″

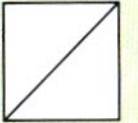

E
9⅞″

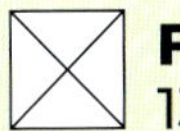

F
13¼″

july 20

ZIG ZAG TRIANGLES

12″ × 12″

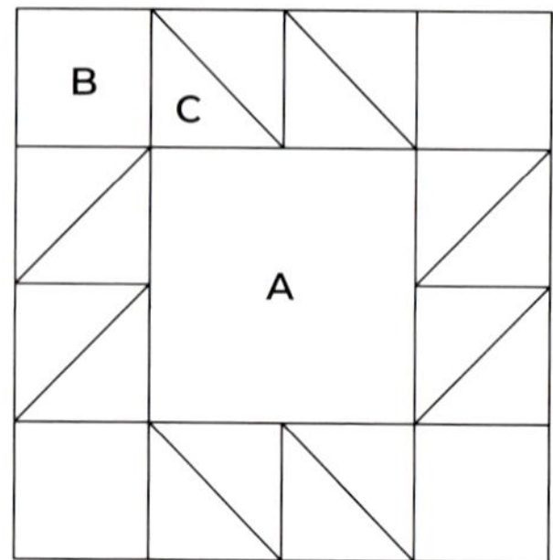

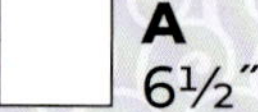

A
6½″

B
3½″

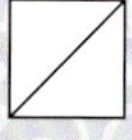

C
3⅞″

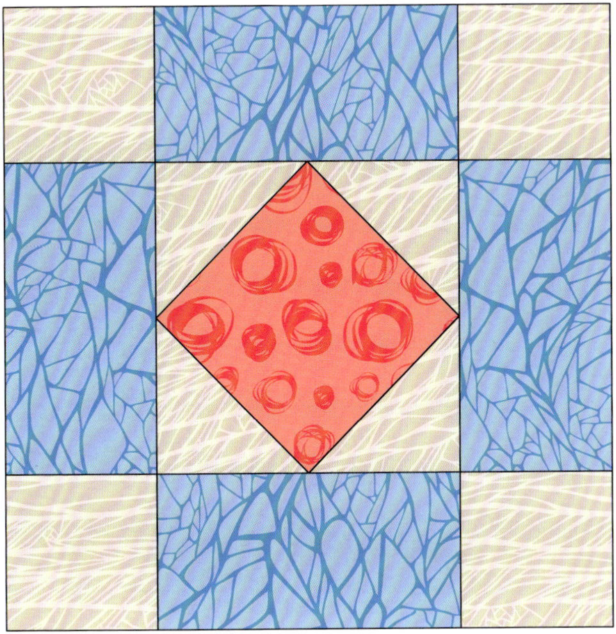

june 14

HOPSCOTCH BLOCK

6″ × 6″

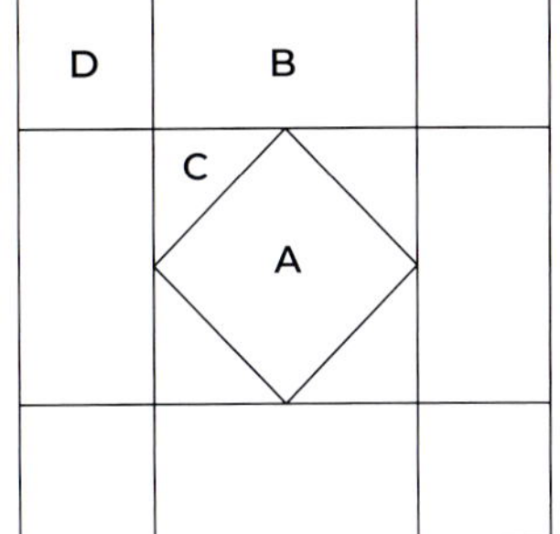

A
2⅝″

B
2″ × 3½″

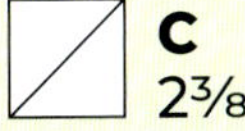

C
2⅜″

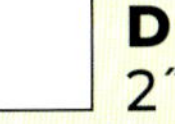

D
2″

july 19

CHEVRON
12″ × 12″

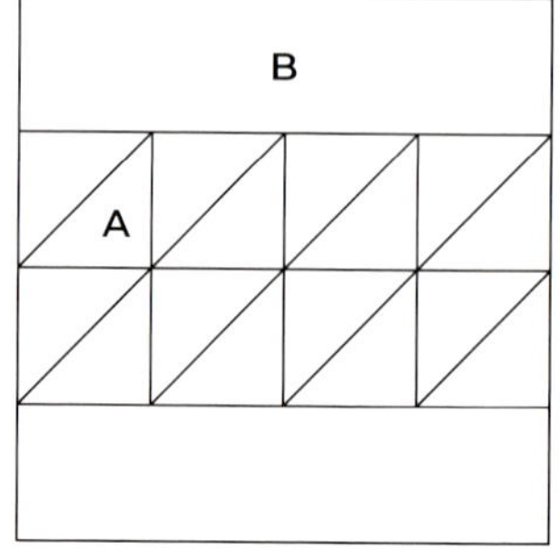

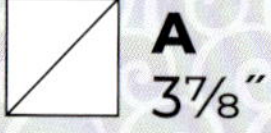
A
3⅞″

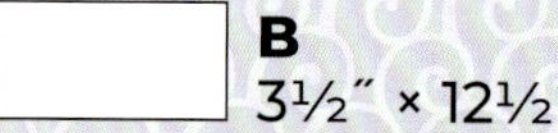
B
3½″ × 12½″

june 15

DOGGY STEPS

12″ × 12″

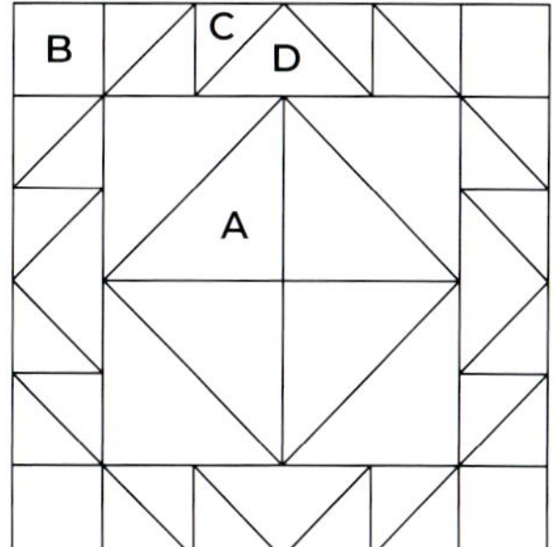

A
4⅞″

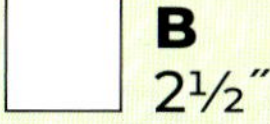

B
2½″

C
2⅞″

D
5¼″

july 18

RED CROSS

8″ × 8″

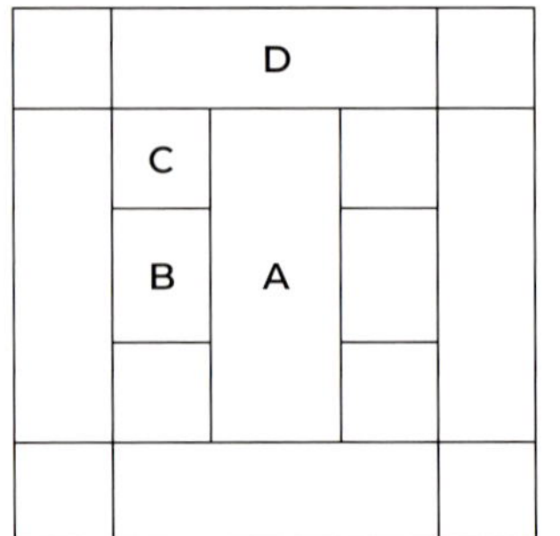

A
2½″ × 5½″

B
2″ × 2½″

C
2″

D
2″ × 5½″

june 16

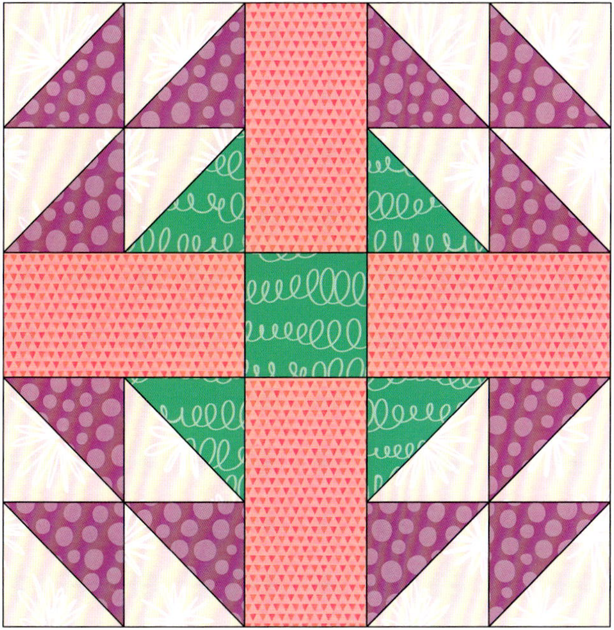

HANDY ANDY

15″ × 15″

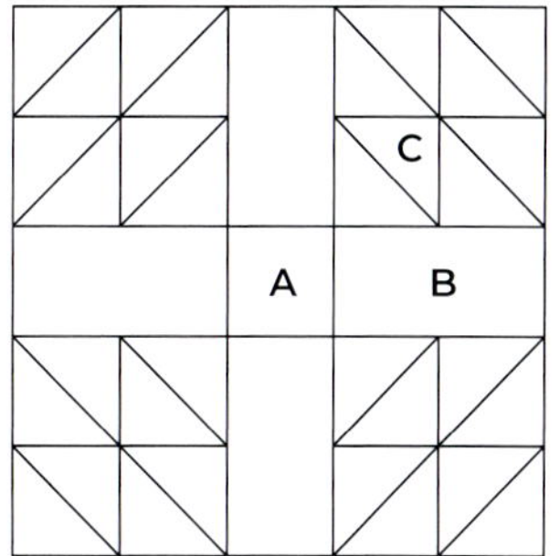

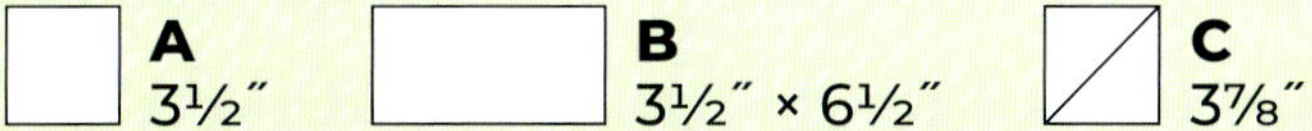

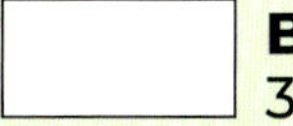

A
3½″

B
3½″ × 6½″

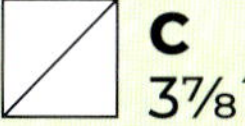

C
3⅞″

OCEAN WAVES

16″ × 16″

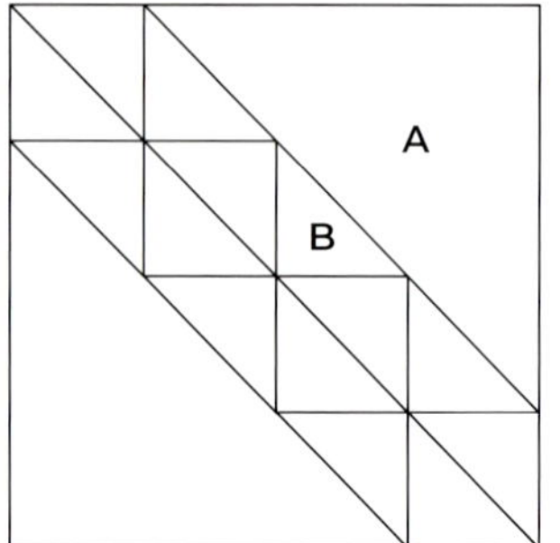

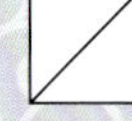

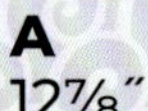

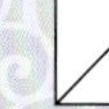

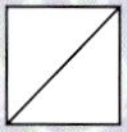

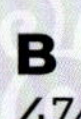

june 17

ALASKA HOMESTEAD

10″ × 10″

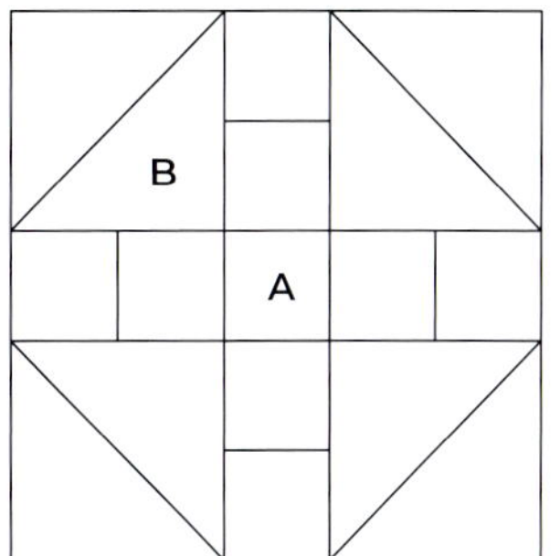

A
2½″

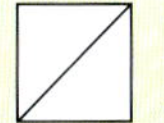

B
4⅞″

july 16

WHIRLING FIVE PATCH

10″ × 10″

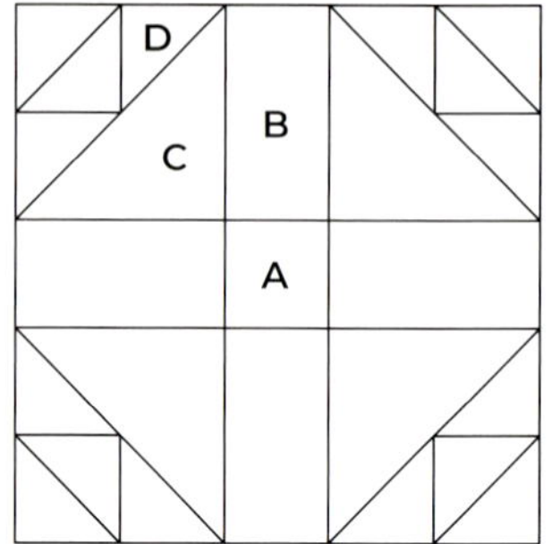

A
2½″

B
2½″ × 4½″

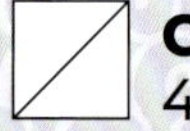

C
4⅞″

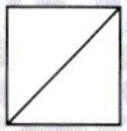

D
2⅞″

june 18

GLORIOUS BLOOMS

20″ × 20″

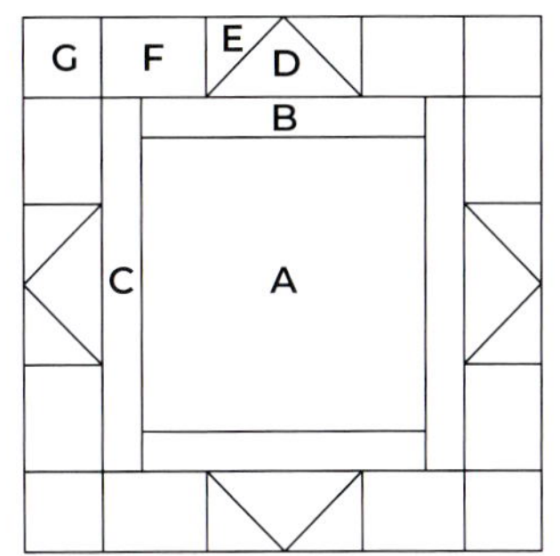

A
11½″

B
2″ × 11½″

C
2″ × 14½″

D
7¼″

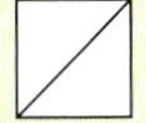

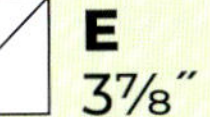

E
3⅞″

F
3½″ × 4½″

G
3½″

july 15

GRANDMOTHER'S CHOICE

10″ × 10″

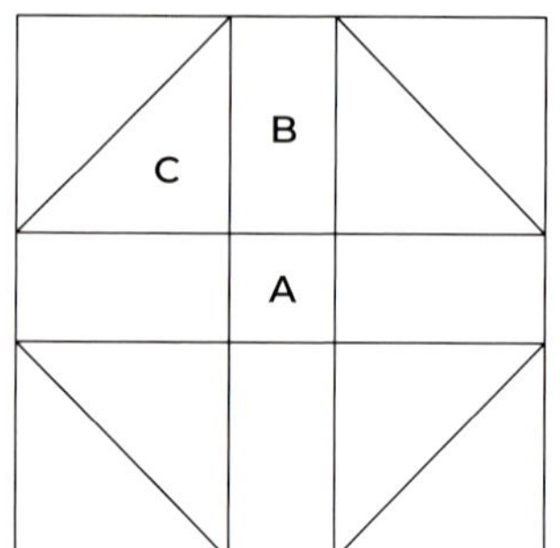

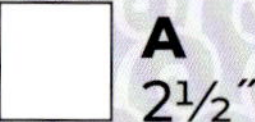

A
2½″

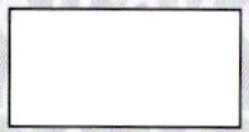

B
2½″ × 4½″

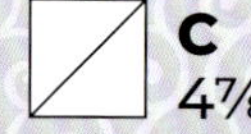

C
4⅞″

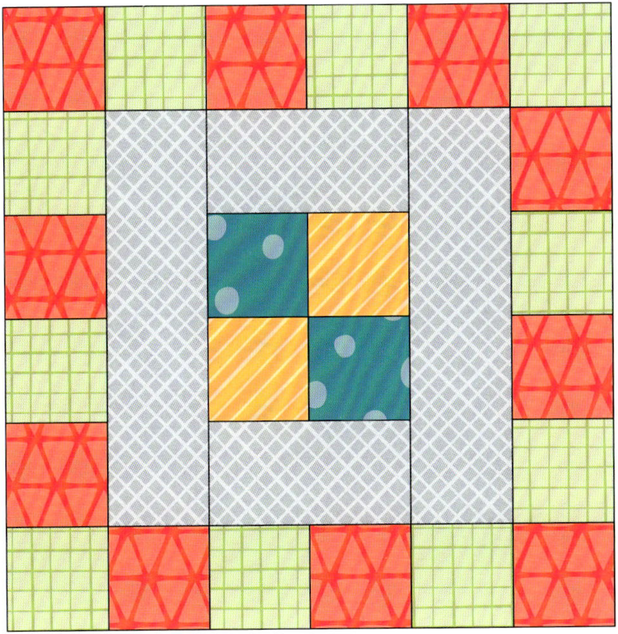

june 19

SCRAPPY 4 PATCH
12″ × 12″

B
A
C

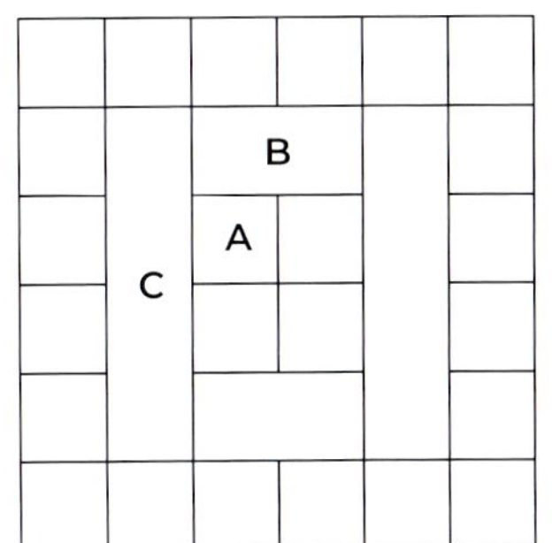

A
2½″

B
2½″ × 4½″

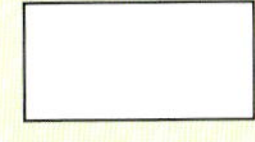

C
2½″ × 8½″

july 14

LOGS AND MORTAR VARIATION

10″ × 10″

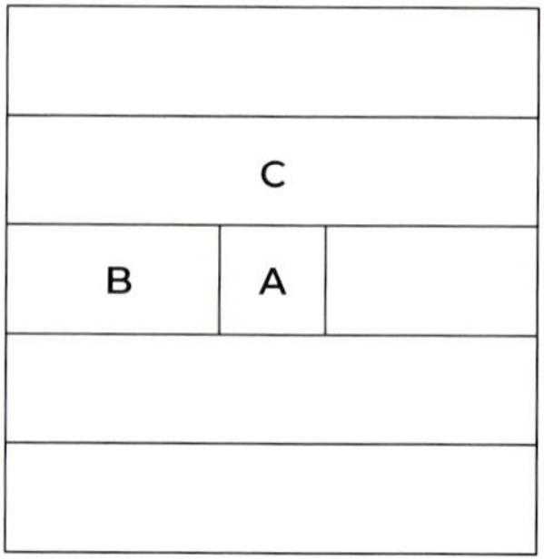

C

B A

A
2½″

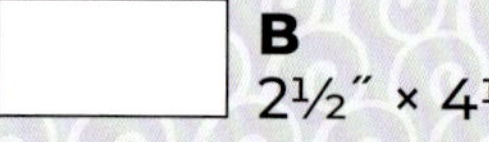

B
2½″ × 4½″

C
2½″ × 10½″

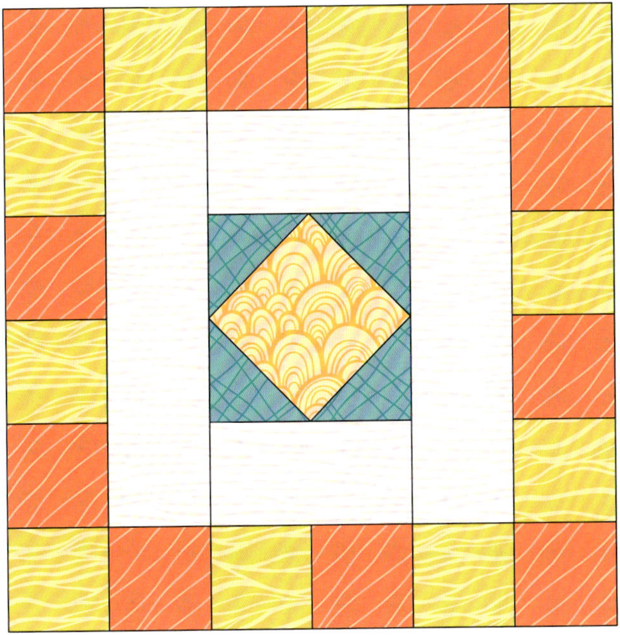

june 20

SCRAPPY SQUARE IN SQUARE

12″ × 12″

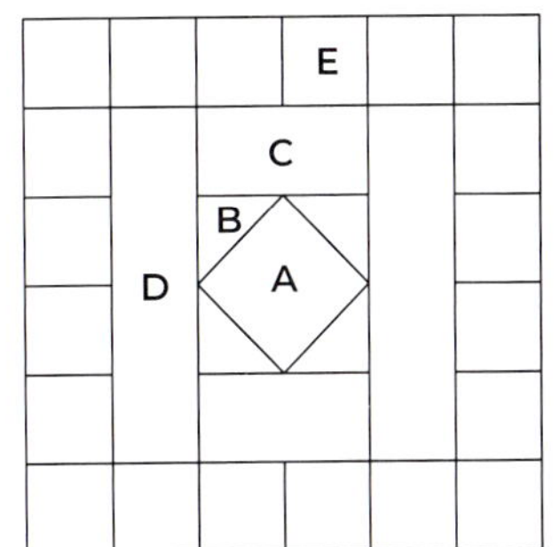

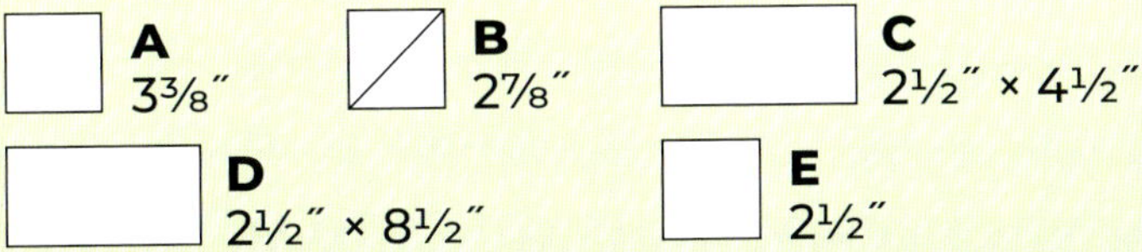

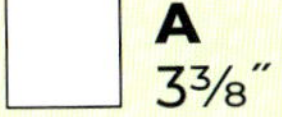

A
3⅜″

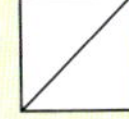

B
2⅞″

C
2½″ × 4½″

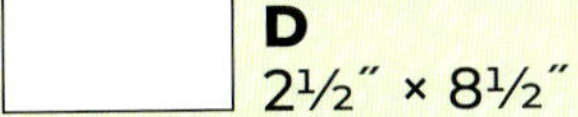

D
2½″ × 8½″

E
2½″

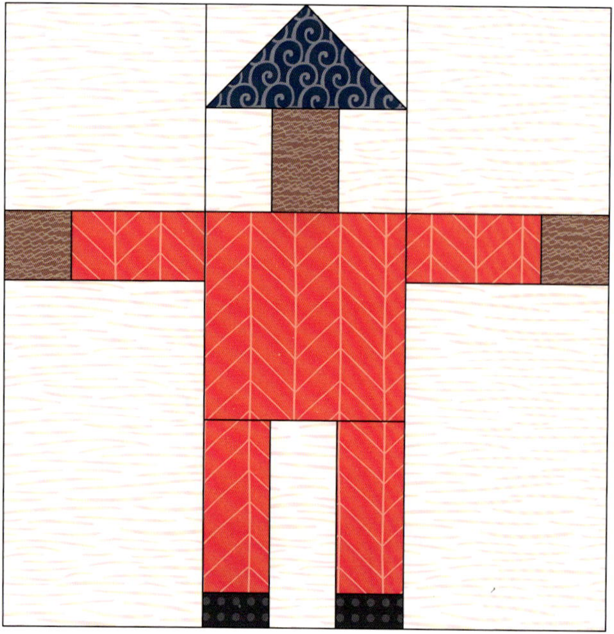

july 13

BOOMER BLOCK

9″ × 9″

A 3½″

B 2⅜″

C 4¼″

D 1½″ × 2″

E 1½″ × 2½″

F 1½″ × 3″

G 1½″

H 3½″ × 5½″

I 1″ × 3″

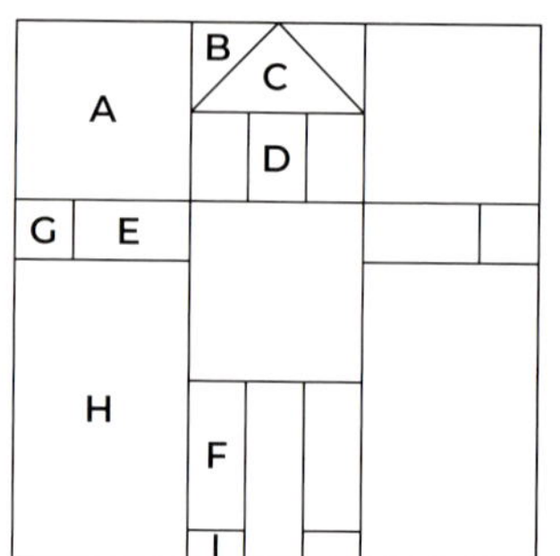

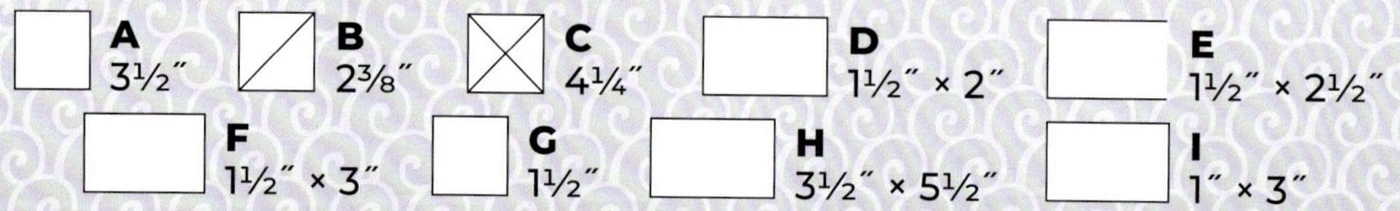

june 21

SCRAPPY BUTTERFLY WINGS

12″ × 12″

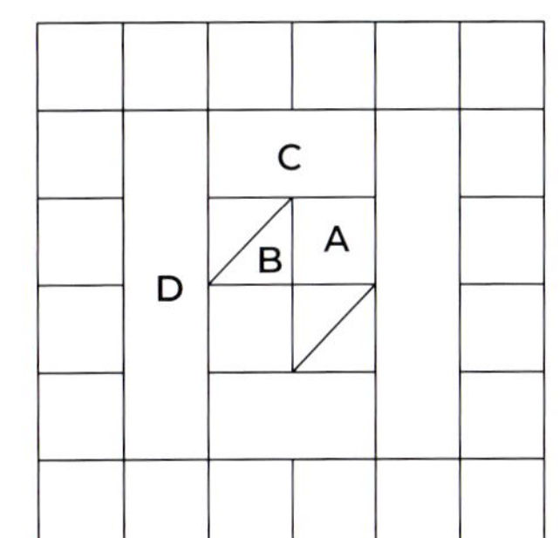

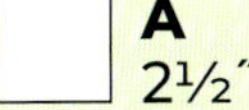

A
2½″

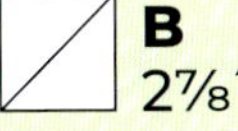

B
2⅞″

C
2½″ × 4½″

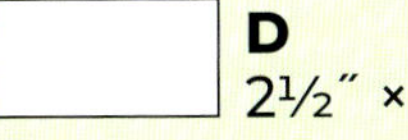

D
2½″ × 8½″

july 12

LAZY DAISY WHIRLIGIG

18″ × 18″

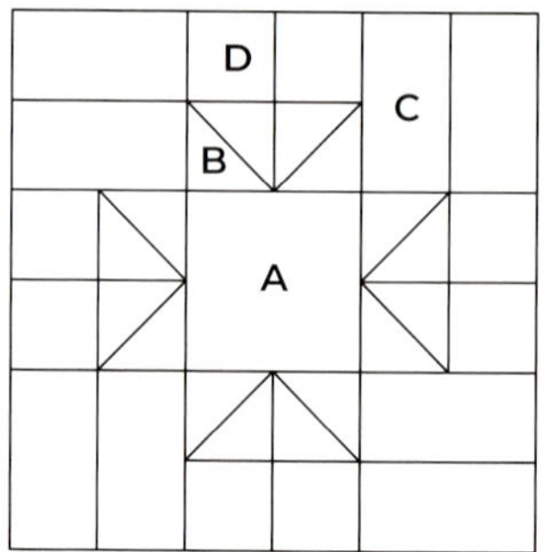

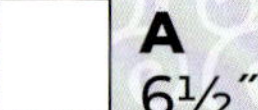

A
6½″

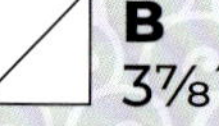

B
3⅞″

C
3½″ × 6½″

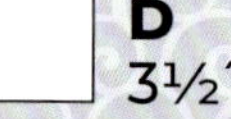

D
3½″

june 22

SCRAPPY WINDMILL

12″ × 12″

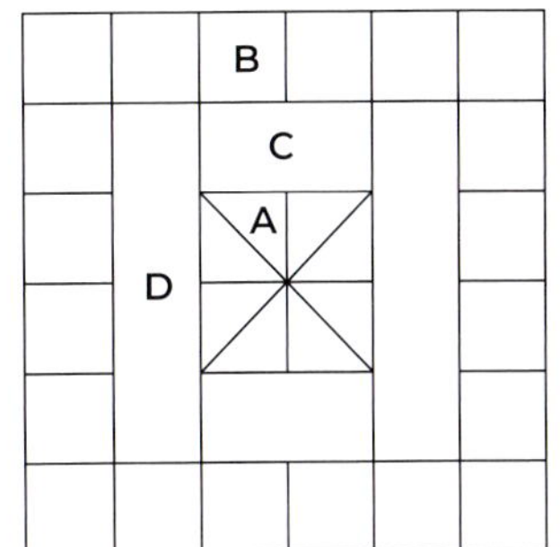

A 2⅞″

B 2½″

C 2½″ × 4½″

D 2½″ × 8½″

july 11

COUNTRY LANES

10″ × 10″

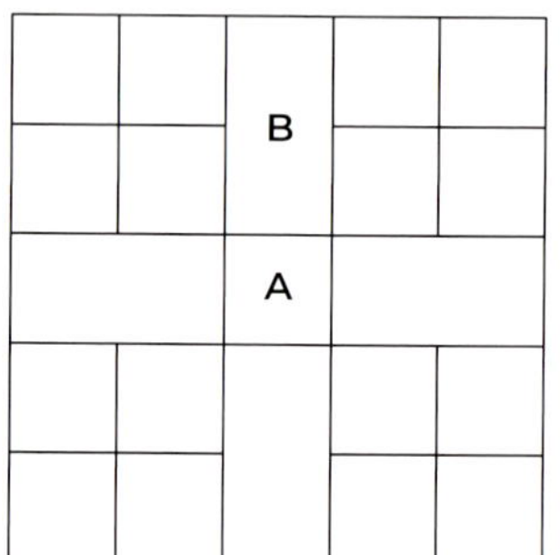

A
2½″

B
2½″ × 4½″

june 23

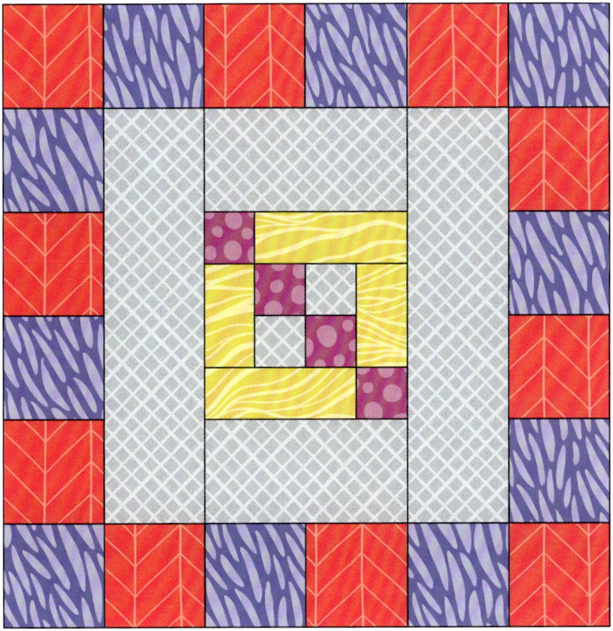

SCRAPPY DIAGONAL SQUARES

12″ × 12″

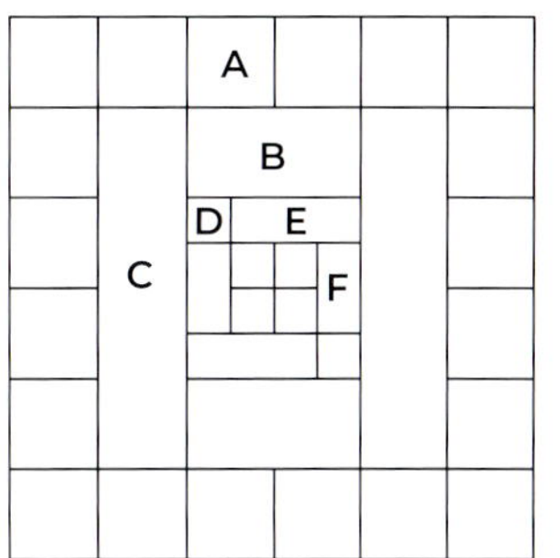

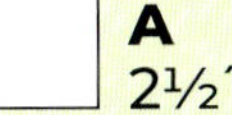

A
2½″

B
2½″ × 4½″

C
2½″ × 8½″

D
1½″

E
1½″ × 3½″

F
1½″ × 2½″

july 10

SHADOW BOXES

12″ × 12″

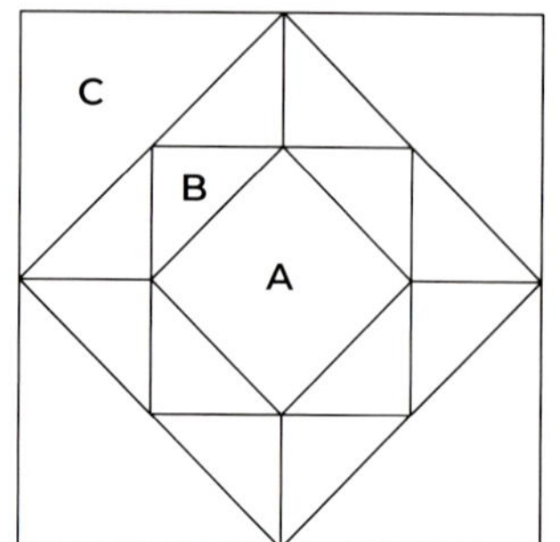

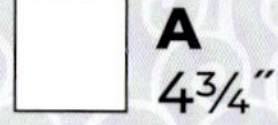

A
4¾″

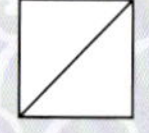

B
3⅞″

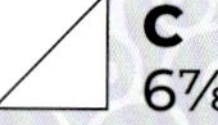

C
6⅞″

june 24

SCRAPPY TRIANGLES

12″ × 12″

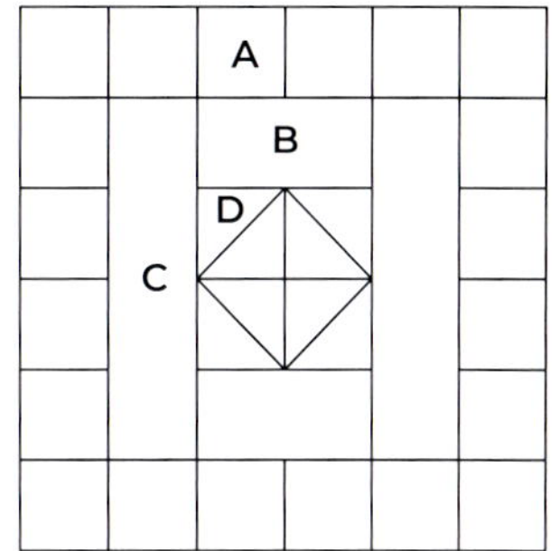

A
2½″

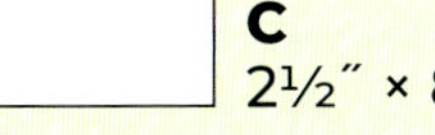

B
2½″ × 4½″

C
2½″ × 8½″

D
2⅞″

july 9

PINEAPPLE BLOCK

12″ × 12″

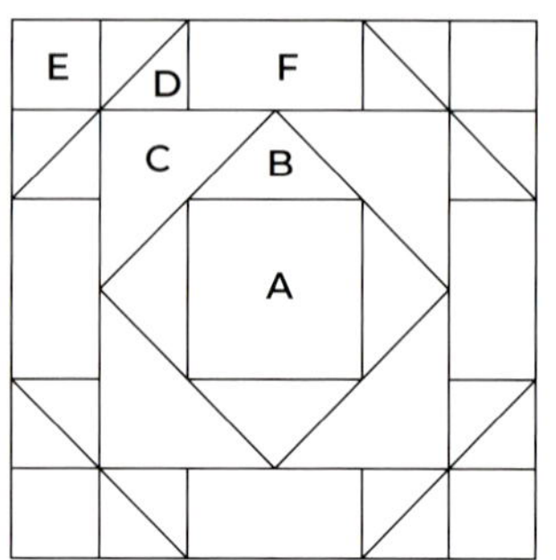

A
4½″

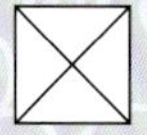

B
5¼″

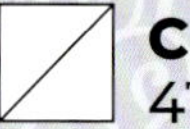

C
4⅞″

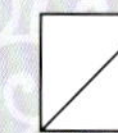

D
2⅞″

E
2½″

F
2½″ × 4½″

june 25

SCRAPPY PUSS IN THE CORNER

12″ × 12″

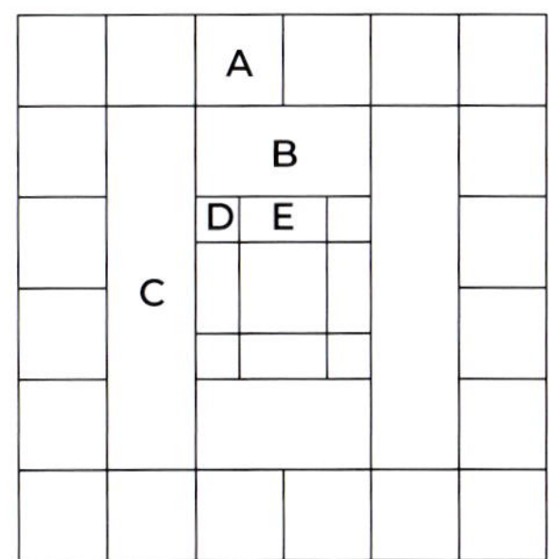

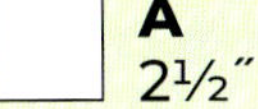

A
2½″

B
2½″ × 4½″

C
2½″ × 8½″

D
1½″

E
1½″ × 2½″

july 8

GEESE GONE WEST

8″ × 8″

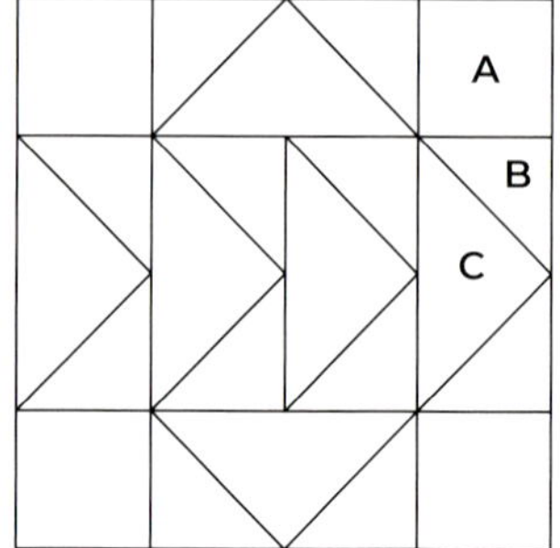

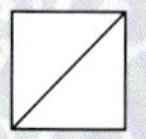

A
2½″

B
2⅞″

C
5¼″

june 26

TUSCAN TRAILS BLOCK

12″ × 12″

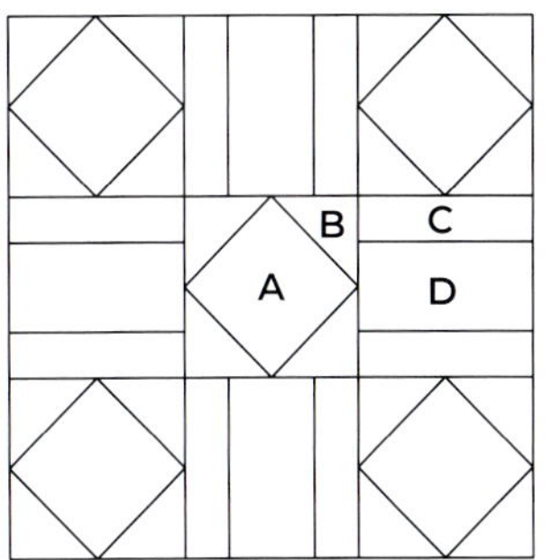

A
3 3/8″

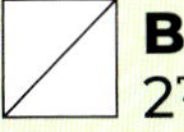

B
2 7/8″

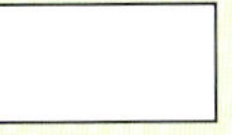

C
1 1/2″ × 4 1/2″

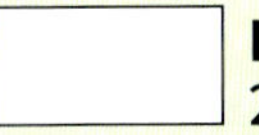

D
2 1/2″ × 4 1/2″

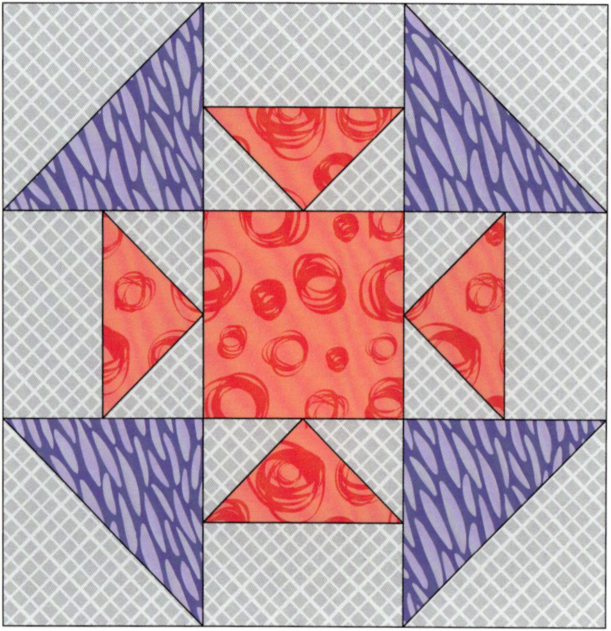

july 7

SHOOFLY VARIATION

12″ × 12″

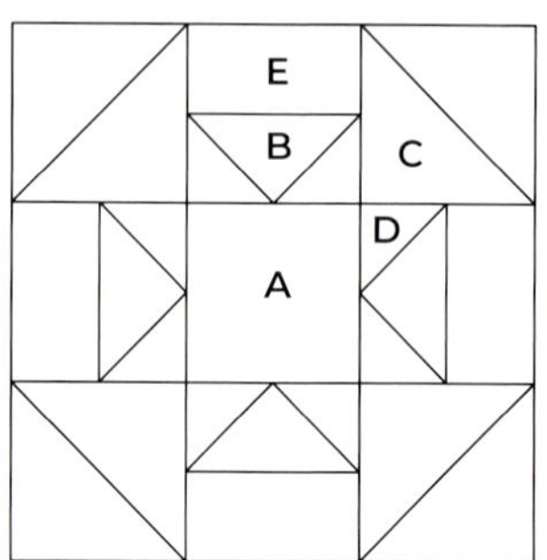

 **A** 4½″

 **B** 5¼″

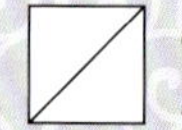 **C** 4⅞″

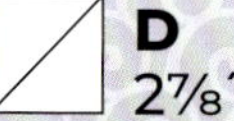 **D** 2⅞″

E 2½″ × 4½″

june 27

MOSAIC TILE BLOCK

18″ × 18″

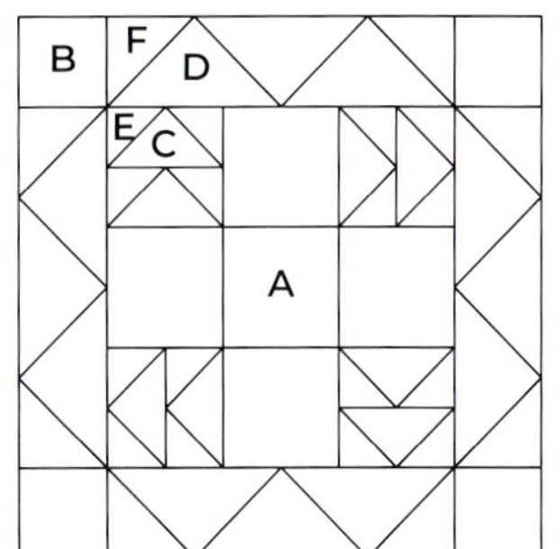

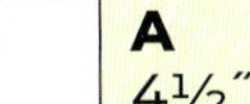

A
$4\frac{1}{2}$″

B
$3\frac{1}{2}$″

C
$5\frac{1}{4}$″

D
$7\frac{1}{4}$″

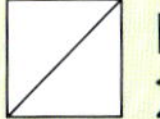

E
$2\frac{7}{8}$″

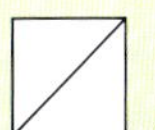

F
$3\frac{7}{8}$″

july 6

STAR CHAIN

16″ × 16″

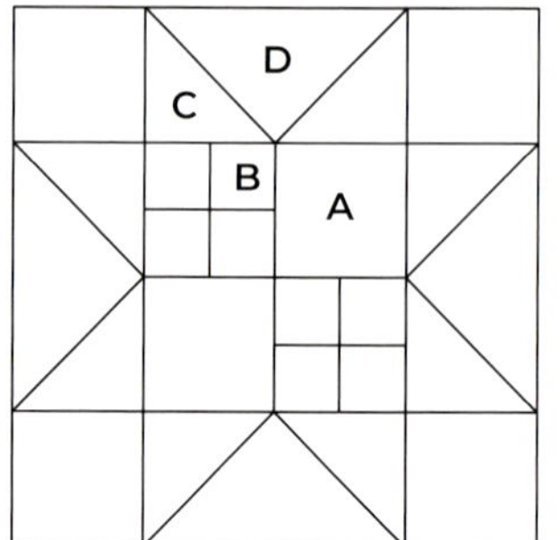

A 4½″

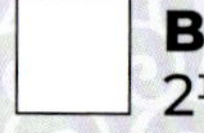

B 2½″

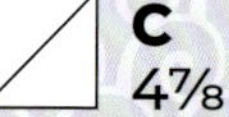

C 4⅞″

D 9¼″

june 28

UNEVEN 9 PATCH

10″ × 10″

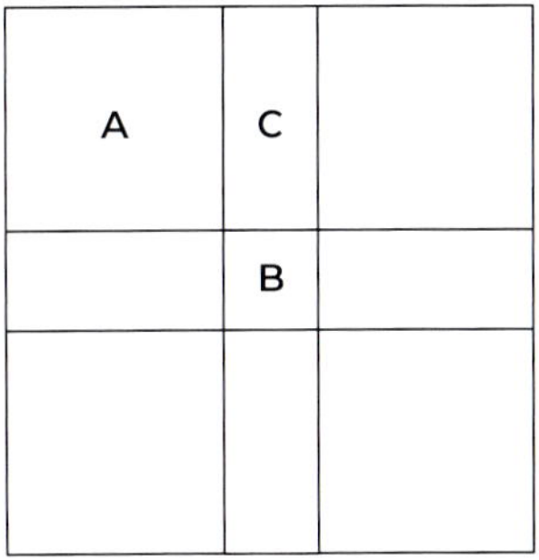

A C B

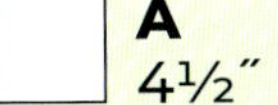

A
4½″

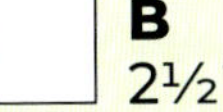

B
2½″

C
2½″ × 4½″

july 5

LIBERTY SQUARES

12″ × 12″

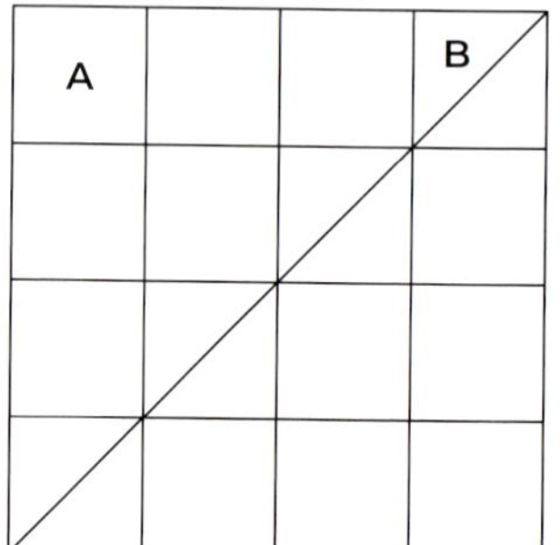

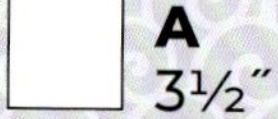

A
3½″

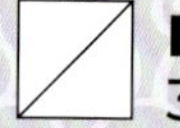

B
3⅞″

june 29

PUSS IN THE CORNER

10″ × 10″

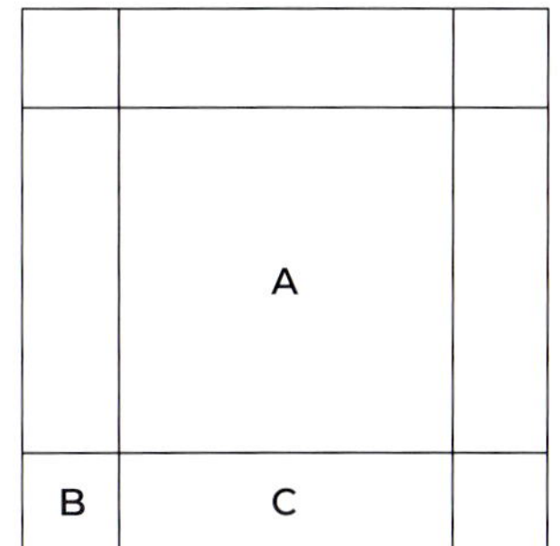

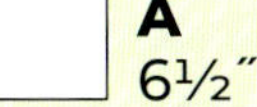

A
6½″

B
2½″

C
2½″ × 6½″

july 4

HEY, HEY USA

18″ × 18″

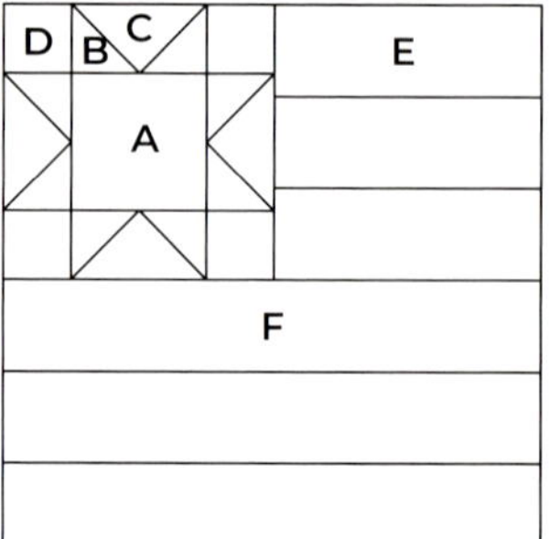

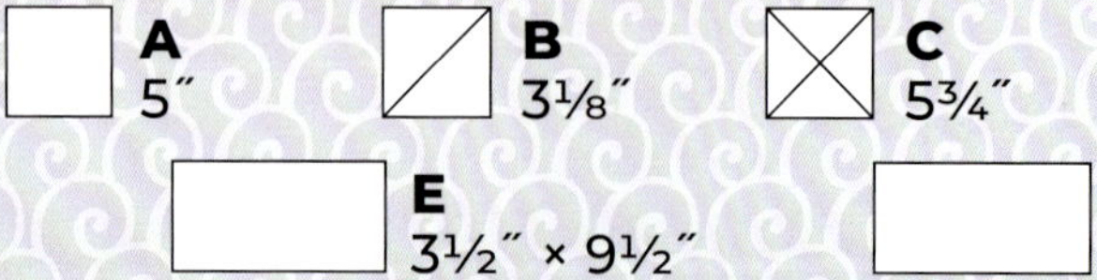

A
5″

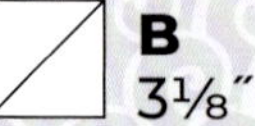

B
3⅛″

C
5¾″

D
2¾″

E
3½″ × 9½″

F
3½″ × 18½″

june 30

SPLIT 9 PATCH

9″ × 9″

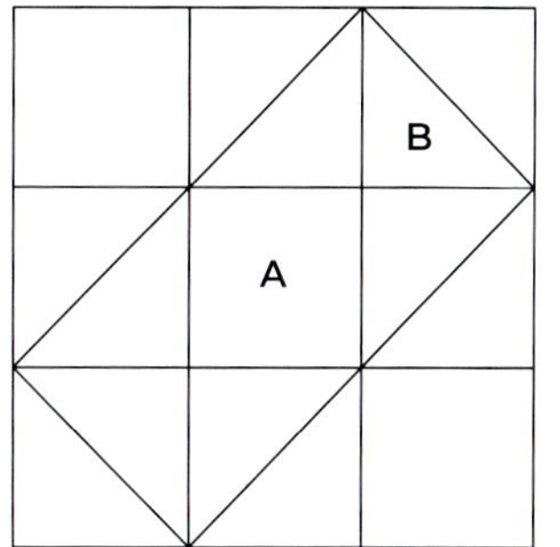

A 3½″

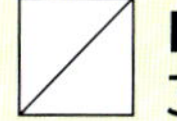

B 3⅞″

july 3

HOURGLASS AND BARS

8″ × 8″

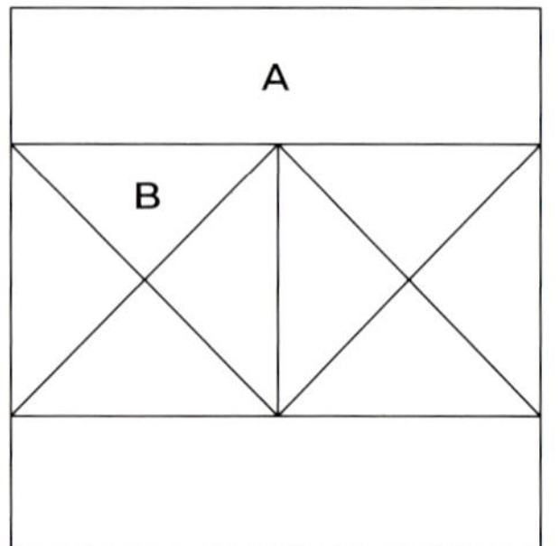

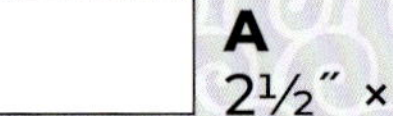

A
2½″ × 8½″

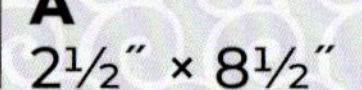

B
5¼″

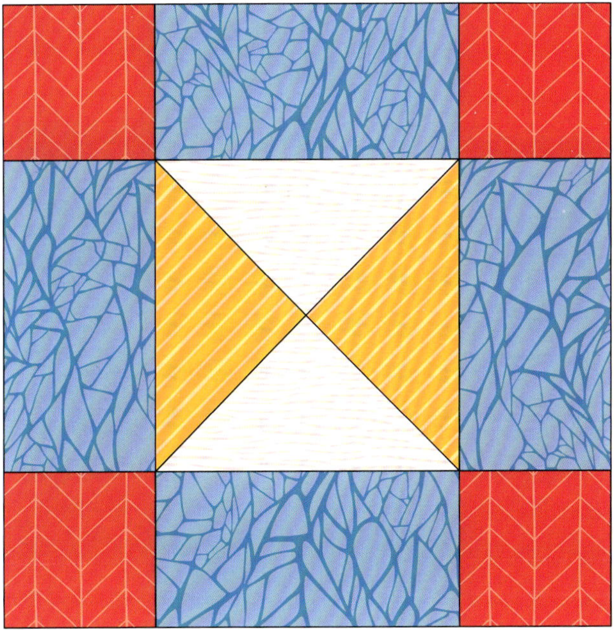

july 1

TRIANGLES AND BARS

8″ × 8″

A
C
B

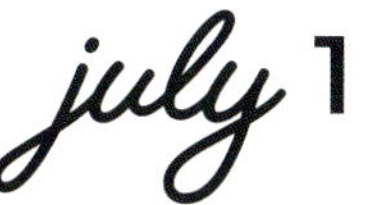

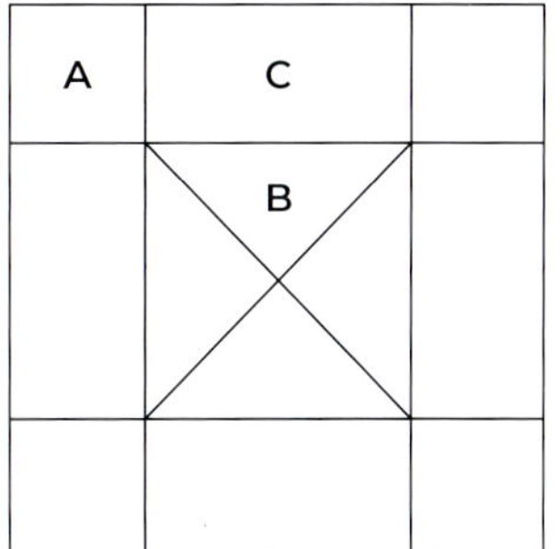

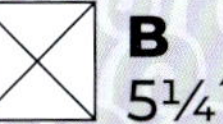

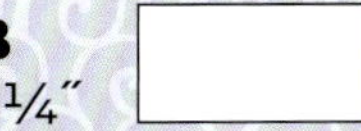

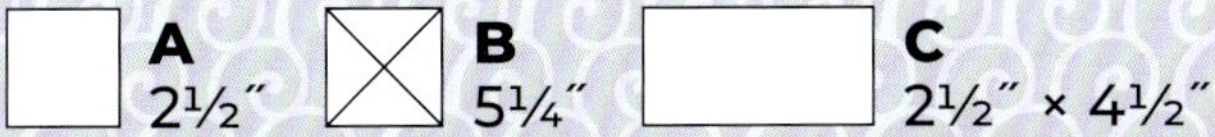
A
2½″
B
5¼″
C
2½″ × 4½″

july 2

FOUR BARS BLOCK

8″ × 8″

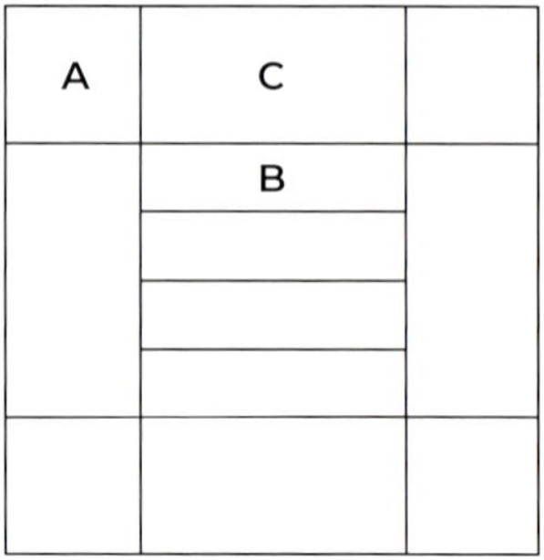

A

C

B

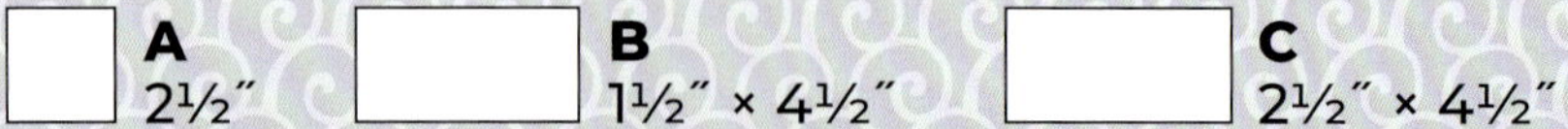

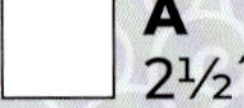

A
2½″

B
1½″ × 4½″

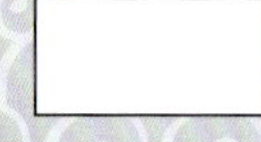

C
2½″ × 4½″

INSTRUCTIONS

Cutting instructions are geared for rotary cutting. Quick-cutting techniques sometimes yield more pieces than needed; save any extras for another project. All measurements for patchwork pieces include ¼″-wide seam allowances. Do not add seam allowances to the dimensions given for each block.

For triangles, cutting dimensions are provided for the square from which you'll cut half- or quarter-square triangles. When you see this symbol ◸, cut the square in half diagonally to yield two half-square triangles. When you see this symbol ⊠, cut the square twice diagonally to yield four quarter-square triangles.

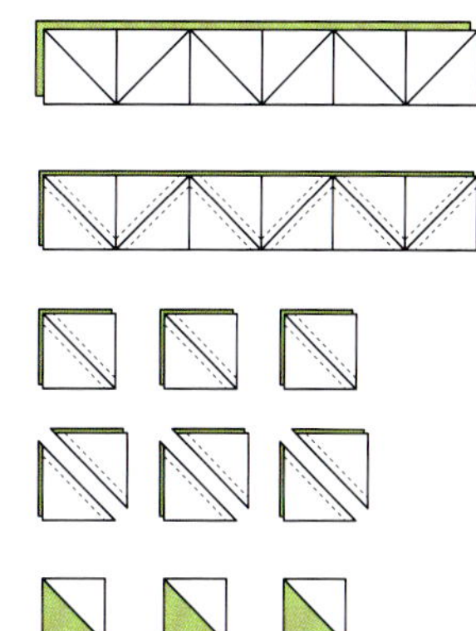

A quick way to cut and piece multiple smaller half-square triangles found in many of the blocks is to use the long-strip method. Let's use an example, where 3⅞″ squares are indicated in the block cutting instructions.

Cut a 3⅞″ strip from each of the two fabrics required for the half-square triangles. Using your rotary-cutting ruler, measure and draw vertical lines every 3⅞″ on the wrong side of the lighter strip. Then draw a diagonal line from corner to corner of each 3⅞″-wide space as shown. Pair the two strips, right sides together, and sew ¼″ away from each side of each diagonal line. Cut on the vertical lines, and then cut the stitched squares along the marked diagonal lines to yield a bundle of half-square triangle units.

Once you've cut all the pieces for a block, it's time to sew the pieces together. Look for the most logical order in which to sew the pieces. Whenever possible, sew the pieces together in rows, and then join the rows as shown at right.

Some blocks, however, cannot be sewn in straight rows. Instead, look for ways to join pieces into manageable units that can then be sewn together. In the block shown at right, join the pieces that make up the center unit first. Then join the pieces to make the triangle units. To complete the block, sew the triangle units to the center unit.

Sew units together;
then join into whole block.

INDEX BY BLOCK NAME

All blocks are square unless otherwise noted.

C

D

E

F

G

H

I

J

K

L

M

N

O

P

T

U

V

W

Y

Z

INDEX BY BLOCK SIZE

All blocks are square unless otherwise noted.

6″

8″

9″

10″

12″

Date	Block	Size
JAN 2	Turnstile	12″
JAN 3	Stepping Stones Cabin	12″
JAN 4	Blues and Whites	12″
JAN 5	Pennsylvania	12″
JAN 6	Art Square	12″
JAN 7	Art Square Variation	12″
JAN 19	Paradox	12″
JAN 20	Shoofly Mosaic	12″
JAN 21	Crowning Glory	12″
JAN 22	Underground Railroad	12″
JAN 26	Town Center Star	12″
FEB 14	Heart Block	12″
FEB 18	Shoofly	12″
FEB 22	Washington Square	12″
FEB 24	Sage Bud	12″
FEB 29	Chicago Geese	12″
MAR 1	T Block	12″
MAR 2	Hole in the Barn Door	12″
MAR 3	Circling Hearts	12″
MAR 4	Double Pyramids	12″
MAR 5	Clay's Choice	12″
MAR 6	Martha Washington Star	12″
MAR 7	Fox and Geese	12″
MAR 8	Variable Star	12″
MAR 9	Ohio Star	12″
MAR 10	Old Maid's Puzzle	12″
MAR 13	The Comfort Block	12″
MAR 14	Crown of Thorns	12″
MAR 15	Jacob's Ladder	12″
MAR 16	Spinning Wheel	12″
MAR 27	Double Pinwheel	12″
MAR 28	Pinwheel Variation	12″
MAR 29	Triangle X	12″
MAR 30	Picnic Patch	12″
APR 18	Double Squares Block	12″
APR 19	Bird Tracks	12″
MAY 20	Contrary Wife	12″
MAY 21	Country Lanes Variation	12″
MAY 30	Crossroads	12″
MAY 31	Memory Wreath	12″
JUN 1	Steps to the Altar	12″
JUN 2	Stairsteps Block	12″
JUN 7	Windblown Square	12″
JUN 9	Bordered Puss in the Corner	12″
JUN 10	Grandmother's Cross	12″
JUN 15	Doggy Steps	12″
JUN 19	Scrappy 4 Patch	12″
JUN 20	Scrappy Square in Square	12″
JUN 21	Scrappy Butterfly Wings	12″
JUN 22	Scrappy Windmill	12″
JUN 23	Scrappy Diagonal Squares	12″
JUN 24	Scrappy Triangles	12″
JUN 25	Scrappy Puss in the Corner	12″
JUN 26	Tuscan Trails Block	12″
JUL 5	Liberty Squares	12″
JUL 7	Shoofly Variation	12″
JUL 9	Pineapple Block	12″
JUL 10	Shadow Boxes	12″
JUL 19	Chevron	12″
JUL 20	Zig Zag Triangles	12″
JUL 21	Tree Everlasting	12″

JUL 22 Ribbon Star 12″
JUL 26 Flying Geese Variation 12″
AUG 13 Four Knaves 12″
AUG 15 Garden Party 12″
AUG 18 Four Seasons 12″
AUG 19 Garden Path 12″
AUG 22 Coverlet Block 12″
AUG 23 Double Four Patch 12″
AUG 28 Hit or Miss Star 12″
AUG 29 Sawtooth Star 12″
AUG 30 Sawtooth Star Variation 12″
AUG 31 Kitty Corner Star 12″
SEP 1 Square and Star 12″
SEP 6 Roundabout Geese 12″
SEP 7 Split Star 12″
SEP 13 Anvil Block 12″
SEP 14 Blue and White 12″
SEP 15 Market Square 12″
SEP 16 Bear Tracks 12″
SEP 17 Ladies Aid 12″
SEP 18 Goose Creek 12″
SEP 19 Lost Goslin 12″
SEP 20 Homeward Bound 12″
SEP 21 Memory Star Variation 12″
SEP 23 Blind Man's Fancy 12″
SEP 24 Sage Bud Variation 12″
SEP 25 Millstone 12″
OCT 5 Jack in the Box 12″
OCT 6 Double Z 12″
OCT 7 Ozark Maple Leaf 12″
OCT 8 Vines at the Window 12″
OCT 9 Ocean Waves Variation 12″
OCT 10 Niña 12″
OCT 11 Pinta 12″
OCT 12 Santa Maria 12″
OCT 16 Big and Little Geese 12″
OCT 17 Coming and Going Geese 12″
OCT 18 Follow the Leader 12″
OCT 19 Day and Night Geese 12″
OCT 20 Geese in Formation 12″
OCT 21 Geese in the Trees 12″
OCT 22 Geese Migration 12″
OCT 23 Geese on the Move 12″
OCT 24 Gosling Go Round 12″
OCT 25 Pinwheel Geese 12″
OCT 26 Railroad Crossing 12″
OCT 27 Three Little Geese 12″
OCT 28 Wild Goose Chase 12″
OCT 31 Pumpkin Patch 12″
NOV 6 Gentleman's Fancy 12″
NOV 11 Double Star 12″
NOV 19 Checkers 12″
NOV 20 Squash Blossom 12″
NOV 22 Puss in Boots 12″
NOV 23 Flying Dutchman 12″
NOV 26 Moving Star 12″
NOV 27 Tic Tac Toe 12″
NOV 28 Building Blocks 12″
NOV 29 Four Patch in Nine 12″
DEC 1 Tesselating Star 12″
DEC 11 Shoofly and Four Patch 12″
DEC 15 Bonnie Scotland 12″
DEC 16 Centennial 12″

DEC 17 Grandmother's Pride 12″
DEC 18 Berkeley 12″
DEC 19 By Chance 12″
DEC 20 Grecian Square 12″
DEC 21 This and That 12″
DEC 29 Brick Road 12″
DEC 31 Delectable Mountains 12″

12″ × 14″

APR 16 Kimono 12″ × 14″

12″ × 18″

OCT 13 Pine Tree 12″ × 18″

14″

JAN 23 Autograph 14″
JAN 24 Logs and Mortar 14″
JAN 25 Southwest Cross 14″
JAN 28 Cross and Crown 14″
JAN 30 Dove in the Window 14″
FEB 12 Lincoln's Platform 14″
MAR 17 Lucky Irish Block 14″
MAR 18 Cobblestones 14″
MAY 28 Album Squares Block 14″
MAY 29 Squares on Point 14″
SEP 10 Hen and Chicks 14″
SEP 11 Criss Cross 14″
SEP 26 Prickly Pear 14″
SEP 27 Mother's Fancy 14″
SEP 28 Grizzly Block 14″
SEP 29 Mosaic Triangles 14″
SEP 30 Bear's Paw Patches 14″
OCT 1 Pieced Ribbon 14″
DEC 10 Bear's Paw 14″

15″

FEB 2 Star and Cross Block 15″
FEB 25 Diamond Facets 15″
FEB 26 Criss Cross Block 15″
FEB 27 Double Hourglass Block 15″
FEB 28 Gems Block 15″
MAR 11 Hilary's Garden 15″
MAR 12 Four Patch Garden 15″
APR 20 Sister's Choice 15″
APR 21 Goose in the Pond 15″
APR 22 Georgetown Square 15″
APR 23 Tea for Four 15″
APR 24 Five Spot 15″
APR 25 Prairie Queen 15″
APR 26 Beginner's Delight 15″
APR 27 Turkey in the Straw 15″
APR 28 Far West 15″
APR 29 Souvenir Block 15″
APR 30 Country Fences 15″
JUN 3 Goose in the Pond Variation 15″
JUN 4 Bird's Nest 15″
JUN 5 Duck and Ducklings 15″
JUN 16 Handy Andy 15″
JUL 24 Garden Star 15″
JUL 25 Star Cross 15″
AUG 25 Young Man's Fancy 15″
AUG 26 Monkey Wrench 15″
AUG 27 Home Circle 15″

SEP 3 Rolling Star Block 15″
SEP 4 Sawtooth Stars 15″
OCT 29 Indian Trails 15″
NOV 7 Churn Dasher 15″
NOV 8 Souvenir Variation 15″

16″

JAN 18 Double Hearts 16″
FEB 1 Snail's Trail 16″
FEB 7 4 Patch and Rails 16″
FEB 8 Hourglass Variation 16″
FEB 21 King's Crown 16″
FEB 23 Double Centennial 16″
MAR 19 Stepping Stones 16″
MAR 20 Blackford's Beauty 16″
MAR 21 Queen's Crown 16″
MAR 26 Cake Stand 16″
APR 12 Double 4 Patch 16″
APR 13 Irish Chain Variation 16″
MAY 22 Antique Album 16″
JUN 11 Stairways Block 16″
JUL 6 Star Chain 16″
JUL 17 Ocean Waves 16″
JUL 27 Interlocked Rings 16″
AUG 17 Castle Mosaic 16″
AUG 24 Next Door Neighbor 16″
OCT 15 Fox and Geese Squared 16″
NOV 24 Four Corners 16″
NOV 30 Star Puzzle 16″
DEC 4 Four and Nine 16″
DEC 5 Star of Hope 16″

18″

JAN 1 Oh, My Stars! 18″
JAN 8 Imperial T 18″
JAN 9 Imperial T Variation 18″
JAN 29 Dove at the Window 18″
FEB 15 Memory Star 18″
FEB 16 Double Geese 18″
MAR 31 Rosebud Block 18″
APR 1 Alabama 18″
APR 2 Antique Tile 18″
APR 3 Flock of Birds 18″
APR 4 Sunshine 18″
APR 5 Squares and Triangles 18″
APR 6 Double 9 Patch 18″
APR 7 London Roads 18″
APR 8 Rolling Gears 18″
APR 14 Rising Sun Block 18″
APR 15 Rising Sun Variation 18″
MAY 1 Baby Bunting 18″
MAY 2 Brave World 18″
MAY 3 Broken Dishes 18″
MAY 4 Butterfly Block 18″
MAY 5 Cheyenne 18″
MAY 6 Cross Patch 18″
MAY 7 Fourth of July 18″
MAY 8 Louisiana 18″
MAY 9 Mosaic Block 18″
MAY 10 Peace and Plenty 18″
MAY 11 School Girl Puzzle 18″
MAY 12 Yankee Puzzle 18″
JUN 13 Old Glory Star 18″

JUN 27	Mosaic Tile Block	18″
JUL 4	Hey, Hey USA	18″
JUL 12	Lazy Daisy Whirligig	18″
AUG 12	Basket of Squares	18″
AUG 20	Double Stars	18″
AUG 21	Double T	18″
NOV 1	Triple Bar	18″
NOV 2	Bars and Triangles	18″
NOV 3	Triple Bars and Squares	18″
NOV 4	Four Patch and Bars	18″
NOV 9	Arizona Block	18″
NOV 10	Arbor Window	18″
NOV 12	Aztec Jewel	18″
NOV 13	Broken Dish	18″
NOV 14	Broken Windows	18″
NOV 15	Big Twinkle	18″
NOV 25	Stepping Star	18″
DEC 25	Christmas Star	18″
DEC 26	Star and Pine Block	18″

20″

JUN 18	Glorious Blooms	20″
OCT 2	Comfort Block	20″

22″

FEB 13	Whitehouse Steps	22″

24″

OCT 14	Tree of Temptation	24″
NOV 5	Woven Star	24″
NOV 21	Diagonal Star	24″

ABOUT THE AUTHOR

DEBBY KRATOVIL has been "sewing for the camera" since 1993, serving as an editor with Quilt Magazine for fourteen years. She's the author of three quilting books and eighteen block-a-day quilting calendars. She's had a web presence since the mid-1990s and has a popular blog, where she shares many tips, free patterns, and other quilting nuggets.

Photo by Matt Meurer

debbykratovilquilts.blogspot.com